DATE DUE			

Western Popular Theatre

Edited by

David Mayer and Kenneth Richards

*The Proceedings of a Symposium
sponsored by the Manchester University
Department of Drama*

METHUEN

LONDON and NEW YORK

First published in 1977 by
Methuen & Co. Ltd
11 New Fetter Lane, London EC4P 4EE
First published as a University Paperback in 1980

Published in the USA by
Methuen & Co.
in association with Methuen, Inc.
733 Third Avenue, New York, NY 10017

© 1977 Methuen

Photoset by Red Lion Setters, Holborn, London
Printed in Great Britain at the
University Press, Cambridge

British Library Cataloguing in Publication Data
Western Popular Theatre (*Conference*), *University of Manchester, 1974*
Western popular theatre. – (University paperbacks; 701).
1. Theater – History – Congresses
I. Mayer, David II. Richards, Kenneth, b. 1934 III. Series
792'. 09181'2   PN 2122

ISBN 0-416-73150-3

Preface

The papers gathered here were delivered at the third University of Manchester International Theatre Symposium, held at Langdale Hall in April, 1974. The theme of the Symposium was 'Western Popular Theatre'. It was a brash attempt to grasp a dangerous nettle. Sooner or later anyone who proclaims interest in the theatre is up against the realization that there are many kinds of theatre and that 'the theatrical event' eludes any easy definition. In most writing on theatre for convenience sake, there is a tendency, usually rather covert, to assume a rough distinction between 'theatre' and 'popular theatre'. The former is invariably supposed to have some pretension to the condition of art and is often defined in terms of its conscious structuring, trafficking in ideas and formal perform-ance location, whilst the latter, in some indeterminate way, is purported to embrace all other performance kinds and to offer its audiences received or traditional attitudes. But the distinction, though merely a working one, begs a multitude of questions. For example, a great deal of 'popular theatre' is as much theatre-building located and may be no less engaged with ideas as is 'theatre'. Indeed, distinctions between 'artistic' and 'popular' are elusive. The ability, willingness and opportunity to provide theatre for the majority is not in itself a guide to artistic merit or the lack of it: Plautus was no less of an artist for entertaining the Roman crowd than the Racine who wrote for the cultivated young ladies of Saint-Cyr. Nor does audience complexion or response necessarily assist in definition, for the heterogeneity of theatre audiences has varied considerably, and often bewilderingly, from age to age and culture to culture. At all levels and in all ways the distinctions intersect, not always to the approval of the practitioners. Common enough to purveyors of both 'theatre' and 'popular theatre' is a desire at once to capitalize upon and to reject the taste of the majority: thus Shakespeare could fashion the most substantial of all theatre careers by pleasing the multitude, but boast that his *Troilus and Cressida* was not 'clapperclawed with the palms of the vulgar', and Charles Coburn could privately deplore the immense popularity of his music-hall song, *Two Lovely Black Eyes*, the success of which helped him to establish his reputation. Such contradiction is characteristic of theatre in all its forms.

Contents

FIGURES

PLATES

Contents

The purpose of this Symposium was to discuss the nature, breadth and durability of what we so loosely and inadequately, but conveniently, call 'popular theatre', yet to acknowledge the contradictions implicit in the subject. To that end fourteen papers were offered over three days, and although to some extent we had encouraged papers on subjects generally conceded to be 'popular theatre' and, further, invited contributions from scholars who had previously expressed interest in 'popular' manifestations, we were not altogether unprepared for divergent thinking. The papers in this volume illustrate that divergence and the fact that 'popular theatre' is a phrase spanning a variety of interpretations of aesthetics, political and social ideologies, and perceptions of culture.

If we have been somewhat headstrong in persisting with a topic so large and amorphous as popular theatre, we have also deliberately imposed a measure of restraint upon ourselves by limiting the scope of the Symposium to the popular theatre of Western Europe and North America. We readily acknowledge that Asia, Asia Minor, Africa, and South America might have made substantial contributions toward supplementing the several statements of theory. On the other hand, to introduce modes and forms of drama without simultaneously being able to provide the necessary explication of the societies in which these drama arose seriously limited our capacity to discuss, certainly to understand, their functions within their social structures. The structures of Western Society, we assumed, were generally accessible to the Symposium participants and are likely to be so to our readers.

What no one attending the Symposium disputed is how ephemeral are the documents of 'popular theatre'. They vanish quickly and are often irrecoverable. Equally ephemeral and beyond our recovery were the discussions which gave thoughtful continuity to these disparate papers. Some papers have been revised in the light of these discussions; others, which were shortened for oral delivery, have been restored to their original state, and two additional papers, by Irmeli Niemi and Viveka Hagnell, were written in response to questions raised during the Symposium.

With gratitude the editors acknowledge the lively contributions of participants, and the assistance from other quarters that enabled the Symposium to develop so effectively. We thank the Department of Drama, University of Manchester, for a grant toward the expenses of the Symposium and for the enthusiastic assistance of department lecturers and postgraduate students. Methuen was similarly generous in its early expression of interest in publishing the proceedings, thereby lending encouragement to the many contributors. The Cultural Affairs Office of the United States Embassy in Paris and London offered assitance to enable conferees to come from France. We are grateful to Mrs Irene Brown, Miss Pamela Titley, and Miss Vera Allen for assistance with Symposium correspondence and for their aid in preparing this volume for the press.

Manchester   D.M.
September 1974   K.R.

Members of the Symposium

Ben Albach	Amsterdam, Holland
Peter Arnott	Tufts University, USA
Kathleen Barker	Society of Theatre Research
Christopher Baugh	University of Manchester
Michael Booth	Guelph University, Canada
Cobi Bordewijk	Leiden University, Holland
William Brasmer	Denison University, USA
Philip Cook	University of Manchester
Eileen Cottis	Polytechnic of North London
Margaret Dale	British Broadcasting Corporation
Robert Erenstein	University of Amsterdam, Holland
Denis Gontard	Université Paul Valery, Montpellier, France
Sinclair Goodlad	Imperial College, University of London
Viveka Hagnell	University of Lund, Sweden
Arnold Hare	University of Bristol
Anthony Hippisley-Coxe	Hartland, Devon
Anthony Jackson	University of Manchester
Geoffrey Joyce	University of Manchester
Gerry McCarthy	University of Birmingham
Patric Mason	University of Manchester
David Mayer	University of Manchester
Monica Murray	British Theatre Association
George Nash	Victoria and Albert Museum
Irmeli Niemi	Turku University, Finland
John Prudhoe	University of Manchester
Kenneth Richards	University of Manchester
Laura Richards	University of Salford
Philip Roberts	University of Sheffield
Sybil Rosenfeld	Editor, *Theatre Notebook*
David Rostron	Worcester College of Education
George Rowell	University of Bristol
Virginia Scott	University of Maine, USA
George Speaight	Society of Theatre Research
George Taylor	University of Manchester
Peter Thomson	University College, Swansea
James Walton	University of Hull
George Wewiora	Ashton-under-Lyne College

VIRGINIA P. SCOTT

The Jeu *and the* Rôle: *Analysis of the Appeals of the Italian Comedy in France in the Time of Arlequin-Dominique*

Popular entertainments are generally so classified because of their appeal and availability to a large audience drawn from all classes and conditions of society. However, the assertion that the Italian Comedy in Paris in the last half of the seventeenth century was available to all classes cannot be supported. The cheapest place, in the *parterre*,* cost 15 sous,[1] a day's wages for many artisans in 1688[2]. Economic necessity dictates that the audience of the *Comédie-Italienne* was drawn from the middle class and the nobility. Can we then regard this form of entertainment as popular theatre?

Yes, if we classify theatrical activities by how they appeal rather than to whom they appeal, by their strategies rather than their spectators.

The purpose of this paper is to defend the assertion that the Italian comedies performed in France by the company known as the *ancien théâtre italien* between 1660 and 1688 can best be understood and accounted for by analysis of their audience appeals; that popular theatre yields to such structural analysis; and that the Italian comedies are most profitably classified as popular theatre.

Conventional dramatic theory does not seem to provide critics with the golden key needed to unlock the strategic mysteries of the *Comédie-Italienne*. Conventional dramatic theory, particularly that devised in seventeenth-century France, is highly prescriptive. It says that a play must do certain kinds of things, that in order to do them it must contain certain elements arranged in certain ways. Since the Italian comedies did not do those things, did not have those elements, and were not arranged in those ways, they were destined to critical condemnation.

*See glossary on p.24 for this and other unfamiliar terms.

Neoclassical comic theory regards the reform of manners as the proper function of comedy. Critics of the period were only too clear about the inability of the Italian comedians to discharge their duty. Saint-Evremond admitted that the comics were inimitable, but declared that 'buffoonery can only divert an honest man for a few moments'[3]. Chappuzeau reported that 'one only goes to see them for pure diversion'[4].

Later critics have taken several positions. The establishment view is that since the Italian comedies cannot be accounted for within the bounds of Boileau's ruling (I like an author that reforms the age,/ And keeps the right decorum of the stage./ That always pleases by just reason's rule;[5]) they need not be accounted for at all. A typical example of this critical posture is a statement found in a rather recent work on theatre audiences in eighteenth-century Paris. 'The only theatre audience is the audience of the *Théâtre-Français*, which finds itself without direct competition (the Italians, the *Opèra-Comique*, the fair theatres are not properly theatre).'[6]

This critical stance was, of course, of no use to those scholars who wished to study the *Comédie-Italienne* in spite of its violation of the norms. Unfortunately many of them have chosen positions which have led to assertions that do not account for the structures and strategies of the genre. For instance, Jules Guillemot, writing in the *Revue contemporaine*, accepted the validity of the neoclassical principles of comedy and solved the resulting dilemma by asserting that the Italians produced 'joyful satire' and corrected manners and morals with seemly neoclassic zeal [7]. This claim led him to classify even the most conventional and scatalogical doctor routines as satire.

Gustave Attinger, whose chapters on the *Comédie-Italienne* have the most carefully reasoned argument I have encountered, fell into still another trap. He did not apply the neoclassical norms, to be sure; rather, he constructed his own normative definition of the Italian *commedia dell' arte* and then demonstrated the deviations of the Italian comedy in France, concluding that it was a sort of messy transition between *commedia* and comic opera[8].

Guillemot asserted that the Italian comedy was something it was not and Attinger regretted that it was not something else. Neither of these stances attracted me.

My principal assumption was that audiences were diverted by the performances of the *Comédie-Italienne*. I looked for the sources of that diversion. My intention was to identify and chart the appeals of the form, describe its structures, and discover its strategies of claiming attention and evoking response. This approach owes much to the theories of Kenneth Burke and other New Rhetoricians who are 'more concerned', as Burke says, 'with *how* effects are produced than with *what effects should be produced*'[9].

The findings of my study form the body of this report. Before I relate those findings, however, I wish to identify the sources which I used and justify the limit which I imposed on my inquiry.

I restricted my curiosity to the period of the career of Domenico Biancolelli, *dit* Dominique, who performed the rôle of Arlequin at the *Comédie-Italienne* from 1660 to 1688. I had two reasons for imposing that restriction. First, Dominique was the principal draw and the rôle of Arlequin came to dominate the productions during his tenure. Second, Dominique's *zibaldone*, or actor's *aide-mémoire*, is in existence.

I had intended, or hoped, to work directly from the Dominique *zibaldone* which describes in great detail his physical and verbal action in seventy-three productions. The primary document available is an holograph manuscript in the hand of Thomas-Simon Gueullette, an amateur of the Italians in the eighteenth century[10]. This manuscript is said to be a translation into French of a document in Biancolelli's own hand which passed to Gueullette on the death of Biancolelli's son, Pierre-François. The Gueullette manuscript is held by the *Bibliothèque de l'Opèra* and has not been edited and published, although many scholars refer to it. I would have used it, but scholarship via overseas post also sets limits.

Fortunately, the Dominique *zibaldone* was the primary source of Claude and François Parfaict's *Histoire de l'ancien théâtre italien*[11]. This work contains thirty-eight production descriptions, most of them slightly revised versions of the Gueullette manuscript. The major revision appears to be a change in voice from first to third person. I have been able to compare only one full example from the two documents; Dominique's *Le Festin de Pierre* has been published in a collection of versions of Don Juan[12]. My judgment, based upon that comparison and the comparison of several fragments as well, is that the differences between Gueullette's version and the Parfaicts' version are not so great as to preclude use of the latter.

Along with the Parfaict volume, I have used material from the Gherardi collection of scenes and scripts written in French by French playwrights for the Italians[13]. I have used only the material which precedes the death of Dominique in 1688. I have looked at and rejected various other possible sources, some useless, some spurious, some unrelated to the period under study[14].

I had some problems using both the Parfaict and the Gherardi.

In spite of a scholarly tendency to refer to Dominique's descriptions as *canevas,* they are nothing of the kind. The entire document is from the point of view of the Arlequin and describes only his scenes. For example, the *Festin de Pierre* begins:

> In the first scene I enter with the King who speaks to me about the debauchery of Don Juan. I say to him: 'you must have patience, Sire. When young men get a little older they change their ways; we must hope that will happen to Don Juan.' The King orders me to tell him some story to amuse him. I take a bench and I sit down beside him; then I tell him the story of Queen Joan.[15]

The Parfaicts changed the point of view and attempted to divide the descriptions into acts in order to give the impression that the full play was being recorded. If this impression stands, one tends to conclude that the Italian comedy was totally without structure and that Arlequin was the undisputed central character of every play.

Fortunately, Gherardi's *Le théâtre italien* corrects any such misimpression. Although many of the early 'plays' in that collection consist merely of the few scenes in French which had been interpolated into the Italian plays, four of the twelve which were first performed in the time of Dominique are relatively complete. Thus, the Gherardi plays give us a good idea of the structure of the Italian comedy and the Dominique *zibaldone* gives us specific, detailed information about the performances.

Of course, the Italian comedies changed over twenty-eight years, and one cannot use the information indiscriminately. Still, in most cases, the Arlequin scenes, especially those dated 1668 to 1674, fit well enough into the structural patterns perceptible in the Gherardi plays of 1682-8.

A brief survey of the evolution of the *Comédie-Italienne* in Paris will help to establish a frame of reference for the remainder of this report. In the beginning — when the Locatelli-Fiorilli troupe began to play in Paris in 1653 — the *commedia dell' arte* was entertainment for an Italianate court. The early productions were Italian in form and language with the traditional love plots and improvised dialogue. The company, as permanently established in 1660, was a conventional *commedia dell' arte* troupe with a Pantalon, a Docteur, a Capitaine, two *amoureux*, two *amoureuse*, a *soubrette* and a first and second *zanni*[16]. Its only eccentricity was Tiberio Fiorilli as Scaramouche, a rôle which defies categorization.

With the death of Mazarin and the diminishing of the Italian influence, the company had to appeal to a wider range of taste.

Around 1668 the entertainments begin to change. *Travesti* plots become common, spectacle and machines become more important, and the *zanni* take focus from the old men and the lovers. In 1680 the troupe took sole possession of the *Hôtel de Bourgogne* after years of sharing various theatres with French companies. It began to experiment with playing in French and in 1684 received official permission to do so over the opposition of the *Théâtre-Francais*. In the next year the Italians began occasionally to perform plays which were largely in French, had been written by a playwright, and were memorized rather than improvised.

The most obvious changes are not necessarily the most material to a study of structure and appeals. The change to French was undoubtedly suggested by the need to increase audiences in order to support a full production schedule at the company's very own theatre. The change to memorization was very likely related to the change to French. I find it improbable that all the members of the company could have improvised with facility in a language other than Italian. Three major actors, in the rôles of Aurelio, Pierrot and Pasquariel, had been in France for less than five years.

The change to French is not, by itself, indicative of any change in structure. Memorization was not a radical departure from the highly formal improvisation of the late seventeenth century. Dominique's *zibaldone* strongly suggests that the performer of the *Comédie-Italienne* went on stage knowing exactly what he was going to do and most of what he was going to say. Increased use of spectacle severely limited any departures from the agreed-upon sequence of scenes.

One result of the changes just discussed — the employment of a playwright — would seem on the surface to be most significant, but even that innovation was less a novelty than might at first appear likely. The plays described by Dominique were also the products of playwrights after 1667; Mario-Antonio Romagnesi, who entered the company in that year, added the duties of resident playwright to his responsibilities as *premier amoureux*: Biancolelli himself, and Lolli, the Docteur, are also named as writers by the Parfaicts. One cannot estimate precisely the extent to which this sort of playwriting meant fully-composed scripts. However, Dominique's descriptions do include some segments of dialogue. The plays were not absolutely fixed; new material was added for new members of the company. However, we have no real proof that the plays of the Gherardi collection *were* fixed. Judging by their structures, they very probably were not.

The change to written plays in French did affect the

performances which became less physical and more verbal; that
development is clear in the Gherardi plays. But so long as such
performers as Biancolelli, Fiorilli and Romagnesi led the company,
the strategies of appeal did not change significantly.

Those strategies developed gradually as the company adapted to
its audiences, capitalized on what was popular and disencumbered
itself of what was not. Instead of the traditional lovers' plot/
zanni's sub-plot, the audience was offered a mélange of magicians,
exotic desert islands, parodies of recent productions at the *Théâtre-
Français* and the Opéra, and — above all — comic love stories of
their old favourite, Arlequin, and their new favourite, Colombine.
The company added more spectacle, more buffoonery, more local
references, and some song and dance. The troupe itself, by 1688,
had changed its composition. It included the Docteur (who had
neither died nor retired), two *amoureux* and two *amoureuse* (one of
each pretty long in the tooth and rarely used), two *soubrettes*, six
zanni, and Scaramouche.

As the entertainments changed, they became less and less like
conventional plays and less and less like *commedia dell' arte* plays.
They became a unique thing, *la comédie-italienne*, in full flight
from the rationalism of Boileau and Saint-Evremond.

I would like to begin my analysis of the Italian comedy with a
detailed summary of the action of one of the nearly-complete plays
from the Gherardi collection. I have chosen to describe *Colombine
avocat pour et contre*[17] because it is the earliest of the four
available (1685), because it is the most complete, offering not only
the French scenes but synopses of the Italian improvised scenes,
and because it is, in my judgment and in Attinger's[18], the most
like the Italian comedies described by Dominique.

Colombine avocat begins with a scene in Italian dialogue
between Isabelle and Cinthio, her lover, in which we discover that
her father is planning to marry her to someone else. Even those
who did not understand Italian could follow the central point of the
scene since the Marquis de Sbrufadelli is mentioned several times.
Sbrufadelli is the patronym which Dominique always used for
Arlequin. Marquis de Sbrufadelli means the Arlequin will be *en
travesti* as a pseudo-nobleman and that his comic routines will be
full of the familiar and popular mockery of the aristocracy and the
commoners who try to imitate their manners.

Scene two introduces Arlequin with Scaramouche as his valet.
We discover that Arlequin is going to desert his fiancée,
Colombine, in order to marry Isabelle and her fat dowry. The scene

is in French. It gives necessary plot information and also cues several comic events to come.

Scene three is a traditional scene of the dressing of Arlequin by three *gagistes* as the tailor, the shoemaker and the hatter. It is partly written, partly improvised. Several similar scenes are recorded by Dominique[19].

Colombine and Pasquariel, *en travesti espagnole*, are introduced in scene four. The scene is written in Italian and establishes that they are looking for Arlequin.

Scene five is between Arlequin and Pasquariel, now speaking a Spanish jargon. The action consists of Pasquariel doing the *rhodomontades* of the Capitaine and Arlequin doing *lazzi* of cowardice. Scene five also sets up scene six, the first of six scenes in which Arlequin encounters Colombine *en travesti*. Colombine speaks Spanish and Arlequin answers as if he understood. The scene ends when Colombine reveals herself and denounces Arlequin who is frightened into a new set of *lazzi*.

Scene seven is a comic routine with Scaramouche and Cinthio as straight man.

Scene eight begins a sequence with a scene in Italian dialogue between Isabelle and the Docteur, her father, in which he insists that she marry Arlequin. In scene nine Isabelle and Arlequin do a traditional routine with Arlequin making a fool of himself at civil conversation. Scene ten introduces Colombine *en travesti* as a maid, applying to Isabelle for employment. Arlequin tries to seduce Colombine who then reveals herself and denounces him again. The scene and the act end with Arlequin, Scaramouche and Pasquariel doing a *lazzi* of the sack.

Act Two, scene one is a solo for Pasquariel, now *en travesti* as a tavern keeper. He explains that he is going to play so many tricks on Arlequin that the latter will die of fright. He then sets up a later episode: 'I know that Arlequin is looking for a mooress to buy for Isabelle. I have warned Colombine to be prepared.'

In scene two Pasquariel sets up Arlequin. Colombine appears in scene three as a Gascon tavern hostess, providing an opportunity for some favourite dialect humour. She once again reveals herself. Scene four is a brief episode in Italian dialogue. The Docteur refuses Cinthio's offer for Isabelle (and Colombine has time to change her costume). Scene five begins the moorish *travesti*, the most extended of all, and also includes a *divertisement*. In scene six Cinthio interrupts and menaces Arlequin. Colombine saves him, but then reveals herself and denounces him as usual.

The next scene, seven, consists entirely of Scaramouche doing his

famous *lazzi* of taking fright. In scene eight Pasquariel tricks
Arlequin with masks of Colombine and the devil which he makes
appear in a mirror and a painting. This scene also includes an
extended routine with Pasquariel as 'the paralytic painter of the
Invalides'.

Scenes nine and ten are improvised, probably in Italian, and
complete the Isabelle-Cinthio plot. Isabelle has discovered
Arlequin's promise of marriage to Colombine and has possession
of the marriage contract he has signed. The Docteur swears to have
Arlequin hanged. Cinthio announces that his uncle is the judge and
that if the Docteur will permit Isabelle to marry him, he will speak
to his uncle about Arlequin. The Docteur agrees.

In scene eleven Pasquariel, who has been eavesdropping, warns
Arlequin that the Docteur has discovered all, but assures him that a
certain professor can save him. Scene twelve is a traditional pedant
routine with Colombine *en travesti* as the professor. The scene ends
with the usual revelation and denunciation.

Act Three begins with Scaramouche disguised as a woman,
afraid that he has been named in the warrant issued for his master.
Arlequin, meeting him, assumes he is a whore. Scaramouche
reveals himself and the two plan to escape. They are caught in scene
two by the Docteur with several officers of the law. Arlequin hides
under Scaramouche's skirt, but gives himself away by talking. In
scene three Pasquariel and Colombine scheme to save Arlequin.

Scene four is an improvised scene in which Pierrot tries to make
love to Scaramouche, still dressed as a woman.

Scene five is a Night Scene with Pasquariel doing the *lazzi* of the
ladder and trying to rescue Arlequin from jail. Scene six is a comic
routine between the Docteur and Pierrot.

Scene seven is the dénouement. Arlequin is brought before the
judge and Colombine accuses him. However, she exits and returns
en travesti as an *avocat*. Her pleading saves him and when she
reveals herself for the last time he agrees that 'heaven has made us
for each other'.

Some facts of the play: it has twenty-nine scenes, five improvised
and twenty-four written out in dialogue. There are three scenes in
Italian, three in mixed French and Italian, three in mixed French
and jargon (Spanish, Gascon and Italian), one in pantomime,
seventeen in French, and two which are not identified by language
but which are probably in Italian because they are part of the
Italianate plot and they are improvised. The play presents no
problems for a French-speaking audience.

I have divided the scenes into four categories: Italianate plot, set-ups, *jeu de travesti de Colombine*, isolated *jeu* of the *zanni*.

'*Jeu*' is a term chosen by Gueullette in translating Dominique and is applied to segments of the theatrical event which appear to be comic routines with complete structures. A *jeu* is not the same thing as a *lazzi*, necessarily, although an extended *lazzi* may make up a *jeu*. A *lazzi* need not have a complete comic structure; a *jeu* must. The notion of the *jeu* is important to my argument; thus, I am going to digress for a moment and cite an example of a *jeu* which contains several *lazzi*:

Arlequin appears at the opening of the scene. He is in a bathtub, waving his arms as if he were swimming, calling for help, saying that he is drowning. Octave assures him that he runs no risk. 'I don't trust what you say,' answers Arlequin, 'for I have often heard of men who are so unlucky they drown in their own spit.' He adds that he is bored and wishes someone would give him a fishing pole so that he could amuse himself fishing for carp. Finally he asks Octave why he is so dressed up. 'It is', says Octave, 'to do you honor and cut a fine figure.' 'But I want to cut a fine figure, too,' replies Arlequin, 'so please show me how.' Octave, after having described several examples of fine manners, adds: 'you have to treat your mistress to some little trinket now and then, a pretty dress or a pearl necklace, or some magnificent bauble for her hair.' 'But,' says Arlequin, 'if I give her all those beautiful things, she'll be cutting the fine figure, not me.' The bath house keeper and his assistants are called to take Monsieur from his bath. They wrap him in a towel and ask him how he found the bath. 'A little damp,' he answers. They put him on the bed and close the curtains. Arlequin leaps to the foot of the bed, calling them traitors and assassins. They ask why he is in such a rage. 'Pigs,' he answers, 'I spend all my money in order to cut a fine figure, and you close the curtains.' Then a brazier and some curling irons are brought and the assistants begin to create his coiffeur. One of them, instead of pinching the curl paper with his iron, pretends to want to pinch an ear. 'Wretch,' cries Arlequin, 'you have burned my ear.' Another assistant comes at him with a hot iron. Arlequin does the *lazzi* of the dwarf; they do the *lazzi* of pulling off the curl papers by force; he cries louder and saves himself from their hands. They run after him, combing him in full flight, and present him with a bottle of scent. He does the *lazzi* of pouring it on their feet. They put powdered chypre on his hair and cover his face with it. Finally, they present him with a basin for washing his hands. He sees a little cake of soap which he puts in his mouth. 'You're joking, Monsieur,' says a bath attendant, 'that's for washing your hands.' 'Oh,' answers Arlequin, 'I thought it was a bit of cheese for my lunch.' The valets take off his dressing gown and dress him as a Baron. Arlequin hears a sudden noise and runs in fright. He falls, fully clothed, into the bathtub.[20]

In English we would call this *jeu* an act or a routine or a turn. It bears no relationship to any other episode in the play and it could be inserted into any other play using Arlequin *en travesti* as a nobleman. A very similar *jeu* occurs in Act 1, scene 3 of *Colombine avocat*.

Analysis of the function of each scene in *Colombine avocat* demonstrates why an understanding of the concept of the *jeu* is essential in comprehending the structure of the piece as a whole. The play contains six brief scenes which embody the Italianate plot. It has five scenes which set up later events. It has seven long scenes of *jeux de travesti de Colombine*, each self-contained but connected by the fact of Colombine's being *en travesti* and by the repetition of Colombine's revelation and Arlequin's increasing terror. Finally, the play has eleven scenes of isolated *jeux de zanni* which have very little connection with either the Italianate plot or the Colombine-Arlequin *jeux*.

A mechanical but quite useful way of determining the principal element of a play is to estimate what takes up the largest share of the always limited time of representation. A nineteenth-century well-made play, for instance, uses vast amounts of time for exposition, point of attack, complication, and dénouement, leading us to the conclusion that plot is the major appeal. A twentieth-century *drame* devotes its time to the exposition and development of character. *Colombine avocat* spends its time of representation on the *jeux*.

The Italianate plot of Isabelle and Cinthio, which would have served as the central structural device in the *commedia dell' arte*, is here reduced to a token. Their story has so little appeal that it ends in Act Two and its resolution is not represented.

The love story of Arlequin and Colombine is also relatively unimportant as plot. Actual plot elements are dealt with quickly; the only significant piece of plot information to be found between the exposition and the dénouement is Colombine's action to save Arlequin from Cinthio in Act Two, scene six. This arouses audience expectation that Colombine will save Arlequin in the end.

Colombine avocat certainly has plots, but since they take up little time of the representation they cannot be held to be very important elements of structure or primary appeals to the audience. I am tempted to quote from the *Goon Show*: 'So much for the tatty plot'[21].

The central structural element of the play, in my opinion, is the repeated *jeu de travesti* of Colombine. We could call this a plot, but to do so would be stretching the term. The *travesti* scenes provide no forward movement and no complication. Five times Colombine tricks Arlequin and frightens him; the sixth time the *jeu* is reversed and she saves him and marries him.

The audience is held not by 'what's going to happen next as a result of what has just happened,' but by 'how are they going to top this?' The *travestis* are chosen for the comic opportunities they provide. Colombine as a Spaniard gives rise to a *jeu* of non-sequitur as Arlequin attempts to converse with her as if he understood Spanish. Colombine as a lady's maid leads to a scene of seduction; Colombine as a Gascon tavern hostess makes a place for dialect humour; Colombine as a Mooress provides opportunities for verbal misunderstandings and ethnic jokes; Colombine as a professor gives occasion for the always-popular parody of learning. The final *travesti* not only brings about the resolution but also gives Colombine the chance to do the *discours*.

This central *jeu de travesti* is supported by several others. Pasquariel appears as a Spanish *capitano*, an innkeeper, a Turkish slaver, and a paralytic painter; Scaramouche disguises himself as a woman; Arlequin is *en travesti* throughout as a marquis.

Travesti is a monumentally useful comic device, especially when played by the masks. The mask or rôle is a series of conventional, carefully established behaviours. The audience member, familiar with the rôle, perceives the comic contrast between disguise and reality. The cowardly Arlequin pretending to be an aristocratic swordsman, the elderly and crotchety Scaramouche dressed as a *fille de joie*, the superb acrobat Pasquariel hobbling in as a paralytic — these are comic because of the inevitability that the rôle will reveal its true characteristics.

Colombine avocat is, then, constructed around the repetition of the Colombine *travestis* and held together by the focal comic device of *travesti*. Still, the play contains several scenes which are not plot scenes and are not part of the *travesti* pattern. How are we to account for Scaramouche's pantomime *lazzi* of taking fright, Pasquariel's Night Scene with the *lazzi* of the ladder, the scene of the dressing of Arlequin, the *lazzi* of the sack, and so forth.

I account for them with the following proposition: the principal appeal of the *comédie italienne* was the performer. The *jeux*, which were not structurally integrated, were star turns — well-known and

eagerly-anticipated routines done by favourite performers. Such
men as Biancolelli and Fiorilli were famous men in the Paris of
their day. Their careers were long and notable, and they were court
and public favourites. When one of these men, or one of the other
special favourites, was announced the audience came to see him do
the expected *jeux*.

In *Colombine avocat* Scaramouche is only minimally integrated.
Fiorilli was nearly eighty and played rarely by 1685. His style,
which was physical rather than verbal, was not easily adapted to the
new *comédie italienne* in French. The audience came to see
Scaramouche with expectations based upon forty-five years of
experience of his *jeux*. No one cared that Scaramouche doing the
lazzi of the sack was not integrated into the structural patterns of
the piece. But if Scaramouche had not done several of the
anticipated *jeux*, the audience would have cared. It would have felt
cheated.

The *jeux* were often determinants of the dramatic structure.
When a featured performer did certain kinds of routines
particularly well, the play had to offer him frequent opportunities
to do them. Biancolelli was a magnificent acrobat before he got fat.
The early plays described in his *zibaldone* offer many chances for
acrobatics and two of them, *Les Quatres Arlequins* and *Les Deux
Arlequins*, have extensive *jeux* based on the contrast between
Arlequin Dominique and his shadow, Arlequin Butord, whose
clumsy imitations drive the real Arlequin into frenzied exhibitions
of leaps and somersaults.

Dominique was apparently also very good at *imbroglio*, a sort of
verbal muddle which occurs when Arlequin means to say one thing
and actually says another. These often appear in scenes of courting,
especially with the *amoureuse*, Eularia. It was worth constructing
the play to include such a scene in order to make a chance for
Arlequin to get off an *imbroglio* like: 'Your cheeks ... used to be as
pink as a freshly-smacked baby's bottom'[22], or 'your teeth are as
white as coral'[23].

No doubt exists in my mind that the performers and their *jeux*
were at the heart of the popularity of the Italians. The next
question, logically, is what were the specific appeals which led to
that popularity?

The *jeu* is principally an opportunity for a performer to exhibit
his physical and verbal skills. By skill I mean more than just
acrobatics or gimmicks like Flautin's ability to mimic several
instruments with his voice. I mean a degree of control of voice and
body which leads to a perfection of action.

Great physical skill is pleasurable in and of itself. The acting teacher, Robert Benedetti, calls this the pleasure of kinetic experience. Speaking of the Asian actor, Benedetti remarks:

> Sad ... that our theatre so rarely provides kinetic and kinesthetic experiences of such potency. Our culture's enormous hunger for such experience is unfortunately satisfied more by Monday Night Football than by the Stage, despite the fact that audiences respond vigorously to any indication that actors are capable of doing more than behaving.[24]

Skill underlies a number of other appeals. First is the appeal of control. Control permits comic response to potentially threatening situations. Skilled performers do not get hurt when they fight or fall from ladders. If there were any danger that they might, the routines would not be funny. Control also permits comedy when apparent clumsiness is based upon absolute proficiency. An example of this occurs in *Les trois Voleurs découverts*:

> Arlequin enters with a sack on his head, looking like a sort of Capuchin monk. Trivelin appears at the window at the agreed-upon signal and asks if he has the sack. 'Yes,' says Arlequin. 'Open it wider,' continues his comrade. 'I can't open it any more,' replies Arlequin. 'Idiot,' says Trivelin to him, 'I'm talking about the sack's mouth, not yours.' Arlequin opens the sack, but he holds the opening to the rear for fear of being bitten. After all these *lazzi* he presents the opening of the sack. Trivelin throws down the packages he has made; each time Arlequin catches one he falls to the ground. Trivelin throws Bologna sausages; Arlequin catches them in his hat and breeches. He sees a baby coming and catches it and puts it in the sack as well.[25]

If there were any doubt that Arlequin would catch the baby the comedy would fail. If Arlequin were to miss a packet or a Bologna sausage after all his pretended difficulty in catching them the comedy would also fail since the opposition of appearance and reality would collapse.

A second appeal based upon skill was the ability of everyone in the company to communicate information physically, even when masked. For nearly twenty-five years these performers played in Italian to a French audience. Would that audience have supported them if the course of events on the stage had been unintelligible? The result of the language barrier was the development of great proficiency in pantomime.

Pantomime has its own appeal; the audience must actively

participate in the event and must interpret the action of the performer. If the pantomime is clear and accurate, the audience will grasp the meaning of the action and derive pleasure from its own accomplishment. Of course, after twenty-five years, some of the pantomime must have been conventional signing. Yet even signing makes an appeal. The initiates who understand it feel superior to the uninitiates who don't (a response which may help to explain the continued support by the Japanese upper class of the Noh play).

The Italians used little pure pantomime; physical action supported and was supported by dialogue. Some notion of the physical action can be reconstructed from the dialogue.

The *jeu* between Arlequin and Trivelin cited above was not conducted in silence, but its comic points could be made by the action even if the dialogue were incomprehensible. Arlequin enters with a sack on his head and gives a signal. Trivelin appears and speaks softly. Arlequin holds up the sack. Trivelin speaks again. Arlequin opens his mouth. Trivelin speaks impatiently. Arlequin answers with his mouth held wide open. Trivelin yells. Arlequin closes his mouth and opens the mouth of the sack. The rest of the *jeu* is comic action.

Some scenes were conducted primarily in pantomime, among them many of the Night Scenes. The gimmick which defined a Night Scene was that the performers behaved as if the stage were dark even though it was brightly lit. The Night Scene was very popular because it gave ample opportunities for *jeux*, including many in which several characters are on stage, each unknown to the others. A good example of a Night Scene with a preponderance of pantomime is to be found in *Les Deux Arlequins*.

He [Arlequin] re-enters after a bit with a ladder which he says he had to borrow from the hangman. Arlequin first does all the turns and *lazzi* of the ladder. Following which he places it against the window of the house, mounts it, and somersaults inside. Darkness causes him to mistake the street door for the door to another room. He comes out and, believing himself to be in a room which he finds extremely large, complains that someone has forgotten to furnish it with chairs. In looking for a way out, he bumps into his ladder. 'Oh, oh,' he says, 'here is my ladder come to look for me in the house.' He does some new turns with the ladder. Trivelin arrives unexpectedly with another ladder; the two valets, without perceiving each other, raise their ladders one against the other and perform different *lazzi* together. Finally Arlequin tries to climb up, but he puts his foot on his comrade's shoulder, is scared, and persuades himself that the hangman has come to take back his ladder. He calls for help, a light is brought, Arlequin recognizes Trivelin, beats him up, and runs away.[26]

Scaramouche was a master of pantomime who played *enfarinée* rather than in mask, thus revealing his eyes and facial expressions. Unfortunately, the available evidence does not permit much reconstruction of the action of Scaramouche since Dominique only described his own and Gherardi published few plays in which Scaramouche appeared.

The performers were not only skilled physically, they were also great verbal comedians doing plays filled with *bon mots*, puns, non-sequiturs, and long verbal routines. Opinion varies on the extent to which the audiences of the 1660's and '70's understood them. Had the majority of the audience been fluent in Italian, however, the pressure to play in French should not have occurred. Also, the verbal comedy shows evidence of adaptation to a French-speaking audience. The plays are full of verbal episodes which gain comic effect from their patterns as well as their meanings.

Patter, monosyllable and jargon are to be found in many of the plays. All of these rely on patterns of sound. A good example of monosyllable is described in *Le Festin de Pierre*. Arlequin, starving as usual, is invited by Don Juan to sit down at the dinner table and tell him all about a pretty young widow:

Arlequin obeys joyfully ... he begins by taking off his hat, which is getting in his way, and putting it on Don Juan's head. Don Juan throws it into a corner of the stage and asks several questions about the young widow. Arlequin, not wanting to lose any time from his food, answers in monosyllables. 'How tall is she?' says Don Juan. 'Short,' answers Arlequin. 'What's her name?' 'Anne.' 'Has she a father and mother?' 'Yes.' 'You say that she loves me?' 'Lots.' 'Where did I see her first?' 'Dancing' ... [27].

Throughout this Arlequin is stuffing food in his mouth as fast as he can. Monosyllable is comic, especially in contrast to Arlequin's usual verbal diarrhoea.

Jargon is often found in the *jeux de travesti*. In the moorish *travesti* of *Colombine avocat* we find several examples, among them the following. Colombine is speaking mostly in Italian with some jargon Turkish.

Colombine: *Mi Patrona chiamara Hallimoroid.*

Arlequin: He has hemorroids?[28]

In *Les trois feints Turcs* Trivelin is a master of jargon Turkish, but Arlequin can only come up with *'got morghen mayer'*[29]. Jargon was such a common device that the word gained usage as a verb. At the end of the scene just mentioned, 'they entered into the Doctor's house, still jargoning'.

An example of patter comes from *Le Chevalier du Soleil*. This is the familiar routine with one character trying to say something and the other continually interrupting. The example was written in French, but is similar to patter scenes described by Dominique. The *Médecin* is Arlequin who has just completed a long tirade making the quick volleys of the patter doubly welcome.

Médecin: [ending his tirade] In short, I make such cruel war on the infirmities of men that when I come across some chronic disease which obstinately resists my treatment, I kill the patient and cure the malady.
Docteur: The cure is admirable.
Médecin: None better.
Docteur: Well, I have given you all the time you wanted for your discourse; now it's my turn to talk.
Médecin: All right.
Docteur: Let's begin with medicine.
Médecin: Willingly
Docteur: Medicine is ...
Médecin: I'm listening.
Docteur: Medicine, I tell you, is ...
Médecin: I'm always willing to learn something new.
Docteur: Will you give me the time to say ...
Médecin: The time is nearly four o'clock.
Docteur: I was saying to you that ...
Médecin: Please, let's control ourselves.
Docteur: Again?
Médecin: Oh, I won't say anything else.[30]

But, of course, he does.

Much of the verbal comedy was undoubtedly lost to the members of the audience who did not know Italian. The puns, the one-liners, the non-sequiturs would all have been impossible. But the structure of the *jeu* was nearly always perceptible through physical action, and the performances were so rich in so many varieties of comedy that the inability of some audience members to follow some verbal sallies was not much of a liability.

So far I have described *jeux* which were designed primarily to exhibit performers' skills. Another group of *jeux* were comic because of subject matter. Certain sorts of human behaviours and conditions were obviously held to be innately funny. Breaking wind was funny; so was defecation. Cripples, freaks, foreigners and men of learning were amusing. The seventeenth century was neither prudish nor compassionate.

The most common of this sort of *jeu* was the extended bathroom joke. Scatology was more popular than obscenity, oddly enough, although perhaps they were united in that omnipresent stage property, the enema syringe, the custard pie of the Italian comedy.

Most of the scholars whose works I have consulted don't care for these 'sordid drolleries', as Attinger calls them[31]. Admittedly, it helps to be eleven years old to fully appreciate them. Much bathroom humour appears in Doctor routines. The grossest one I have encountered comes from *Le Médecin volant*:

> *Arlequin*: ... but I must see the urine of the invalid. Madame, do you know how to make pi-pi? I see perfectly that the illness of Madame comes from an obstruction. Therefore, she must take a little walk, say from here to Lyon.' Eularia re-enters followed by Diamantine, her maid, carrying some urine in a glass and saying that her mistress is worse than ever. Arlequin brings the glass of urine to his nose and says, 'If the meat is as tasty as the broth, I'd like to have a slice.' He then drinks the urine and blows it into Pantalon's face.[32]

Some of the scatalogical *jeux* were very extended. In *Le Collier de perles* Arlequin steals a pearl necklace and swallows it. Retrieving the pearls accounts for most of Act Two and all of Act Three. The enema syringe is brought fully into play.

I suggest that the root of the comic response to this sort of thing is pleasure in another's loss of control. The response was not the prurient giggle of modern times but the hearty laugh of the Greek who found the involuntary functions of the body a perfect scream and adored watching those leather phalluses flip up and down. The enema makes defecation an entirely involuntary function, particularly ludicrous if the victim should be about to use the *chaise-percée* in which Arlequin is hiding. Scatology was so popular at the *Comédie-Italienne* that I believe the reason for the vast number of *travestis en médecin* was that such *jeux* gave the best opportunities for enemas.

Obscenity is scarcer. The plays themselves are not really lewd as far as the available evidence shows. They contain a good many *double-entendres* and some cuckold jokes, but very few *jeux* with purely sexual subject matter. My own opinion is that the written evidence is misleading and that the performances were, indeed, obscene. The iconography gives at least one clue to possible phallic comedy. Several engravings of both Dominique and his successor Evaristo Gherardi show Arlequin in profile with the slapstick held so that its handle, visible across the body, and with a rounded knob on the end, appears in precisely the position of the phallus[33]. Perhaps the slapstick, like the enema syringe, did double duty. It certainly came into play when that other hysterical human habit, breaking wind, took place.

My guess is that the real obscenity was filtered out of the written evidence by Gherardi, who compiled his collection after the ascendency of the great prude, Mme de Maintenon, and by Gueullette and the Parfaicts working over the *zibaldone* of Dominique in the eighteenth century.

Other *jeux* with comic subject matter mocked human distortion; there were *lazzi* of giants and dwarfs, *jeux* of cripples and wounded soldiers. Many of these also exhibited the physical skills of the performers. Still other *jeux* focused on hicks (usually Gascons) and foreigners (often Germans). The Polish joke was alive and well and living in Paris.

The list of types of *jeux* is not endless, I suppose, but it is long. It must be since the *jeu* was what this form of entertainment was all about. The plays did not progress from event to event; they leapt from *jeu* to *jeu*. The exposition signalled not what could be expected to happen to the characters but what *jeux* could be expected to appear on the stage.

The performers, whose skills were so aptly displayed by the *jeux*, were also the source of another set of appeals — the appeals of the rôle. Each performer constructed his own rôle, partly from tradition and partly from his own abilities and in response to the tastes of his particular audience. By and large the performer retained his rôle throughout his career and the rôle retained its characteristics. The result of this condition was the establishment of what Kenneth Burke calls a conventional form, the appeal of form as form[34]. This appeal is based upon categorical expectancy; anticipation is anterior to experience.

The rôle is not dramatic character but a form. It consists of a set of behaviours demonstrating fixed responses to stimulae. The form of Dominique's Arlequin was as invariable as the form of an Italian sonnet or James Bond thriller.

Arlequin-Dominique was a coward, a glutton and a *naïf*. If he was threatened he hid or ran; if food was available he stuffed himself; if the misperception of reality was possible he misperceived it. The audience, after twenty-eight years of experience of the rôle, anticipated everything. It could instantly predict Arlequin's behaviour in any situation and, perhaps most appealing, it was always ahead of him.

Arlequin's *naïveté* was his dominant characteristic. It went beyond the dictionary definition of simpleness and artlessness. Arlequin was unable to perceive reality accurately, especially cause and effect both in action and in language. The following *jeu de naïveté* shows why Arlequin's schemes always fail. He is unable to perceive and correct the logical fallacies in his behaviour.

Arlequin enters in the first scene. He has a sword and a leather collar and says that he is returning from the army where he served at Porto Longone. He ends a scene of fantasy saying that he hasn't a sou and that he is resolved to ask charity from the passers-by. Cinthio happens by. Arlequin raises his hat and says: 'Sir, how about a little donation for a poor mute who is deprived of the use of speech.' Cinthio answers, smiling: 'Are you the mute, my friend?' 'Yes, sir,' continues Arlequin. 'But how can you be mute,' replies Cinthio, 'when you have just answered my question?' 'Sir,' answers Arlequin, 'if I hadn't answered your question you would have thought me very badly brought up.' ... Arlequin then realizes his blunder and adds: 'You are right, sir, I made a mistake. I meant to say that I am deaf.' 'Deaf,' answers Cinthio. 'Nonsense!' 'Oh, I assure you, sir,' answers Arlequin, 'I can't even hear the⁻noise of a cannon.' 'But you can hear me,' answers Cinthio, 'when I speak to you. Could you hear if someone called to you and offered you some money?' 'Oh, yes sir,' answers Arlequin. Cinthio's laughter makes Arlequin aware of his stupidity and he excuses himself by saying: 'Ah, sir, I don't know what I'm saying; I am so lightheaded from lack of food. I meant to say to you that I am blind; a cannon shot in the Italian war carried off both my eyes.' Cinthio, wanting to unmask this scoundrel, pokes his fingers at Arlequin's eyes, but Arlequin backs away and fends him off. 'You can see everything,' says Cinthio. 'You lie like a pig.' 'Pardon me, sir,' answers Arlequin, 'I am usually blind, but whenever someone tries to hurt me I can see.' Cinthio laughs again. 'Oh, sir,' continues Arlequin, 'I swear I don't know what I'm saying. I wanted to tell you that I am crippled in the arm and the leg.' Cinthio, going through with it to the end, backs away from Arlequin doing the *lazzi* of offering money. Arlequin reaches out his hand and runs after Cinthio. Cinthio returns and gives Arlequin a kick saying: 'You are a fraud!' 'Yes, sir,' says Arlequin, 'you're absolutely right. That's jusf what I wanted to say to you, but I couldn't think of the word. I am a fraud. I am a poor soldier who has just returned from Porto Longone ...'[35]

The appeals of the rôle are quite clear in this *jeu*. Audience anticipation is anterior to the event throughout. Everyone knows from the moment that Arlequin announces he is mute that he will continue to imbroil himself in ridiculous statements which are observably untrue. The audience also anticipates that the *jeu* will be cleverly developed and concluded with a good kicker. One of the disadvantages of conventional form is that the audience has a clear set of critical criteria based upon long experience.

The appeals of conventional form are more complex than one example can demonstrate, but the basic principle holds throughout all the variations. Expectations are anterior to the event and based upon learning or previous experience. That anyone studied the *comédie italienne* is unlikely; the reliance on conventional form in this case indicates an audience of some constancy. The expectations are fulfilled. On those occasions when a rôle appears to be violating a fixed characteristic, one can be certain that as the *jeu* develops the anticipated behaviour will eventually occur.

Granted that most dramatic form involves the audience in a gradually increasing ability to anticipate character behaviour, usually that ability is based upon the experience of the event itself. The advantage of the rôle is that no time need be spent providing the audience with the information needed to predict behaviour. The Italian comedy is absolutely without character exposition. Like most highly conventional forms, it is also relatively unintelligible to the uninitiated.

Familiarity does not breed contempt as far as popular entertainment is concerned. Familiarity breeds a pleasurable ability to predict and a relaxed assurance that favourite events are going to occur sooner or later. When the set-up begins, the audience leans forward in happy anticipation. It knows what's coming and, thanks to the skill of the performers, it knows that the routine is going to be just as funny as it was the last time. The situation is precisely that which obtained with the old Jack Benny radio programmes; at some point in each programme we heard the *jeu* of the Maxwell car or the *jeu* of the underground bank vault. These *jeux* were inextricably tied to the rôle of Jack Benny and if they did not occur, we were disappointed.

Another way to define rôle is that a rôle is a clown persona.

Thus, part of the appeal of the rôle is the appeal of the clown. My contention that the performers of the *Comédie-Italienne* were clowns is based upon the extensive appearance in the evidence of one principal form of clowning which I am going to call bully-patsy. The tradition of the first and second *zanni* is a bully-patsy tradition. First *zanni* is a clever, lazy bully; second *zanni* is a dumb but willing patsy. First *zanni* thinks up illegal and immoral things for second *zanni* to do. Second *zanni* gets into horrible trouble but (and this is a key appeal) in the end first *zanni* is left holding the bag. The pattern is like a symbolic daydream arising from human dominance games. The little guy comes out all right in the end, and the big bully gets put in his place. It is all very reassuring. In the Trivelin-Arlequin *jeu de volant* which I cited above, one might expect that Arlequin, who is catching the stolen merchandise, will be the one who is caught, but in fact Trivelin gets greedy and grabs the sack away so he is the one to be arrested.

First zanni was not the only bully of the *commedia dell' arte.* Pantalon and Capitaine were also bullies and losers. The bully-patsy tradition continued even though the company was without a first *zanni* of sufficient skill to play with Dominique from the death of Locatelli in 1671 to the arrival of Constantini (Mezzetin) in 1682. The plays of that period lack traditional first and second *zanni jeux*, but Arlequin remains the patsy, everybody's patsy.

Dominique had no choice but to create an Arlequin who was a patsy since Locatelli as Trivelin, a first *zanni*, preceded him in the company. But Arlequin could be a bully. This duality was very apparent in the performances of the Italians since Trivelin actually was an Arlequin, flat cap, black mask, patches, *batte* and all.

This adds an interesting complexity to the patsy-bully clowning of the two *zanni*. On several occasions the potential duality of Arlequin formed the basis of a *jeu*, as in the following scene from *Les Deux Arlequins.* Trivelin is the Balourd.

In the third act Arlequin appears on the stage with a bottle in his hand. He perceives Arlequin Balourd who holds a bottle just like it. He runs; the Balourd follows him. He raises the bottle; the other does the same. Arlequin, astonished, thinks he is seeing his shadow. 'I am going to make him break that bottle,' he says aside. He turns a somersault holding his bottle in his hand. The Balourd puts his down and does the somersault clumsily. Arlequin, still trying to make the other break his bottle, executes several perilous leaps; the Balourd imitates him, heavily. Finally Arlequin gives the other a blow on the back with his bat; the

Balourd returns one to Arlequin's stomach. 'Ohime,' cries
Arlequin. 'I am dead.' ... The true Arlequin, tired of this
badinage, says to the other: 'Stop mocking me or I'll clip you
one.' The Balourd repeats the same words and, adding action to
the threat, gives him a slap. 'Here's a rogue who's a man of his
word,' says Arlequin and begins to cry. 'You're not Arlequin,'
he continues, 'you're too bold. You must be the Devil.' 'Yes, I'm
the Devil,' answers the other. Arlequin, extremely frightened,
runs to Diamantine's door and pounds on it. The Balourd, who
is hidden behind him, takes Diamantine's hand when she appears
and goes into the house with her, making the sign of the horns.
'Ohime,' cries Arlequin, 'the Devil has cuckolded me.'[36]

When Arlequin tries to bully, Trivelin turns the tables on him with
that classical torment, exact mimicry of everything the victim says
or does. The evidence does not, in this case, tell us if Arlequin
eventually triumphs and reaps the just reward of the patsy.
Normally he does even if his reward is only escaping his due
punishment for some idiotic *fourberie*.

The appeal of bully-patsy is only one of clowning's many
appeals. Clowns display rôles rather than impersonate characters;
they are free to comment on the behaviour of their rôles. This
performer-persona relationship has a distancing effect. The
performer stands between the audience and the action giving the
audience permission to laugh at the extravagances of human
behaviour being displayed. The comic take is probably the most
important device by which the clown grants this permission. It
seems to say: 'You and I would never do anything as dumb as that.'
The audience remains relaxed, never asked to perceive its own
behaviour as consubstantial to the action of the rôle. Rather, it
shares judgmental status with the performer. When a behaviour
was mocked within an Italian comedy the intent was not corrective.

Clowning has still other advantages besides its distancing effect.
Clown personae inhabit the ideal moral universe as envisioned by a
child, a world of 'serves him right' and 'me first'. The most
grotesque and eccentric behaviour is permissible because clowns
only display human behaviour, they do not represent it. The hero is
the *zanni*-patsy who observes none of the restrictions society
enforces on human beings. He defecates in public, passes wind,
gobbles his food and yells for more, bashes everyone in sight with
his noisy slapstick when he's feeling brave but runs away in tears
from bigger people, loud noises, and ghosts. He pretends to be all
sorts of wonderful things he isn't — marquises, barons, princes,
even the Emperor of the Moon. He laughs at the halt and the blind.

He has marvellous ideas for playing all sorts of wicked tricks on other people and though he always gets caught he never gets punished. The people who pick on him always get into trouble.

Perhaps the best way to account for the appeal of Dominique's Arlequin-Clown to that predominantly male audience of the seventeenth century is to suggest that he was the memory of a lost paradise, the world-as-it-ought-to-be of any small boy.

This discussion of two of the principal sets of appeals of the Italian comedy — the appeals of the *jeux* and the appeals of the rôle — does not account for the many other appeals which the Italian comedians provided for their audiences. Limits of time and space make a full charting impossible. My study, although not exhaustive, has led me to certain conclusions.

First, the *comédie italienne* was a form of popular theatre. Its function was to divert, relax and reassure its audience. Its appeals were centred in the performer, his skill, his rôle, and his status as a clown. Its structures were conventional, from the structure of the one-liner to the full articulation of the play. The principal structural device, the *jeu*, achieved that status because it best suited the exhibition of the performer. The Italian comedy offered no surprises but faithfully kept its promises. Like most forms of popular theatre it changed as audience tastes changed. If the audience wanted Dominique, it got Dominique. If it wanted French, it got French. If it wanted spectacle, and the *Théâtre-Français* was offering too many *chambres à quatres portes*, the Italians were only too happy to specialize in spectacle.

The basic appeals, however, did not change. They were constant throughout the twenty-eight years I have studied, and I am tempted to suggest that they may be constant throughout the history of popular comedy.

Popular theatre is not an easy, trivial or inferior form of the literary theatre. It is a thing in itself and should be studied as such. Critical methodologies based on theories designed to account for the literary theatre will not make the popular theatre accessible to us. Popular theatre of the seventeeth century in France was not a thing of plot, character, thought and language. Decorum and verisimilitude, the Siamese twins of neoclassicism, had nothing to do with it.

The popular theatrical entertainment is an event designed to divert, offering highly-skilled performers the opportunity to display themselves. It elicits a high degree of audience involvement because its structural strategies depend upon a high degree of anterior expectancy. It is difficult to reconstruct and account for.

The process of doing so is easier if we cut loose from prescriptive theory. There exists a portrait which Duchartre identifies as Dominique, although the subject of the portrait is clearly costumed as a Docteur. Oreglia identifies him as Giuseppe Biancolelli[37]. Whoever he is, what we see is a big, fat man with a little, cynical smile on his face. He is clearly giving us the finger. May his spirit prevail among those who study the popular theatre.

Glossary

amoureuse: female lover.

amoureux: male lover.

ancien théâtre italien: the old Italian company as opposed to the *nouveau théâtre italien*, a troupe led by Luigi Riccoboni, which was invited to establish itself in Paris in 1716.

balourd: numskull, dunce.

batte: a slapstick.

canevas: *sogetto* or scenario, outline of the action.

Capitaine: a braggart soldier; a mask.

chaise-percée: close stool or commode.

chambre à quatres portes: conventional scenery for neoclassical comedy in the seventeenth century.

Comédie-Italienne: the Italian Theatre in Paris.

comédie italienne: the genre of Italian comedy.

commedia dell'arte: literally, the professional theatre. A form which originated in Italy in the sixteenth century. Best known for its use of masks, continuing characters, and improvisation.

discours: long set speech with rhetorical and stylistic flourishes.

dit: under the name of, known as.

divertisement: interlude with music and dance.

Docteur: a pedantic old man, usually a lawyer in France; a mask.

drame: a serious play.

enfarinée: in white face: from *farine*, flour.

fille de joie: prostitute.

fourberie: piece of trickery, deceit.

gagiste: minor comic; hireling not sharer.

Hôtel de Bourgogne: Parisian theatre built in 1548 and used by various companies until 1783.

jeu: a discrete comic unit with a complete structure — a beginning, middle and end. A routine or turn.

lazzi: verbal or physical comic bit.
médecin: physician.
Opèra-Comique: The Comic Opera.
Pantalon: an irascible old man; a mask.
parterre: the pit.
premier amoureux: more important of the two actors playing male lovers.
rhodomontades: vainglorious brags or boasts, as rodomontade.
rôle: usually a dramatic character. In this study the term refers to a continuing character played by an actor throughout his career.
soubrette: female servant; love interest for *zanni*.
Théâtre-Français: the company usually known today as the Comédie-Française.
travesti: disguise, also implying parody or burlesque.
zanni: lead comic; a mask.
zibaldone: record of his performances kept by an improvisatory actor for his own use.

Notes

1 J.N. DuTralage, *Nôtes et documents sur l'histoire des théâtres du Paris au xvii*^e *siècle* (Paris, 1880), 62.

2 John Laurence Carr, *Life in France Under Louis XIV* (New York, Capricorn Books, 1966), 142.

3 Charles de Saint-Evremond, 'De la comédie italienne', *Oeuvres* (Amsterdam, 1739), III, 268-9.

4 Samuel Chappuzeau, *Le théâtre français* ... (Paris, 1674), t. I, ch. xxi.

5 Nicolas Boileau-Despréaux, *The Art of Poetry*, trans. Sir William Soames in Barrett H. Clark, *European Theories of the Drama* (New York, Crown Publishers, 1947), 162.

6 Maurice Descotes, *Le Public du théâtre et son histoire* (Paris, 1964), 7.

7 Jules Guillemot, 'La comédie dans la vaudeville: le théâtre italien', *Revue Contemporaine*, 2nd series, 51 (May 1866), 92-119.

8 Gustave Attinger, *L'esprit de la commedia dell' arte dans le théâtre français* (Neuchatel, 1950), 167-212.

9 Kenneth Burke, 'Lexicon Rhetoricae', *Counter-Statement* (Los Altos, Calif., Hermes Publications, 1953), 123.

10   Thomas-Simon Gueullette, *Traduction du scénario de Joseph Dominique Biancolelli* ..., Bibliothèque de l'Opèra, Rés. 625 (1-2). The manuscript has been microfilmed and is available from the Service Photographique of the Bibliothèque Nationale.

11   François and Claude Parfaict, *L'histoire de l'ancien théâtre italien depuis son origine en france jusqu'à sa suppression en l'année 1697* (Paris, 1753).

12   G. Gendarme de Bévotte, *Le Festin de pierre avant Molière* (Paris, 1907), 335-53.

13   Evaristo Gherardi, *Le théâtre italien* (Paris, 1700).

14   As, for instance: [Cotolendi], *Arliquiniana* (Paris, 1694); Angelo Constantini, *The Birth, Life and Death of Scaramouche*, trans. Cyril W. Beaumont (London, 1924). Both of these are highly suspect.

15   Gendarme de Bévotte, 339-40.

16   Information about the first appearances of individual performers and the composition of the company at various points in time is taken from the Parfaicts, 1-130. This information was compiled by T.-S. Gueullette and published by the Parfaicts as a refutation of Du Gerard's *Tables alphabétique et chronologique des piéces représentées sur l'ancien théâtre italien* ... (Paris, 1750).

17   Monsieur D*** [Nolant de Fatouville], *Colombine avocat pour et contre*, in Gherardi, I, 327-420.

18   Attinger, 192.

19   See esp. *Le Baron de Fœneste*, Parfaict, 422-4.

20   *Ibid.*

21   Spike Milligan, 'The House of Teeth', *The Goon Show Scripts* (New York, 1972), 185.

22   Monsieur D*** [Nolant de Fatouville], *La Matrône d'Ephèse*, Gherardi, I, 22.

23   *Le Baron de Fœneste*, Parfaict, 433.

24   Robert L. Benedetti, 'What we Need to Learn from the Asian Actor', *ETJ* (December 1973), 463-7.

25   Parfaict, 165.

26   *Ibid.*, 244-5.

27   *Ibid.*, 276-7.

28   Gherardi, I, 372.

29   Parfaict, 229.

30   Monsieur D*** [Nolant de Fatouville], *Arlequin Chevalier du Soleil*, Gherardi, I, 264-5.

31   Attinger, 188.

32 Parfaict, 220.
33 See Pierre Louis Duchartre, *The Italian Comedy* (New York,
    Dover, 1966, rpt. of London: Harrap, 1929): engravings of
    Biancolelli, 130, Locatelli, 158, Gherardi, 104 and 106-7. See
    also Giacomo Oreglia, *The Commedia dell' Arte*, trans.
    Lovett F. Edwards (New York, Hill & Wang Drama Books,
    1968): sixteenth-century engraving, p.13, but note revised
    carriage of the *batte* in an eighteenth-century lithograph,
    pp.46-7.
34 Burke, 126-7 and 204-12.
35 Parfaict, *La Fille desobéissante*, 145-7.
36 Parfaict, 242-3.
37 Duchartre, 153; Oreglia, 88.

ROBERT L. ERENSTEIN

Satire and the
Commedia dell'Arte

No one can study the *commedia dell'arte* for long without encountering the word satire. Many scholars apparently find the two notions related. Constant Mic, equating caricature with satire, says that Italian *commedia dell'arte* actors would habitually introduce into their performances unmistakable satirical allusions to real-life situations, persons or issues[1]. In his quest for the origins of the *commedia dell'arte* Toschi points out — among other things — the influence of medieval carnival satire on the new genre[2], while Kindermann holds that quite soon after the rise of the *commedia dell'arte* the prevailing interest in satire gave way to the art of pure acting skill[3]. Clearly opposed views on this point are held by Allardyce Nicoll[4] and A.K. Dshiwelegow[5]. The latter sees the *commedia dell'arte* as concerned solely with socio-critical satire whereas the former writes that the true *commedia dell'arte* 'shows not the slightest trace of social satire' and, further, that the *commedia dell'arte* masks, 'confessedly taken from actuality, were selected for their comic potentialities and not with any social-political objective'. These examples, which could be multiplied at will, will suffice to show what dire confusion prevails with respect to the notions of *commedia dell'arte* and, particularly, satire. Hence the welter of conflicting opinions sketched above.

In the past three or four decades there have been a number of studies which attempt to describe and explicate the phenomenon 'satire'[6]. With the results obtained so far it ought to be possible to arrive at a well-defined notion of satire which will provide the theatre student with a suitable tool and help reduce drastically these misunderstandings. However, the scope of these studies is generally restricted to satire in literature, i.e. to satire in written texts regarded as finished structures. In drama, on the other hand, the written text is merely a component in the genesis of an artistic production which achieves its ultimate completion in performance. True, some of these studies also deal with examples of satire taken from dramatic writings, but they do so without going into the problem of how this satire works in performance and without suggesting the conditions that must be fulfilled if the satire is to get across as such to the audience. So far scant attention has been paid to the question of what is added to, or taken away from, the satiric content of a dramatic text by all those who contribute to the actual stage presentation for which the dramatist is presumed to have written his play. It is quite conceivable, for instance, that an overly droll production of a piece written in a satirical vein will work havoc with the original intentions of its author. The different manifestations of satire in various literary forms go to show that satire is not bound up with any particular art form but is determined by the author's intentions. As far as the staging of a satiric play is concerned we must add: and by the intentions of director and actors as well.

These studies agree that the satirist's intention is to hold up to ridicule, to expose or criticize certain individuals, prevalent beliefs, ideological fashions, topical events or situations. The devices used are mockery, irony, exaggeration. The tone may vary from light-hearted and cheerful to bitter and cynical, but there is invariably an element of Horace's *ridens dicere verum*. For satire to be effective, its target must be identifiable and familiar to the reading public or audience. This implies that a satirist writes primarily for his contemporaries, that he directs the shafts of his criticism at the here and now. A satiric text is intended for immediate consumption, and actors may join in the satirical attack through their style of acting, costumes, make-up or mime. The topical nature of the undertaking, the concern with actual events and current fashions, tends to make satiric plays a kind of instant drama which will rarely survive the fleeting day. If highly talented dramatists have occasionally written satiric plays that have remained popular and held the stage to this day, their survival is due not so much to their being satires as to the total dramatic impact of the plays. Since the intervening centuries have seen shifts in what are regarded as legitimate targets of satire, present-day audiences will be aware only of a form of satire from the past. In performance, the satirical element of such plays assumes a much milder aspect so that it becomes almost akin to parody, the distinction between parody and satire being that a parody ridicules, but does not denounce, certain individuals, situations or events.

It is entirely possible, however, that a modern director will adapt an old satiric drama to present-day conditions and bring both setting and *mise en scène* up to date, thereby revitalizing the satire. Even when in the past more universal human follies and foibles were being satirized, dramatists would give their critical onslaught a form and context recognizable to their contemporaries, but here later ages will find more to recognize and chuckle over. Every period has its *nouveaux riches*; all the same, a number of scenes in Molière's *Le bourgeois gentilhomme* will strike a modern audience as comedy or parody rather than as satire. To a later age a satiric scene becomes comic if it no longer retains its original relation to historical reality. Directors and actors have been apt to hasten this process by exploiting the comic aspects of such scenes to the hilt. A good example is the fencing-master scene in Molière's play.

Criticism implies an underlying system of standards and values on which an author (or actor) bases his criticism. Inevitably, it seems to me, an author will in his criticism react to actuality from the perspective of an ideal world which he has projected for himself and from which he derives his standards. A satirist may be aware to a greater or less extent of this ideal projection, but even when the process is largely unconscious, the satire derives its being from the tension existing between the ideal projection and its reflection in actuality.

This tension must therefore be present also in the performance of a satiric drama, at least if the director and actors are intent on putting the satire across in a recognizable manner. This means that in staging a satiric play they will be guided by their own ideal projection, which may correspond in greater or less degree with the author's. Unlike the author, they must always be aware of this tension between ideal and reality in order to control its effect in the performance. Another condition that must be fulfilled if the satire is to be recognizable to audiences is that it must influence the main action or at least be linked to it through a subplot, thus assuming a readily ascertainable function within the entire performance. It is only then that the criticism derived from a conscious or unconscious set of standards underlying the author's work will become visible. Again, it is only then that the actor's attempt to stimulate the audience to adopt a critical attitude towards the target of their criticism, or more fundamentally, to make the audience change their scale of values, will stand any chance of success. If the satire is confined to an isolated crack, without contributing to the developing structure of the play or without being in some other way related to it, the possible satiric effect dies with the laughter which the witty crack provokes. It is then no more than a hilarious moment without any consequences, insufficiently revealing the author's or actor's intentions. Its effect is much the same as that of a joke made by a politically uncommitted entertainer at the expense of, say, a well-known politician who has launched a widely unpopular measure. Cashing in on the widespread resentment against the measure, the entertainer will use this mood to draw a laugh. All he wants is to get this laugh; his aim is not to induce his audience to adopt critical attitudes towards the politician or his proposed measure. On the strength of the above considerations I now arrive at the following definition of satiric drama in performance:

Drawing on a well-defined frame of reference based on an explicit or implicit set of values underlying the text, a satiric performance ridicules and criticizes by means of mockery, irony or exaggeration certain individuals, prevalent beliefs, ideological fashions, topical events and situations or human vices, familiar and recognizable to the audience.

As the outcome of these reflections, I now propose to examine the satiric dimension of the *commedia dell'arte* in the period from 1560 to 1640.

The rise and growth of the *commedia dell'arte* saw the birth of the first professional troupes and simultaneously the first woman took the world stage as an actress. But it also ushered in actors' theatre. This means that, in examining the satiric dimensions of the *commedia dell'arte*, we shall — because of the absence of authors — be concerned solely with the intentions of the actors.

With the aid of the material that has come down to us, and taking into account the conditions under which the performances took place, we must try to form a picture of these performances and of their effect on the audiences of the time.

The rise and growth of the *commedia dell'arte* took place in a country torn by civil strife and largely occupied by Spain; after the Council of Trent the Church of Rome had launched a counter-offensive against the Reformation and, mainly under the auspices of the Jesuits, sought to get a firmer hold on the faithful. In a country undergoing such upheavals and a prey to chaos and lawlessness, overt criticism was tantamount to suicide. Anyone intent on voicing dissent and criticism was forced to do so in covert terms. The times seemed ripe for a genre like satire. But a troupe putting on satiric plays must of necessity address itself to a particular section of the public susceptible to, and appreciative of, such critical attitudes on the part of the actors.

However, there is nothing to show that the *commedia dell'arte* troupes did in fact address themselves to any particular section of the public. They drew their audiences from every stratum of society. Plays were acted in the open air or indoors for the common people, at the courts of Italy and France, but also before Spanish audiences in North and South Italy, as well as before liberal cardinals in Rome. Actors enjoyed no social security at all, and as professionals they were dependent on the favour of this widely varying public. Although improvisations by standard characters on certain set themes or *scenarii* remained their speciality and formed the nucleus of their repertoire, the same actors would appear at court in completely different plays such as tragedies, pastorals and *intermezzi*. Patronage was an all-important factor in those days. The numerous letters from actors' companies to princes, requesting permission to come and play at court or invoking their gracious protection, seem to bear out the supposition that courts provided the main source of income. Besides, the strolling companies needed royal protection from the incessant attacks by the clergy, to whom, as Barbieri wrote in *La Supplica*, actors (*istrioni*) were synonymous with witches (*stregoni*), and who saw the theatre as the favourite haunt of the devil[7]. Still, the fierce ecclesiastical onslaughts on professional actors were never organized or inspired by Rome and were confined to incidental harassment, though never so incidental that professional actors could afford to disregard them.

Their dependence on courts, where generous patrons could be found, the constant denunciations and harassment by ecclesiastics and the broad spectrum of audiences made it impossible for *commedia dell'arte* actors to indulge in anything like revolutionary or anti-establishment sentiments. Their struggle for life and the constant battle they had to wage to win recognition for their profession demanded so much effort that they could not at the same time set out deliberately to effect changes in public attitudes and awareness, not even — at least until the publication of Barbieri's *La Supplica* in 1628 — where the standing of their own profession as a form of art was concerned.

As regards their repertoire, few complete texts have come down to us. Of their *commedia all'improvviso* all we have is *scenarii, lazzi*, illustrative material and spectators' comments. Of the other genres we know a number of plays, such as Isabella Andreini's pastoral, *Mirtilla*, the tragedies and tragicomedies by her son G.B. Andreini and the comedies of Niccolò Barbieri. Of the plays by non-actors which they performed, we know for instance Tasso's *Aminta*, which the Gelosi presented in 1573, having rehearsed for two months under Tasso himself. All these were plays without a trace of satire; they were included in the repertoire simply because there was a demand for plays of this kind among courtiers.

For their improvised performances we must make do with the meagre material that has survived. The *scenarii* set out timeless plots involving young men in love, who are thwarted by their parents and sometimes even have to contend with their own fathers as rivals in love. Their entanglements are unnecessarily complicated by a stupid *zanni* and subsequently solved by a clever *zanni*.

The *scenarii* contain no indications of conscious attempts at satire. But this does not of course rule out the possibility that the actors introduced satire into their improvizations as an integral part of the performance. If they did, we might expect to find traces of satire in the *lazzi*, or in preserved dialogues or monologues by characters like the *innamorati*, the Capitano, Pantalone and Zanni or Pantalone and the Dottore. But again we find no trace of satire. The *lazzi* are comic *intermezzi* which bear no relation to the context. That they were purely comic is confirmed by the fact that the most frequently found *lazzi* are those of fear, alarm, greed and gluttony. Even Isabella Andreini's elaborate literary lovers' dialogues on a variety of themes, published posthumously in 1618, contain no satire. They are no more than virtuoso demonstrations of her mastery of the language and of witty variations on *concetti*.

Nor did the masks, the *tipi fissi*, of the *commedia dell'arte* lend themselves readily to satire. They were abstractions from certain character types, with a single trait developed to grotesque proportions. The mask became the symbol of one prevailing passion and compelled the actor to act out that passion. At the same time each mask made a well-defined contribution to the plot line through its own highly specific and personal resources, visual as well as verbal. The *scenarii* show that comic possibilities were exploited to the hilt in a number of often ludicrous and highly unrealistic situations. Within such a framework a satirically intended remark would fail to produce the desired effect, since it had no function within the totality of the performance.

Another indication that satire in any guise or form was lacking in the *commedia dell'arte* can be found in the denunciations by the clergy of these performances *all'improvviso*. The charge was invariably corruption of morals, never the propagation of ideas regarded as a threat to the established order. In the face of attacks by the clergy the actors maintained that the avowed object was precisely to promote morality. They emphasized their beneficial influence, pointing out that their performances kept people off the streets where they would gamble, drink, whore and otherwise be tempted to leave the straight and narrow. Pier Maria Cecchini even claimed that wherever they gave night performances he had always heard the courtesans curse the actors and their plays, because they were losing customers[8]. This warrants the supposition that what the Church as the guardian of morality objected to was the manner in which such recognized taboo subjects as marriage, woman's honour and sex were mocked.

And yet the *capitano* mask could have provided the *commedia dell'arte* with a splendid opportunity to inject satire into its performances by ridiculing the Spanish usurpers, perhaps even encouraging resistance against the foreign tyrants. But the *capitano* does not go beyond the occasional adoption of a Spanish name like Mattamoros and knows but one passion: bragging about his utterly fantastic exploits. Either these *capitani* cherished their lives too much to indulge in any criticism of the Spanish regime or there was simply no room for this kind of satire in the *commedia dell'arte*.

All these findings suggest that *commedia dell'arte* performances were in the nature of rollicking farce much more than of comedy — satiric or otherwise. Their entertainment value lay in the appeal they made to lower instincts in their scoffing at established taboos.

This type of drama is devoid of topical interest; it is not restricted to any particular time or place and can without any form of adjustment be played in Mantua, Milan or Paris. This also accounts for the lack of development in *scenarii* or *lazzi* which, because they were not bound to any one place or time — and therefore never adapted to local conditions — could be played over and over again. The important thing was not what was acted but only the manner of acting. This same bias we also observe in critical notices, where it is always the individual acting that counts, never the play itself. With emphasis laid squarely on individual roles and the partial elements of the play, these performances tended to uphold existing structures rather than to question accepted standards. The Italian *commedia dell'arte* performance is therefore best defined as an improvised farce played by actors who for their bread and butter were prepared to act anything else required of them, depending on the fashion of the time. Critical attitudes towards the world around them are altogether absent and this critical stance is precisely a necessary condition for satire.

How then was it that the *commedia dell'arte* farce became satire: how did the verbal joke turn into a verbal weapon? For this change to take place, the *commedia dell'arte* had to be shorn of an essential characteristic, and this happened not in Italy but in France, where the Italian way of life and world of ideas were juxtaposed to the French. The influence of the *commedia dell'arte* on French comedy is unmistakeable, and Molière's indebtedness to the Italians is common knowledge. But all these impulses from the *commedia dell'arte* were harmoniously integrated within a specifically French tradition of comedy reflecting the French national character.

As long as the Italian *commedia dell'arte* troupes paid only brief visits to France, they were able to uphold their own tradition. Always on the move and always playing to fresh audiences, they found their own Italian repertoire entirely adequate, and tended more than ever to emphasize visual and mimic aspects in order to overcome the language barrier.

Things changed, however, when in 1660 the *Ancienne troupe de la Comédie Italienne* settled permanently in Paris. Under the influence of French taste the masks changed to conform more closely to the French way of life. This was manifested, for instance, in the servants' parts. Thanks to the individual talent of Domenico Biancolelli — both as manager of the troupe and as actor — Arlecchino achieved a successful transformation into Harlequin and won a place for himself in the Paris theatre. New masks, such as Colombine, Pierrot or Mezzetin, were created or evolved in conformity with French taste, while Scaramouche, introduced by Tiberio Fiorillo about 1640, became so popular that he completely ousted the Capitano from public favour.

In its early years the *Comédie Italienne* continued to be entirely Italian. Its emphasis was on verbal and mimic jokes, and the miming of plot elements became a regular part of the endeavour to put the story across. These attempts to achieve maximum audience understanding led to the inclusion of French texts within Italian performances. At first this practice would be restricted to one or just a few scenes, but once there was this break-through, French authors eagerly started writing plays for the Italian actors. This repertoire, acted between 1682 and 1697, is well represented in Gherardi's edition of the *Théâtre Italien*.

Once written dramas or scenes by French authors came to be a regular feature of the repertoire, improvisation, one of the fundamental characteristics of the *commedia dell'arte*, was on the way out, even though a suggestion of improvisation persisted in the French dialogues. When they had become established in Paris, where they permanently took over the *Palais Royal*, the Italians ceased to be strolling actors, ever in search of fresh audiences. Also, they began to conform more and more to French taste with a resulting refinement of the *commedia dell'arte* masks. All the same, we must have no unduly high expectations of the sophistication of the plays, as appears from the following *lazzi* in *L'Empereur dans la Lune* dating from 1684, in which the Docteur has to bow low before Arlequin, who plays the Emperor in the Moon:

> The Docteur lifts his hat and makes his bow. Arlequin who faces him also bows, turns round and says to the Docteur: 'Lower, Sir, lower.' The Docteur bows even lower and at the same time Arlequin lifts his backside so that the Docteur pokes his nose into it. After this Italian *lazzi*, etc.

This type of broad humour was not peculiar to the Italians, as can be seen from an unpublished stanza which Lesage wrote twenty years later for the *Théâtre de la Foire*, where not a single word of Italian was spoken and French *esprit* entirely set the tone. Arlequin sings:

> Il faut une pièce farcie
> De couplets gras, de tours gaillards,
> Et nous aimons à la folie
> Les pots de chambre et les pétards:
> C'est cela seul qui nous fait rire,
> Talalerire.[9]

While the introduction of French texts from 1682 onward certainly promoted intelligibility, it was almost inevitable that the various masks should lose their distinctive individual character which each actor had evolved for himself and made his trademark. The primary passions symbolized by the different masks no longer determined the content and form of the shows; they retreated before an alien form of entertainment imported from outside the *commedia dell'arte*. Arlecchino no longer remained a greedy and stupid servant whose main passion was 'guzzling' but was transformed into a shrewd servant, 'un grand diseur de bon-mots', given to publicly philosophizing about life. Arlequin — recognizable only by his costume — was no longer a clearly defined rôle within which the actor improvised, devising *lazzi* and creating ever more complex plot-entanglements, but he became an actor playing many parts, preferably in one and the same play, in order to demonstrate, in addition to his protean character, his superb prowess. Improvisation on a given scenario by a number of masks who each in turn were allowed their big scene was superseded by the acting of a set text, still permitting some scope for improvisation but on a greatly reduced scale, and always requiring new rôles which, with the exception of the servants, often had little to do with the original stock characters. Arlequin acted as Arlequin in just one or two scenes and for the rest filled in with whatever the plot called for: lawyers and pedants, old gentlemen and young lovers, Olympic gods and foreign princes. And whether he fulminated or cracked rather obvious jokes, his main task was still to exploit comic effects through his *lazzi* and whatever other opportunities the text offered. By now the original Italian *commedia all'improvviso* no longer led a life of its own, having been reduced to *intermezzi* in French comedies and farces.

The introduction of French-speaking scenes cleared the way for far more extensive topical allusions to Paris life. Gherardi's collection contains innumerable allusions to contemporary events and situations, and universal human foibles and vices also came in for their share of censure.

For Attinger this was a sufficient reason to speak constantly of satire in the *Comédie Italienne*[10], while Kindermann wrote that improvisation as the main ingredient was relegated to the background and comic action infused with local colour and trenchant social satire became all the rage[11]. Again it is to be regretted that both Attinger and Kindermann have failed to state precisely what they understand by satire. A study of the contents, structure and, where possible, manner of presentation of the texts has made me rather sceptical of a qualification like 'trenchant social satire'; while Attinger is only too apt to call texts 'satiric' on the strength of isolated topical allusions.

Satiric content in the texts of Gherardi's collection cannot be denied, the question being merely, how much? To Gherardi himself the satire was so self-evident that in the 'Avertissement' of his edition he wrote: 'Je passe sous silence la satyre fine et delicate.' Even before these texts were published, the *Mercure Galant* of 1684 had corroborated Gherardi's view by speaking of these 'scènes Françoises, pleines d'une satire agréable, et très-finement tournées' [12]. These accounts by an actor (Gherardi took up the Arlequin role upon Biancolelli's death in 1688) and by an eyewitness suggest that the satire went beyond text and author's intentions alone. Accounts like these have led scholars to assume that satire was the regular thing in every performance and in every play and, depending on their own ideas about satire, to add such qualifications as 'trenchant', 'sociocritical' or 'grotesque'.

Since this satiric intention is not always so self-evident in these texts and stage presentations to me as it was to, say, Gherardi — who after all was in a better position to judge — I have had recourse to the *Dictionnaire de l'Académie Françoise* (Paris, 1694), which defined 'satyre' as a work in prose or verse written to denounce and criticize vices, uncontrolled passions, follies and hubris. A secondary meaning given is 'tout discours piquant, médisant', i.e. any stinging or backbiting discourse or speech. This is clearly a much broader interpretation than our current definition of satire and my formulation derived from recent studies. Let us therefore return to the texts and the performances and inquire more closely into their satiric nature.

The use of French and the advent of French text writers established the *'esprit gaulois'* as a regular feature of the performances of the *comédiens italiens*. Even a superficial analysis of the texts that have come down to us makes it quite clear that this *'esprit gaulois'* and the *commedia dell'arte* were fundamentally incompatible in spite of the adaptation of the masks to French taste and of increasing sophistication of the repertoire and *lazzi*. This is hardly surprising in performances by Italian actors of works by French authors who had not been nurtured in the *commedia dell'arte* tradition. The Franco-Italian way of acting and the French style of writing — taking for its two main sources of inspiration daily life in Paris and the works of Molière — continued to exist side by side as distinct entities, even in stage presentations, although these suggested a high degree of integration. It was in fact the combination of these two elements which gave the performances their peculiar charm and comic effects.

In the texts we can distinguish two kinds of scenes, each serving its own distinct purpose: scenes that refer to, and sometimes criticise, topical matters, and scenes that aim at exploiting the comic talents of the *comédiens italiens* and which seek to entertain by means of farce-like entanglements and effects.

These scenes were combined with a fairly straightforward plot, which in the majority of the fifty-five pieces collected by Gherardi is basically to the effect that a young daughter is betrothed to an old man whom she does not love, having bestowed her heart on someone else. The wily pranks of Arlequin, Colombine and/or other servant types like Pierrot, Scaramouche and Mezzetin are enlisted to discredit the old man and unite the young lovers. The elements of farce and especially the topical scenes may take up so much of the play that the love intrigue is relegated to a mere subplot.

Strikingly, these subplots always feature personages outside the stock characters of the *commedia dell'arte*. Since these peculiarly French personages are in fact acted by the stock characters, often without any form of disguise, a comic dimension is added to the play. When, for instance, Arlequin adopts the part of family lawyer as a perfectly straight rôle, his very appearance on the stage produces a comic effect because of the mask he is wearing as well as the motley legs protruding from under his black topcoat. No character dressed like this can be taken wholly seriously, and no matter how stinging his denunciations may be, their effect is inevitably much milder because of the context in which the satire figures. It is in this kind of scene, which leaves no room for the original mask, and in which Arlequin has ceased to function as *zanni*, that we find most references to actuality and the most frequent attempts on the part of the author to induce critical attitudes in his audience.

It seems to me that today we can no longer dub each and every allusion to French conditions 'satire'. Many of these allusions, particularly isolated ones, were thrown in only to raise a laugh. *The Banqueroutier* contains a scene in which Pasquariel in utter dismay comes rushing on with bad news which he can hardly bring himself to tell. The dialogue which unfolds between master and servant has this joke: 'Persillet: Est-ce que ma femme est morte? Pasquariel: Le ciel ne vous aime pas assés pour cela.' Even those who are unwilling to accept my definition of satire will find it hard to interpret this as a piece of satire on the position of women in Paris of the 1690s. Such jokes on marriage, on adulterous, coquettish or over-fastidious women are scattered thick through the texts. Not least because of their frequently incidental character, I find it extremely hard to see them as attempts to stimulate critical attitudes or bring about changes in public awareness with respect to woman and her desire for emancipation, or regarding marriage or coquetry: rather, it seems to me, these jokes use an established institution like marriage or the phenomenon 'woman' with her potential for good or evil merely to raise an easy laugh.

Here author and actors alike were not in the least concerned to attack human failings by exposing them in a critical spirit, as Molière did in *Les précieuses ridicules* and *Les femmes savantes*; rather, they seized gratefully upon these foibles to entertain by ridiculing them. Because they set out to show up eternal and basically unchanging vices in stock situations involving characters who seemed more like types than persons of flesh and blood, these stage presentations assumed the character of farce rather than comedy. For comedy, dealing as it does in more fully human characters and more readily recognizable situations, is essentially satiric because it seeks to entertain by holding up to ridicule universal human failings and thoughtless adherence to certain patterns of behaviour, and because it seeks thereby to teach implicit lessons. Comedy thus leaves no room for unduly droll effects which distract attention from its purpose to teach as well as to delight.

Molière, besides being a great comic artist, was an eminent satirist, who sincerely appealed to his audiences to adopt critical attitudes towards the objects of his ridicule. This sincerity of purpose is lacking in most pieces written for the *comédiens italiens*.

On the contrary, on reading these texts I cannot help feeling that the authors would have evinced heartfelt regret if what they denounced had really been remedied, since this would have put paid to their livelihood as well as to their easily won laughs. This same lack of commitment, with which they expressed their *'esprit gaulois'*, also appears from the eagerness with which in their plays they seized on the rivalry between the Italian actors and the *Comédie Française* and the *Opéra*. This rivalry grew as the *comédiens italiens* put more French texts in their performances and drew larger audiences than their rivals.

All the same, allusions to this competition do not go beyond making fun of the rival actors and parodying their styles. The purpose of the jokes is never to direct basic criticism at existing conditions from an ideal projection of what the Paris theatre should be like, and thereby to change the present situation. Every single well-known passage in *Le Cid* was parodied. There was also familiar parody of Racine's *Bérénice* in *Arlequin Prothée*, where we find the following variant of *Bérénice*, Act II, scene I:

ARLEQUIN as Titus, SCARAMOUCHE as Paulin.
Arlequin: A-t-on vu de ma part, le roi de Comagene?
  Sçait-il que je l'attends?
Scaramouche: Si signor, si signor.
Arlequin: Parle François. Je dis que tu n'es qu'un butor.
  Répons, âne: Que fait la reine Berenice?
Scaramouche: La reina Berenice ... la reina ... Ber ... Berenice,
  elle est la haut qui pisse, signor ... et ... per se ben ...
Arlequin: Parle, acheve! fy donc. Quel Paulin! quelle bête!
  Diable soit de Paulin, et de sa confidence!
  Cheval, âne bâté, va hors de ma presence.
  Cours apprendre ton rolle, évite ma fureur,
  Indiscret confident d'un discret empereur.
                                    (*Scaramouche s'en va.*)
(*Aux auditeurs*)
  Ce début n'est pas mal, messieurs, et sur ce ton
  Je m'en vais effacer Floridor et Baron.

Here too satire seems to me too big a word; it would be used inappropriately.

In my opinion the same thing goes for most of the topical allusions of the time. The generally isolated cracks and brief verbal jokes do not aspire beyond the level of parody or comic effect. The absence of a context providing a wider frame for the jokes militates against satiric intent. Whenever a text shows evidence of such satiric intent, we must still answer the question whether the Italian actors deliberately tried to act out the satire. A good example is found in what is generally regarded as the most satiric piece in Gherardi's collection, Fatouville's *Le Banqueroutier*, which savagely denounces the speculative mania of the day and the sharp practices by which one speculator enriched himself at the expense of others. This social satire even provides the main theme of the play, the lovers and their problem being relegated to a subplot. The satire is mitigated by scenes that bear little relation to the main plot and are scattered through the play as a kind of *intermezzi*. In these scenes Arlequin, to demonstrate his prowess, plays a wide variety of rôles, while in the main plot he is also the lawyer Ressource, who for ample remuneration devises the knaveries and carries them out. It is surprising that in this play, which shows evidence of the author's intention to promote critical attitudes towards the disastrous practices of speculators, the author should not have carried his disapproval to the point where he has the malpractition-ers come to a sticky end. There is no poetic justice rewarding the goodies and punishing the baddies. On the contrary, the evil designs of the villains are entirely successful, and I'm very doubtful whether in devising this ending Fatouville deliberately sought to show what actually happens in real life. If the satire had been seriously intended, the author would have upheld his ideal projection and its attendant standards in having the false lawyer's tricks miscarry, thereby giving the play an exemplary effect. With the ending as it stands, he stimulated rather than discountenanced these malodorous practices, all the more because the subplots and the Italian manner of presentation were bound to temper the satire and take some of the sting out of his attack. Possibly he had to contend with his Italian actors, who perhaps were not prepared to see the satire carried to that length. Another conspicuous feature of the play is that for his satire the author made no use whatsoever of the *commedia dell'arte* masks in their original functions.

Thus we see that when after 1682 French scenes came to be included in their stage presentations, the *commedia dell'arte* masks became increasingly devitalized as they more and more tended to become the mouthpieces of French authors.

The extent to which the *comédiens italiens* were prepared for the sake of success and gain to frenchify their repertoire and increasingly place their comic talents at the disposal of French dramatists seriously antagonized others in the profession. This resentment grew until the actors of the *Comédie Française* and the *Opéra* left nothing untried to discredit them with Louis XIV. Their efforts were finally crowned with success when in 1697 the mere rumour that Madame de Maintenon was the target of their mockery in *La fausse prude* induced Louis to revoke the licence of the *comédiens italiens* and order them to leave Paris.

But the actors had reaped too much success with characters like Arlequin, Mezzetin, Scaramouche and Colombine to be consigned to oblivion. Their memory lived on and was constantly revived by the many reprints of the plays collected by Gherardi and in the paintings and drawings by Gillot, Watteau's teacher. Small wonder then that the *Théâtre de la Foire* took over their most popular masks and made these the central characters in their plays. As a result, another peculiar characteristic was lost, since from that moment these characters were played by French actors.

The struggle between these illegal fringe theatres and the established and privileged *Comédie Française* and the *Opéra* lasted till 1791 and gave rise to new genres like *vaudeville* and *opéra comique*. It was not an evenly matched contest and public sympathy was with the underdogs, who again and again found legal loopholes that enabled them to provide fresh theatrical fare. In the main this was no more than farcelike entertainment because of the handicaps under which the actors laboured. Here again the purely comic effects were entrusted to Harlequin whose main business it was to parody the established troupes who sought to have their performances stopped. The struggle for existence and recognition determined the character of their performances, which indeed were not noted for their topical interest. In one of his earliest plays Le Sage might have Mister Vaudeville sing:

Bonne musique
Fine critique
Tout y pique.[13]

But the collection of plays by Le Sage and D'Orneval[14] falls far short of the critical level of the Gherardi collection. Their only concern was parody, as many stage indications explicitly stated. Even the *nouvelle troupe des comédiens italiens*, who from 1716 were licensed to perform in Paris, were parodied by Harlequin and his fellows. The fact that *commedia dell'arte* performances were parodied by characters derived from the *commedia dell'arte* shows clearly that Harlequin and his mates in the *Théâtre de la Foire* had, apart from their outward appearance, severed all their bonds with the original *commedia dell'arte* masks. They had degenerated into mere stereotypes, utterly dependent on authors, and they could be used for any purpose from droll entertainment to trenchant satire.

To what extent French actors possibly made a deliberate effort at satire in their style of acting is virtually impossible to ascertain. One thing was certain, however: whenever an author used these characters, his play was bound to have a farcelike undertone. This was exactly the reason why, e.g. in Germany in 1737, Gottsched symbolically banished the Harlekin-character from the theatre; this character developed under the influence of the *commedia dell'arte* and the *Théâtre italien*, and wherever Harlekin appeared sheer comic effects tended to be pursued at the expense of moral teaching[15].

How easily these stereotypes could be used for almost any purpose can be observed quite clearly in a country where the Italian *commedia dell'arte* had never become established and where its only influence had been through French strolling companies. This was the case in Holland, which after about 1680 tended to imitate French culture almost slavishly and where every Parisian fad or fashion was faithfully copied. Early in the eighteenth century Holland saw French companies touring in a repertoire based on the performances of the *comédiens italiens* and the *Théâtre de la Foire*. Via printed texts as well as performances Dutch authors became familiar with Arlequin, Scaramouche, Colombine and other masks. Because the Dutch knew nothing of their background, the characters could readily be used for various types of comedy but also for slapstick farces as well as for biting satires.

A series of sixteen engravings by G.H. Xaverij of scenes from one of these unpretentious farces still survives and is reproduced in the French edition of Duchartre's *La comédie italienne* (Paris, 1925). In this farce Arlequin is indisposed and the Docteur diagnoses the cause as pregnancy. Arlequin lays six eggs, which he proceeds to hatch out, but five of the six children die. Assisted by his servant, Piro, he undertakes to raise the little one, changing his nappies, complaining about all the filth and even suckling it. In the teeth of all mockery he persists in his nursing effort, and the last scene shows little Arlequin conning his ABC. A scatterbrained plot which only deserves mention because of the engravings, which date from some time after 1718, and because of Arlequin's double rôle of father and mother.

Far more interesting is the manner in which in 1720 the most original eighteenth-century Dutch dramatist, Pieter Langendijk (1683-1756), launched a savage attack on the promoters of the South Sea scheme, introduced in France by John Law and subsequently copied in both England and Holland. The speculative fever of investors in South Sea shares and Mississippi Company stock rose to an unprecedented pitch, and in Holland, as in France, enormous sums changed hands. The gambling urge, as deepseated a national characteristic of the Dutch as their tendency to moralize, set many pens scratching. Pamphlets, songs, broadsides and sonnets inundated the country. No fewer than nine plays were written in which the excesses were denounced or sometimes lightheartedly satirized. Of these nine plays, which clearly showed the authors' concern over this social frenzy, Langendijk wrote two, one an original comedy in three acts, *Quincampoix of de Windhandelaars*[16], and a one-act play, *Arlequyn Actionist*, which the author himself called a free imitation of a presently unknown French model. The original play must have been written between 1715 and 1720 for the *Théâtre de la Foire*. This can be inferred from the character of Gille in Langendijk's play, which was inspired by the French character of Gilles, who was an original creation by the *Théâtre de la Foire* and in Paris was a tremendous popular success. In view of the subject matter and the character of Gille, I believe that Langendijk erroneously stated in the 1720 edition of the play that it was 'in imitation of the *Théâtre italien*'.

In this one-act play Kapitano untruthfully gives out that he will sail with a whole shipload of shares to Southland to make his fortune there by trading. Scaramoes is his first mate, Kolombine is the cook and Mezetijn the barber. The purpose of this ruse is to make share prices soar. When Arlequyn, who poses as a ship's chandler, has supplied a chest full of windbags in exchange for half a pound of shares, a grotesque fight ensues between Kapitano, who behaves in a very cowardly manner, and Arlequyn. The Kapitano's forces win and Arlequyn, taken prisoner, is locked into a chest. The Kapitano has fainted but is revived by the smell of a burning share. While in the chest Arlequyn has disguised himself as Mercury, and on his release from the chest he delivers a philippic against the South Sea promoters. His disguise is penetrated, however, and he is forced to surrender all his shares in exchange for his freedom. Having done so, he demonstrates in a sublime piece of acting, at Kapitano's request, what will become of the share trade: He sells a burning candle end to Kapitano in exchange for a coin. Kapitano in turn sells the candle end to Scaramoes for a number of shares. By singing the praises of his candle end and the light it gives, Scaramoes manages to dispose of it for still more shares. Thus the candle end passes from hand to hand, but as its price rises its life span decreases until finally Gille, having paid for it with a whole armful of shares, burns his fingers and drops the guttering wick. It falls into the pile of shares, which goes up in flames. No more convincing object lesson on the worthlessness of the shares could have been given on the stage. A ballet concludes this one-act play, which was acted ten times in a single month to great public acclaim.

We see here how the author deliberately denounced the speculative mania, ridiculing it by reference to a well-defined set of values. From first to last this critical stance governs the developing structure of the play. The Dutch characters, harking back to the *Théâtre de la Foire*, helped to set the comedy tone needed for effective ridicule of the target of satire. Played as it was by Dutch actors, who were entirely innocent of all experience of the Italian *commedia dell'arte* that might have tempted them to overdo the comic effects, the satire was effectively conveyed in the actual performance. It was possible for the *castigat ridendo mores* adage to be successfully put into practice because there was no chance of the Dutch audiences, any more than the actors themselves, being distracted by memories of the *comédiens italiens*. With their *lazzi* and improvised Italian *intermezzi*, these latter had inserted purely farcelike elements in the written French texts and thus impaired the sometimes satiric intentions of the authors, distracting attention from what was being denounced.

This shows that the shift from verbal joke to verbal weapon becomes possible only as more and more elements of the original Italian *commedia dell'arte* were being abandoned. The more the *commedia dell'arte* lost its 'arte' aspect of pure art and theatrical skill — the game played only for the sake of the game as an expression of the play instinct and zest for life — and the more the masks degenerated to meaningless stereotypes, the more this genre became adapted to conveying the satiric intentions of authors, who could fashion the characters to suit their intentions.

The decay of the *commedia dell'arte* gave rise to new genres which made possible new developments in the theatre. As such this decay is a normal phase in a continuous process of change. Thanks to these changes first authors, and at a later stage actors also, were given a chance to use devitalized *commedia dell'arte* masks to write and act satires for which there had been no room in the Italian *commedia all'improvviso*.

Notes

1 Constant Mic, *La commedia dell'arte* (Paris, 1927), 66.
2 P. Toschi, *Le origini del teatro italiano* (Torino, 1955), 723.
3 H. Kindermann, *Theatergeschichte Europas* (Salzburg, Otto Müller Verlag, 1959), vol.III, 277.
4 Allardyce Nicoll, *The World of Harlequin* (Cambridge, U.P., 1963), 150*ff.*
5 A.K. Dshiwelegow, *Commedia dell'arte* (Berlin, Henschelverlag, 1958), *passim.*
6 I.e. David Worcester, *The Art of Satire* (New York, Russell & Russell, 1960² (1940); Northrop Frye, *The Anatomy of Criticism* (Princeton, N.J., Princeton U.P., 1957); Robert C. Elliott, *The Power of Satire* (Princeton, N.J., Princeton U.P., 1960); Gilbert Highet, *The Anatomy of Satire* (Princeton, N.J., Princeton U.P., 1962); Alvin B. Kernan, *The Plot of Satire* (New Haven, Conn., Yale U.P., 1965).
7 Nicolò Barbieri, *La supplica. Discorso famigliare a quelli che trattano de' comici con studio critico, note e varianti di Ferdinando Taviani* (Milan, Il Polifilo, 1971), 71, and Ferdinando Taviani, *La fascinazione del teatro* (Rome, Bulzoni, 1969), LII.
8 Quoted in Taviani, LXIII.
9 Quoted in Eugene Lintilhac, *Lesage* (Paris, 1893), 128.
10 Gustave Attinger, *L'esprit de la Commedia dell'arte dans le Théâtre Français* (Publications de la Société d'Histoire du Théâtre, Librairie Théâtrale, 3, Rue de Marivaux, Paris, A la Baconnière, Neuchatel (Suisse) 1950), 165-212.
11 H. Kindermann, vol.IV, 76*ff.*
12 Quoted in Oskar Klinger, *Die Comédie-Italienne in Paris nach der Sammlung von Gherardi* (Strassburg, 1902), 177.
13 Quoted in Lintilhac, 130.
14 Mrs. Le Sage and D'Orneval, *Le Théâtre de la Foire ou l'Opéra comique* (Amsterdam, 1722-31, 6 vols).
15 Horst Steinmetz, *Der Harlekin. Seine Rolle in der deutschen Komödientheorie und — dichtung des 18. Jahrhunderts* (Groningen, Wolters, 1965), 5*ff.*
16 Rue Quincampoix in Paris was the bankers' quarter where trading in the shares of the Louisiana and Mississippi Companies took place. It was also the nickname of a coffee house in Kalverstraat, Amsterdam, likewise a centre of this share trade.

KENNETH RICHARDS

The Restoration Pageants of John Tatham

As *finale* to the second of the four pageants John Tatham prepared for the Lord Mayor's Show of 1664, *London's Triumphs*, the poet had St Katherine, patron saint of the Haberdashers and surrounded by the emblems of her martyrdom and her company, welcome Charles II and observe:

> *We hope Your Majesty will not suppose*
> *Your with your* Johnsons *and your* Inigoes.

Had Charles seen no other civic pageant, in the four years since his restoration, and had he only the barest recollection of the court masques of his childhood, it is doubtful that he could, by any licence of his imagination, have supposed that the *mélange* of emblematic devices, industrious 'mechanicals' and crude doggerel that Tatham had contrived for the occasion could have been a spectacle prepared by Ben Jonson and Inigo Jones. Yet this was by no means the least ambitious of the seven or eight Lord Mayor's Shows Tatham prepared between 1657 and 1664, when the Great Plague and the Fire of London put a stop to the traditional ceremonies for some six years.

Of course, the adverse valuation of Tatham's work implied in these remarks must be much qualified, for the dramatic, visual, and intellectual substance of pageant shows is notoriously difficult to determine, and there is constant danger of doing gross injustice to a pageant-maker's work when so little is available on which to base even tentative comment. The popular English pageant shows of the seventeenth century are even less accessible than the court masques, and survive for the most part only in brief printed descriptions and formal speech texts prepared for sale on the day, and in a scattering of illustrative materials — and the shows of the early Restoration period are particularly remote, for information is negligible. Further, the shows were composite efforts and combined the diverse talents of a number of men. When we speak of 'Tatham's pageants' the phrase for the most part embraces only the 'design' of the pageants, the emblematic elements and the

formal speeches as set down in the descriptive pamphlets[1]. But
the finished shows were as much, and in many respects more, the
work of artificers whose skills and contributions are barely
recorded. The subject, then, is peculiarly elusive. Yet descriptions
and contemporary reports intimate something of the quality of
these spectacles, and while many details remain obscure, and much
of the appeal of the popular land and acquatic pageants is
irrecoverable, there seems little doubt that pageantry after the
Restoration rarely, if ever, achieved the occasional but striking
unity of tone and pertinence and complexity of symbolic statement
that characterized a number of the pre-Commonwealth displays[2].

That London pageantry received no second lease of life after the
Restoration may be thought curious, for the times were in some
respects propitious for a revival of pageantic spectacle: the relieved
rejection of an austere Parliamentary rule; the self-assurance of a
newly restored court; the political desirability of asserting in wide
public terms both national unity and central authority; and the
burgeoning taste for show that the theatre proper was quick to
exploit — all operated in the pageant-makers' favour. Certainly the
street and water pageants were popular with the Restoration crowd:
John Evelyn, Thomas Rugg, and the Venetian Resident, Francesco
Giavarina, are among those who attest to this[3]. Samuel Pepys
despised the shows, but watched them nonetheless; and on one
occasion resisted the temptation to wear his 'new velvet cloak ...
the first that ever I had in my life,' for fear it be mussed by the
throng of spectators[4]. Something of the excited response of
ordinary London citizenry to these occasions is suggested in the
Lord Mayor's instructions to the City constables: that carts,
coaches and other impediments be cleared from the pageant routes,
children and servants be prevented from letting off fireworks and
discharging guns in the streets, and particular care be taken that
lanthorns with candles be hung out at night[5].

Pageant shows provided festival occasions for all, as much after
the interregnum as before it. In fact Charles II's reign began with a
burst of ceremonial and pageant splendour that augured well. It
was, furthermore, pageantry of a kind that had lost ground in the
decades immediately before the Civil War. Increasingly in the
Jacobean and Caroline periods Lord Mayor's Shows came to
assume a primacy in spectacle that had hitherto been reserved for
civic entertainment of the monarch. It has frequently been
remarked that the Stuart courts found the intimate and exclusive
masques more attractive fare, and in the Caroline period
particularly the personalities of Charles I and Henrietta Maria,

both of them sensitive, austere and inclined to shun the vulgar, were alien to public carnival in whatever form. But the restoration of the monarch in 1660 promised to reverse this trend. Charles II took full opportunity to exploit by personal appearance and celebratory display the popularity of his return, and for a time he made the London streets his stage, as if by public pomp and spectacle he were intent to banish from memory forever his father's last 'memorable scene'. Pageantry in the first two years of Charles II's reign is of the earlier and Continental tradition of entry and fête in being monarchy-inspired: it is organized in all its essentials to greet and compliment the sovereign, to banish the ogres of the past, to assert the regenerative force of the new king, and to weld and inspire the nation.

It did so in a wealth of spectacle which we may briefly rehearse. The King's first entry into London on Tuesday, 29th May, 1660, is justly accounted one of the great processional occasions in English history. Pageantry proper seems to have been wanting, but there were speeches, popular side-shows of the fairground type, bonfires and banners, and, of course, the great parade itself. In July, Charles dined in state at the Guildhall and was triumphed in the streets with lavish pageants: the entertainment costing the City the formidable sum of £7,888.2.6d[6]. The Lord Mayor's Show on 29th October of that year inevitably veered somewhat from its customary matter to centre on the fact of the king restored, and was appropriately entitled *The Royal Oake*. April 22nd and 23rd, 1661, saw perhaps the most splendid of these royal occasions, the King's progress through the City of London from the Tower to Whitehall, and his consecration and crowning at Westminster, a two-day event accomplished, says the Venetian Resident, 'with all possible splendour and decorum, no one sparing his money to make it exceptional and memorable for ages to come'[7]. Apparently, even the French were 'forced to acknowledge' that it eclipsed their own sovereign's nuptial entry into Paris the previous year[8]. Finally, in 1662, there was the *Aqua Triumphalis*, the most conspicuous water pageant of the reign, mounted to celebrate the first entry into London of Charles' bride, Catherine of Braganza.

But although impressive and costly, popular and instructive, to people and sovereign alike, these royal pageant theatres of the streets and waterways do not signal any effective and sustained revival after the Restoration of the traditional art of pageantry. Nor did the example of the royal shows stimulate any resurgence of artistic vigour in the annual Liveried Company pageants which, although they continued to be produced in a form that united the visual and the verbal into the early eighteenth century, seem to have possessed little inspiration or cohesion[9]. The reasons for the failure of poets and artificers effectively to revive London pageantry and to capitalise upon apparent political and social opportunities are complex and ultimately no doubt intangible. Yet the career of John Tatham, a writer today almost wholly ignored but the most prolific deviser of pageant shows in the years immediately before and following the return of the King, offers some indication as to why Restoration pageantry failed to recapture the spirit and match the achievement of the great age of civic pageantry that runs from George Peele to Thomas Heywood. Examination of the post-Restoration decline of popular pageantry cannot finally be divorced from the broad political and social pressures of the period, but for reasons of space this paper will focus more specifically upon the verbal, preparational and presentational aspects of Tatham's work[10].

In the first four years of Charles II's reign, all the London civic entertainments were fashioned, in terms of their literary and emblematic elements, by only two men, John Ogilby and John Tatham. Ogilby, although a man of considerable and multifarious talents, was principally a geographer and cosmographer, and contributed only one piece, though that a distinguished one — the coronation Progress of 1661[11]. Incomparably the more important of the two as far as pageantry is concerned was John Tatham, for he devised probably all the civic pageants in this five-year period, save for the royal Progress. An indifferent versifier and possibly an erstwhile Red Bull playwright of the Caroline period, little is known of Tatham's work before the closure, and although he published two plays during the interregnum, unacted and arguably unactable, he brought out only one straight play after the reopening. *The Rump*, a personal and political satire on the last years of the Commonwealth, which was performed at Dorset Court in June 1660 with a success ascribable more to its topicality than to its intrinsic merit. His *forte* immediately before and after the Restoration was pageant work, and he prepared both aquatic pageants for royal occasions and, possibly with one exception, all the Lord Mayor's Shows of the period we are examining. But unlike his predecessors in pageant making, he was not a distinguished working dramatist engaged in the contemporary life of the theatre proper, nor did he bring to his task their poetic vision and theatrical flair. His poetic talent was thin, and his ability to establish subtle and complex associations within the allegorical, mythological and historical materials traditional to the pageant form was limited. What he possessed in the main was a certain talent to assist in organizing the diverse elements that went to make up a pageant show. It is instructive that his most successful piece was the *Aqua Triumphalis* of 1662, for it is of the nature of water processions, with their heavy, stately, slow-moving barges, that calculated timing and ordering is of the essence; and it is equally pertinent that such aquatic shows tend to emphasize a few salient features rather than many densely interrelated elements and to rely on visual communication rather than verbal, for they are seen at a distance and in motion.

Before he came to prepare the *Aqua Triumphalis*, Tatham had acquired some experience in handling water shows. After Ogilby's coronation entertainment for Charles II on Monday, 22nd April, 1661, the King and nobility returned to Whitehall and from a balcony overlooking the Thames had rounded off the day by watching a 'night Triumph' in the form of a water pageant of Tatham's devising, the *Neptune's Address*. It seems that well in advance of the great day Charles himself had seen and approved the models for this show, which consisted of a sequence of four pageants, simple in conception and in visual and verbal statement. The first was a floating replica of the Tower of London manned by soldiery, intended to be, says Tatham,

> the Emblem of Your People's love,
> From whose united Strength Your Actions move.

The second took the form of a turning circle in the water, composed of three ships pursued by three whales on whose backs sat three

> Prey-Men, with Dudgeon Daggers in their hands (like those of Pigmies), Hats on their heads buttoned up, and Monchatoes like *Switzers*, smoking Tobacco, their Mouths wide, ready to swallow the Ocean.

In the midst of this circle was a rock from which rose 'the Royal Oake, adorned with Crown and Scepters'. The whales, Tatham tells us, represent the enemies of the King and the nation, and their pursuit of ships signifies the ruin of trade by the Commonwealth's men who preferred waging war to engaging in profitable commerce, while the emblematic rock offers the promise of emergent monarchy setting all to rights. The third presentment was even more transparent in meaning, if only that for decades in various guises it was a recurrent emblem: three garlands setting forth the crowns of England, Scotland and Ireland, and also

moving on the water in a circle. The final pageant was a floating
castle from which Neptune issued 'Mounted on a Whale', from
whose belly came the sound of loud hautboys: musical prelude to
Neptune's farewell address to the King. The show concluded with
all four pageants bursting spectacularly into flame, an effect
brought off by a naval gunner, one Zacheus Juat, to suggest that

> the Elements of Water and Ayre had been invited
> to the Celebration of His Majesties *Coronation.*

There is, of course, nothing new in the details of this water
triumph, and pleasing to monarch and crowd as it no doubt was, it
does not compare in variety and inventiveness or dramatic content
with many of the great water pageants of the past, like the shows
for Elizabeth at Kenilworth and Wanstead, or some of the Lord
Mayor's Show water pageants mounted before the Civil Wars.
What it seems to have possessed was a naive *brio*, no doubt relaxing
for Charles at the end of an exhausting day of adulation, and part
at least of its simplicity must be seen in this context, for it was very
much an after-piece to the day's main proceedings. No more
inspired in detail was the water show Tatham prepared two months
later as the opening pageant of the Lord Mayor's Show of 1661.
This is distinctive in that it was the first of its kind since Heywood's
Londini Status Pacatus of 1639, and of particular interest is the
amphibious nature of its pageant, for after it had greeted the Lord
Mayor on the river as he passed in his barge to Westminster:

> the aforesaid Ship, Furniture and annexed Sceans return, and are
> received at the place where the Ship first launched, and from
> thence are conveyed through *Pauls* Church-yard into *Cheapside*,
> where they make a stand near St. *Lawrence* Lane.[12]

Both these shows were useful preparatory runs for the more
notable entertainment Tatham conceived for the City's reception of
Catherine of Braganza when she was brought by water from
Hampton Court to Whitehall on Saturday, 23rd August, 1662 —
the *Aqua Triumphalis*. As the last great Stuart spectacle this show
merits more extensive examination.

From Tatham's descriptive pamphlet we learn at least the names
of some of the artificers responsible for mounting the pageant: 'the
Management and Ordering of this dayes Triumph' was in the
charge of Peter Mills, the City Surveyor, and 'Mr. Malin, Water
Bayliff'; also mentioned are 'two City Painters', 'Excellent in their
Quality', and Thomas Whiting, Joiner, and Richard Cleere,
Carver. The 'City Painters' were Captain Andrew Dacres (or

Dakers) and William Lightfoot[13]. Both of these men had worked with Tatham, and with Whiting and Cleere, on the 1659 and 1660 Lord Mayor's Shows and, along with Whiting and Cleere, worked with Peter Mills on Ogilby's Coronation Progress[14]. Although Tatham's *Neptune's Address* does not give the names of the artificers, it is highly likely that all these men were responsible for mounting that show, for they had prepared the same day's land triumph. What in fact emerges from the scant information we have about the technical preparation of pageants in these years is that by the time of the Restoration there had been a significant shift in the way pageantry was commissioned and organized by the City and the Livery Companies. Where in pre-Commonwealth times poet and artificer would submit a proposal against the competition of other, similar teams, and the winning team would sub-contract work, by the close of the interregnum much of the organization of shows had been centralized. Thus the same poet, Tatham, prepared all the royal and possibly all the company pageants of the period, except for the royal Progress, and in the known cases he worked with the same team of master artificers; and on the one occasion when another poet was employed (Ogilby for the Progress), he too worked with the regular team of senior craftsmen. The effects of such centralization were not necessarily all to the good, for it concentrated major work into comparatively few hands and may well have excluded younger and original talent. But in the case of the *Aqua Triumphalis* the familiarity of poet and artificers with each other's work was advantageous.

In preparing the water pageant Tatham and his colleagues seem to have been under some pressure, for the poet laments:

> the shortness of the time allowed me, and the uncertainty of their Majesties Arrivall

the last a recurring hazard for organizers of royal shows. But the complaints were justified, for the pageant-makers had no more than three weeks to conceive and execute the spectacle, and indeed the time at first threatened to be much shorter. A circular letter of 29 July 1662, from the Lord Mayor to the Masters and Wardens of the Livery Companies, advises that the King and Queen will make their water entry into London on Thursday week, barely nine days ahead, and instructs each company to prepare for the occasion:

> with your Barge Standards Streamers Colours Drumes Trumpetts and other Musique & all the Ornam[ts] appertaining in the greatest Pomp and beauty, so as to be ready at halfe a dayes

warning to attend us on this Service, in such manner and order as
shall be directed by Mr. Water bailiffe to whom the Marshalling
of the Companies upon the water is Committed.[15]

A further letter of 4 August noted that the passage had been
deferred to a later date, but urged that there should be no
slackening of preparations. On 29 July an order was issued
delegating overseer responsibilities for the Company pageants:

> In order to the preparations to bee made for her Mat^ies Reception
> upon the River of Thames Mr Mills Capt Dacres and M^r
> Lightfoote are appointed to view the Pageants of any of the
> Companies of this City and to make choice of and fitt and trim
> upp wth all expedition such Pageants as they conceive most
> proper to bee used on this occasion. And they are to make use of
> the ground Galleries in Gresham Colledge for this service.[16]

In the early weeks of August the busy activity of the Companies in
mounting the show provided gossip for London letter writers[17],
and when Saturday, 23 August, was finally chosen for the great
occasion all appears to have been ready[18].

On the early morning tide the ceremonial barges of the twelve
companies were taken up river and anchored off Chelsea, until
between eight and nine in the morning they continued to Putney to
meet the royal barges coming down from Hampton Court. Then,
with the Lord Mayor's barge leading the way, the companies
escorted the 'Royal Trayne' down-river again to pass the three
'Grand Pageants' awaiting them *en route* to Whitehall. Before each
company barge was a boat bearing a minor pageant that expressed
the activity or associations of the guild, and the most important
emblem in each pageant was elevated on a small wooden 'stage'
approximately twelve feet long and eight feet wide. Thus the
Mercers, who led the companies, presented on their 'stage' a Virgin
beneath 'Canopy of State', clad in a 'Silver Mantle' and about her
head a 'silver Coronet', while, off-'stage' at her feet she was
attended by three maids of honour, and three pages standing either
side of the boat. This was followed by the Drapers', on whose
'stage' beneath a canopy sat 'a Grave *Roman* Magistrate', holding
in his right hand a sword and in his left a 'Triple Crown', and
attended by Loyalty, Truth, Fame and Honour. The figures on
these two pageants made traditional allusions to the company
saints and patrons, but they further served to image the royal
couple being brought in to London: the virgin bride, Catherine of
Braganza, and the omnipotent ruler, Charles II, the emblems of his

pageant showing him to be the embodiment of national order, military might, the unity of the three kingdoms, and possessor of all the qualities associated with wise rule. The other pageant barges portrayed only their companies: thus the Merchant Tailors' presented a 'Wildernesse' with seated Pilgrim and two camels with Moorish attendants, allusions to the Company's patron saint, St John the Baptist, and to its extensive trading interests, and the Goldsmiths' raised the figure of Justice, clad in garments of gold, coronet of gold, and holding in one hand 'a Ballance, in the other a Touchstone'.

A vivid and detailed illustration of the entire entertainment is available in a contemporary engraving made by Dirk Stoop (see Plate 1). The last of seven scenes covering the entire passage of the Queen from her departure at Lisbon to her entry into London, this is the most complete visual record we possess of an English water pageant of the period[19]. Stoop was peculiarly well placed to provide this: a Dutchman, he had been resident in Lisbon for some years, where he had been Court painter, and he accompanied Catherine on her voyage from Lisbon to London. Of course, such engravings must be approached with caution, for they often distort and embellish on what they represent, but Stoop's illustration is surprisingly faithful in its detail. It includes nearly all the elements described by Tatham in his pamphlet, but details too that Tatham omits for he was, as he repeats, 'strieuthned in point of time'. That Stoop's picture is essentially reliable is suggested by a comparison of it with Tatham's account and with surviving records of the companies. For example, those of the Goldsmiths' show that approval was given for the construction of a 'staye' to include:

(1) a place for Justice, with a canopy over her head; in her right hand a balance, in her left a touchstone.

(2) at the feet of Justice, two attendants, each holding in their right hands cups of gold and in their left gold ... [words illegible]

(3) an open space with a forge; three persons forging, a furnace with others filing and raising plate.[20]

The first two of these entries are described by Tatham, although with slight additions and modifications. But the third is not mentioned. In Stoop's engraving, however, although the number of persons the entry specifies is reduced, otherwise the activity is very faithfully depicted. Again, Stoop illustrates with great delicacy the royal barge as it was described by John Evelyn, 'an antique-shaped open Vessell, covered with a State or Canopy of Cloth of

Plate 1. Dirk Stoop's engraving of the Aqua Triumphalis

Gold, made in forme of a Cupola, supported with high Corinthian pillars'. The engraving is a composite illustration of the entire show and depicts, in addition to the royal barge, the Lord Mayor's barge, eight of the company pageants, and all three of the 'Grand Pageants' which were the high feature of the spectacle.

The first of these, anchored at Chelsea, showed Isis in a 'Sea Chariot drawn with Sea-Horses' scattering flowers from a *cornucopia* in her right hand, and with her left holding a watering pot denoting that she is wife 'to *Tham*'. She spoke the first address of welcome as the royal barge passed. A lively droll of singing watermen was presented between this pageant and the next, which was moored at Lambeth and took the form of a Floating Island with Tham as its principal figure represented as 'an old Man with long Hair and Beard, which may signifie the Weeds and Sedges of the River: on his Head he wears a Crown of Flowers'. He held a trident in his right hand, symbolizing that he is 'King of Rivers', and in his left a pitcher of water pointing his association with all seas and rivers and that he is 'Grandchild to *Oceanus*'. Two nymphs at his feet bore on their heads replicas of Greenwich and Windsor Castle. At the front of the pageant stood a Lion and a Unicorn, on their backs 'two bigg *Boyes*' representing Scotland and England. Tham's speech was a fulsome assertion of the friendship between England and Portugal. A second droll followed, this time of singing and dancing Indians and Seamen, reinforced in the background on the Thames embankment by several side-shows where 'tricks of Ability [were] performed, both on the Stage and the Rope.' The final pageant was at Whitehall Palace steps, where Thetis sat in a '*Sea Chariot* made in a manner of a *Scallop Shell*, drawn with two *Dolphins*, on whose backs are placed two *Tritons*'. On her head was a '*triple Crowne* to denote and distinguish her *three Estates* as she is supposed to be *Mother of all the Gods, Goddess of the Sea*, and *Empress of all Rivers*'. In her speech of welcome, like Tham, she extolled the might and virtues of England and Portugal, London and Lisbon, and anticipated a prosperous union for the royal couple and the two nations.

Of the visual magnificence of this water show there can be no doubt. It far exceeded, wrote Evelyn, 'all the *Venetian Bucentoro's* etc. on the *Ascension* when they go to Espouse the *Adriatic*' and had

> innumerable number of boates and Vessels, dressd and adornd with all imaginable Pomp: but above all, the Thrones, Arches, Pageants and other representations.

Pepys watched it from the top of the Banqueting House and estimated '10,000 barges and boats, I think, for we could see no water for them, nor discern the King nor Queen'[21]. The size of the flotilla is a conspicuous feature of Stoop's engraving. The preparation and management of the spectacle reflect well on the Surveyor, Mills, and the water bailiff, Malin, but are a tribute as well to Tatham, whose conception of the pageant effects had a simplicity and directness appropriate to the occasion. The decoration of the company pageants seems largely to have been in the hands of the companies themselves and their advisers, Mills, Dacres and Lightfoot. Precise instructions issued by the Goldsmiths show that the poet was allowed to direct only 'the habits of the several persons', and these, together with the emblematic devices worn or carried by the figures, were substantially laid down by a long tradition of association. Most of the poet's invention was centred on the preparation of the three 'Grand Pageants', on the composition of their pictures and of the formal speeches.

Conceiving all three as conventional tableaux, Tatham made no attempt to introduce dramatic elements, even of the most rudimentary kind. The scenes are live sculptures, theatrical only in their visual splendour. Such dramatic conflict as there is, is implicit in the contrast between these static and stately compositions and the vigorous mimetic antics and colloquially familiar songs of the droll interludes. A certain thematic unity and development is perceptible between the three pageants: from Isis, the tributary river, through Tham, the King of Rivers, to Thetis, ruler of all waters; and further implied is the character and potency of Charles' Kingdom itself, a land of streams and rivers, all flowing to a centre of wealth and power, then spreading out to mingle with and control all seas and oceans. At the same time, however, there is a certain naivety and inappropriateness about some of the deeper associations which Tatham attempts to draw out. For example, the point is emphasized that Thetis is wife to Peleus, and thus represents the antiquity of navigation. On one level of the show's statement the reference is right, but on another it is slightly discordant, for a central fact about Thetis' marriage was that it was an enforced one — not an altogether happy analogue in the context of this royal matrimonial celebration. Again, Thetis is given 'hair long and grey, disshevel'd', by which, as Tatham says, he wished to indicate the cares and fears of a sea-man's perilous life. The idea is valid but, one feels, rather elusive.

Such glosses in Tatham's descriptive pamphlets serve to point up one of his major limitations as pageant poet. Where earlier poets would glance at the complex meaning of a visual symbol in the verbal elements of their composition, Tatham's speeches and songs are unable poetically to encompass subtle explication nor to subsume the details of the visual statements. His verse is content to operate on the level of jingling doggerel that states the simple and obvious. A quite typical example of his verse at its best is the following lines from Tham's address to the King and Queen, which combines the compulsory note of mild belicosity with professions of Anglo-Portuguese unity:

> Britain *is by this* Floating Island *meant*,
> . . . .
> *The name of* England *shakes 'em, Warr, and it,*
> *Strikes 'em into their* Mother-Ague *fit.*
> *And that your ample glories may encrease,*
> Portugal *claps you with the Arms of Peace.*
>
> . . . .
> Lisbon *is* London, Tagus Thames, *and then,*
> *The* Portugues *are become* Englishmen,
> *The* English, Portugues, *both meet in hearts,*
> *Thus* Providence *unites remotest parts.*

Clearly, the quality of this water pageant lay wholly in its spectacle, and not in any fusion of visual and verbal statement. Of course the importance of the verbal element in a water show is marginal, the form of its nature defeats other than short and direct statement. Yet the thinness of Tatham's poetic utterance here cannot be altogether discounted, for it is characteristic of all the songs and formal speeches he composed for pageant shows. In the later court masques the artificer supplanted the poet — the bays, says Shirley, was 'thrust out to let the plush in'. In late pageantry the poet was not so much forced out as found wanting in the talent that would have enabled him to hold his own with the artificer. Where earlier the union of the poets, Jonson and Dekker, and the artificer, Stephen Harrison, in the preparation of James I's coronation entry in 1604, or the collaboration of Middleton and Christmas on guild pageants, had produced spectacle dense in its visual and verbal meanings, the absence of any such mutually fructifying union in the preparation of Tatham's pageants, and those of his successors, is marked. In the *Aqua Triumphalis* the inadequacies are concealed by the water-pageant form and its tendency to enhance the 'body' rather than the 'soul' of the spectacle; in Tatham's other pageant work the case is different.

Tatham's poetic limitations as pageant-maker are more apparent in his Lord Mayor's Shows, all of which he composed between 1657 and 1664 when he held a position tantamount to that of official City poet. With the outbreak of the Civil War these annual shows, like the theatre proper, ceased; but their revival pre-dated the re-opening of the theatres by five years, a single Mercers' pageant being paraded in 1655, and two Skinners' Company pageants in 1656. In the 1656 Show there was strong emphasis on lively and varied entertainment to re-enforce the formal pageants, with a water battle on the Thames, a twelve-foot giant, and 'green men' clearing a way through the crowds; but the frivolity accompanied and contributed to, rather than disruptively intruded upon, the pageant scenes proper — a distinction Tatham was less able to preserve when he commenced pageant writing in 1657. It is difficult to get any real purchase on the quality of Tatham's shows with the records we possess, for his descriptive pamphlets are insubstantial, and again we know virtually nothing of the work of the artificers who collaborated with him[22]. But it would seem that the pageants he devised over the next seven years contained little that was really fresh or striking. As one would expect in so traditional a form, all the customary scenic motives of the pre-Commonwealth Lord Mayor's Shows recur: naval fabrics, manned and rigged as for sea, arbours in wooded groves, triumphal chariots, fountains, Britain imaged as mountain, island or rock, together with all the time-honoured figures and devices that bespoke the Livery Companies. In many respects Tatham's pageantry carried over into the Restoration traditions of popular spectacle running back to the Middle Ages. Like pre-Commonwealth practice, too, the utilization of some scenic units, or elements of them, from year to year, suggests judicious cannibalization of constructs, both Lord Mayor and Royal; Tatham's descriptive pamphlets invariably conclude with remarks on the careful dispersal and storage of decorations and properties.

Evident, too, is some concern for unity of presentation. Tatham is not always successful in avoiding the danger inherent in multi-part shows working a variety of locations — fragmentation into quite disparate units — but his best work does endeavour to establish interconnections between individual pageants within a complete Show. We may take as example the Show Tatham prepared for Sir Anthony Bateman and the Skinners' Company in 1663, *Londinium Triumphans*. The absence of an aquatic pageant was compensated for by the provision of five land pageants. The first to greet the Mayor on his return from Westminster presented 'two Leopards richly set out' carrying on their backs two sumptuously clad negroes. The negroes, and two girls who stood at either end of the stage, carried banners bearing the arms of the City and the Company. The second pageant depicted a detailed Skinners' Company scene on a stage fourteen feet long and eight feet wide: a 'Wood or Wildernesse' at the front of which, beneath 'a Wilde Arbour', sat a figure representing Faunus, clad partly as forester, partly as hunter, wearing a fur-lined robe and attended by three satyrs; on stage were 'several Boyes in the shapes of Bears, Monkeys, and several other beasts relating to the Companies Trade'. At Cheapside, the third pageant was 'a stately Fabrick' bearing a figure representing Albion at whose feet was figured the City of London with on either side representatives of York, Bristol, Worcester and Norwich, while the pageant was decorated about with painted landscapes of these cities. The fourth pageant was in the form of a Chariot bearing a Turk and slaves, tribute to the new Lord Mayor's Levantine trading interests. The final pageant in Soper Lane showed 'a stately Building' before which sat Minerva, holding a lance and a shield (on which was painted books and instruments) to bespeak her quality as Goddess of Arts and Arms.

Clearly Tatham was attempting here to establish a developing and meaningful interrelationship between the scenic units of his Show: from a simple and direct image that signalled the Company being fêted, through celebration of that Company's activities, then a triumph of England, London and the cities, to particular compliment of the Mayor entering into office, and concluding with a plea not only for his support of trade, but of arts and sciences too. It is interesting that whereas earlier Restoration Lord Mayor's Shows had understandably made frequent reference in scene or word to the restored monarchy and the nation's expectations of it, the tone here is closer to that of the pre-Commonwealth Shows in drawing out a distinction between City and Court. Thus Minerva's speech in support of learning:

> If she address her self to *Court* (the place
> Where she should find acceptance, and a Grace)
> The wanton leere of a betraying Eye
> Bespeaks her (straight) a scornful Injury.
> The *Country* knows her not; they wish all right
> But hardly to her Help will add a Mite;
> To what place must her Miseries repair,
> But unto *Athens?*

But unified though the show is, we do not find the subtlety and complexity of statement and vivid dramatic life that had been features of many pre-Commonwealth Shows, where the skill of the artificer was extended and enriched by the imagination of a dramatic poet. Rather, what Tatham tends to emphasize are organizational matters, the ordering of the processions and the grouping and precedence. Indeed, in his 1661 pamphlet he rather plaintively laments that some people have objected to his obsession with 'the marshalling of companies', and defends his practice 'because every year there are some alterations in their routes and procedures'. The attitude seems symptomatic of the integrity but paucity of poetic vision that characterizes much of his work. We cannot, of course, take Samuel Pepys's response as representative, but when he described the Shows as 'silly' and 'but poor and absurd', he may not have been wholly wide of the mark. Tatham's pamphlets leave the impression that all too often the Shows did little more than unimaginatively rehearse overly familiar and perhaps largely exhausted materials. They are verbally undistinguished and for the most part scenically derivative.

But if Tatham was unable to exploit the literary possibilities of the received pageant form, and failed to explore original variations within the traditional materials, he did develop pageantry in ways which substantially determined the future shape of the Lord Mayor's Shows. His friend and successor as City pageant-maker, Thomas Jordan, is usually held responsible for vulgarising the form by introducing cheap comic effects and excessive fairground elements: in short, for failing to maintain a balance between formal compliment and lively popular entertainment. But Jordan was merely following a tradition laid down by Tatham. It is true that the Lord Mayor's Shows came partly out of folk-materials, that crowd-catching buffoonery is found in early pageants in the mid-sixteenth century, and that in the Caroline period Thomas Heywood, then the leading and most prolific pageant writer, included comic 'interludes' or anti-masques in his shows. But in Tatham these elements take on a quite new importance. Heywood was fully conscious of the extent to which he was, in his own eyes, debasing the pageant form. We know little of the composition of his 'interludes' because he expressly avoided describing them; they were, as he says, 'contrived only for Pasttime, to please the vulgar'[23].

In Tatham's Lord Mayor's pageants these pastimes for the vulgar are not brief and incidental concessions to an undemanding taste, functioning as after-pieces to the main business, but form a substantial part of a pageant scene, or can indeed comprise the whole of a scene. In *London's Glory*, prepared as part of the

Guildhall entertainment of Charles II, 5 July 1660, and not strictly a Lord Mayor's Show, but in structure, content and organization closely analogous, we find that two of the five pageants presented to the King were of this kind:

> At Pauls Chain a Pageant in the Nature of a Droll; where is presented the figure of Industry, and the Carders and Spinners, in relation to the Clothiers Company.
> At Cheapside Crose another droll, where *Pretty* and the Tumblers play their tricks.[24]

The Lord Mayor's Show of 1661 is particularly rich in such entertainment, and no less than three of its pageants either contain or are closely linked to the antics of 'drolling Americans', 'disporting and throwing their fruit about' and 'making musick on the tongs and other antique instruments'. In *The Royal Oake* of 1660, the fairground entertainer Diamond appeared; in 1663 satyrs playing 'rude instruments' performed wild dances, and in 1664 a number of figures are shown 'wantonly tumbling'[25]. At least some of these elements, as remarked, can be found occasionally in earlier pageants but they are comparatively rare. What is striking here is the extent to which the spirit of the drolls and of fairground entertainments, their characters, dialogue and business, come increasingly to pervade the shows. In *The Royal Oake*, the main pageant telling the story of Charles's escape from 'Bosco-bell' employs a number of woodsmen who 'disport themselves, dancing about the *Royal Oake*' and provides dialogue of which the following is a sample:

> *1 Woodsman*: what done o mean wullo beezen the vine zight, ho ho, what pestilent gay vellow's yon.
> *2 Woodsman*: tis the Lord Mayor
> * * * * * * * * * * * * * * * *
> *1 Woodsman*: A Meezle take thee, Neame cham glad to zee thee. Give me thyn hond, how done mine Aunt I prithee.
> Had Iche but known o this zame gaudy Noone, Chad don'd o viner Clothes and viner Shoone.

Encouraged, too, is the kind of extravagance we encounter in the principal figure of the final pageant in the 1661 Show: 'an European, every part of him figured and habited in the fashion or manner of severall nations which trade and relate to Europe'. Pointing to his dress he says:

Although my shape may seem ridiculous,
Unsuitable, rude, and incongruous,
Contemne me not; there's nothing that I wear
About me, but doth some relation bear
To th' Customes of those Countryes with whom
You Traffique in all parts of Christendome.

On occasions there is an apparent organization in the use of
such comic materials. In this 1661 Show most of the lighter matter
formed the 'Afternoon's Business', after the Lord Mayor's
banquet at Guildhall, thus it functioned rather as 'anti-masque' to
the morning's more formal spectacle. But such structuring seems
more fortuitous than purposeful and what these fairground
elements amount to is a corruption of the received form and
materials of pageant show as these had been refined by the
Jacobean and Caroline dramatists. They imply, too, a shifting
presentational aesthetic. This was to threaten the basis of pageant
statement and is nowhere more apparent than in the most engaging
of the Shows, the *London's Triumph* of 1662, for John Robinson,
Clothworker.

This Show is usually ascribed to Tatham and may well be his
work as he composed all the other Lord Mayor's Shows from 1657
to 1664. Slight doubt is occasioned, however, by the absence of his
name on the title-page and the epistolary address, and the curious
disclaimer of this epistle:

> besides my own *Incapacity* and *Discomposure*, the *Employment*
> it self was so wholly *Strange* to me, that it never till now fell
> within my Disquisition. And now the more I *reflect* on it, the
> more I conceive it a *Design* fit for Persons of far greater *abilities*
> than I am *furnished* withall or dare *pretend* to.

Further, nowhere else in Tatham's work do we find so extreme a
movement in pictorial representation away from the traditional
high abstractions of pageantry and towards the realistic depiction
of familiar activities and locations. Whether or not it is by Tatham,
it is indicative of a trend. The first pageant provided a fortification
like the Tower of London, with cannon firing and 'persons Flatting
and Coyning of Money, others as Warders standing at the Gate'. A
common soldier delivers some plain citizen advice:

We have good *Laws* enough, and need not make
The *Gentry* for their reputations sake,
To be chose *Members* spend a thousand pounds.
Let them keep home, and mind their *Hawks* and *Hounds*.

Another showed clothworkers at their trade with a smiling but grave overseer watching with satisfaction 'his servants about him diligent in their distinct callings'. The overseer delivered a formal speech in praise of the skill and industry of clothiers, and as the Lord Mayor's procession moved on, two old weaver women rendered a part song, the burden of which was picked up by 'the whole body of the Work-folk'. A third pageant was a representation of St Paul's, with speeches to the Lord Mayor and the King telling its history and drawing attention to recent neglect and the need for renovation:

> My roofe, half Patcht, half ope', As if a Prayer
> Could not ascend without a freer Ayre;
> My Altars trampled on, my stalls are turn'd
> To Faggot-sticks, my holy vestments, burn'd;
> My Pavement, dirt and trash: nor wonder; when
> You hear, I'd more to do with Horse, than Men;
> O cleanse it (Royal Sir) ... [26]

Of course the Tower and the Clothmakers at work are scenes which appear in earlier pageants but the tone and treatment here suggest the beginnings of something new — reproduction of the actual: provision of quasi-realistic vignettes of the working life of the City, its mariners, soldiery, artisans and merchants, and the spirit of the City as located in its people and places. Naive and in little, it is a handling of citizen life more in the manner of a Shadwell or a Ravenscroft. It is a retreat from, and a denial of, the strategies and materials of traditional pageantry.

Consideration of John Tatham's work as pageant-maker, elusive though that work is, and cautious, tentative and hedged about with qualification as any comment must be, suggests that a complex of factors worked against the effective revival of traditional pageant forms after the Restoration. It is tempting to suppose that something fresh in civic pageantry could have emerged if the Royal and Lord Mayor's Shows had been in the hands of devisers with more dramatic and poetic imagination than Tatham possessed. Certainly his monopoly of the form helped in part to seal its fate: not merely because his talent was limited, but because his ascendancy initiated a greater divorce between the pageant theatre of the streets and the working theatre proper than had prevailed before the closure. Whether responsibility for effecting this divorce must be laid on the City or the indifference of contemporary dramatists is hard to determine. The revival of the Lord Mayor's Shows while the theatres were still closed partly accounts:

presumably the number of dramatists available for employment on pageant-making was limited. Of the major dramatists who survived the interregnum, there is no indication that James Shirley or William Davenant had interest in pageant shows[27]. The professional dramatists of the day appear to have stood aloof. Perhaps they had no choice, for the pre-Commonwealth practice of teams of active dramatists and artificers competing against each other for the reward, above all financial, of devising the shows, was abandoned in favour of the regular provision of civic pageants by a man who, the evidence suggests, no longer had close connection with the theatre, and who worked in collaboration with what appears to have been a standing team of City craftsmen. It was an arrangement that became accepted practice. Again, before the Wars not only dramatists cultivated the pageant show, but occasionally we find prominent actors from the regular theatre performing in pageants, as did Burbage, Lowen and Rice. After the Restoration, although the theatres seem to have been closed on pageant days, the only named players we encounter are fairground entertainers like Pretty, Nash, Diamond, and later, the rope-dancer, Jacob Hall[28].

But monopoly work conditions and the separation of pageant theatre from regular professional theatre were not the only determinants. The increase in sophisticated spectacle at the roofed and artificially lit Restoration theatres also adversely affected the survival potential of traditional emblematic pageantry, for the revolution in scenic presentation initiated by Inigo Jones in Jacobean and Caroline Court spectacle invaded the public playhouses and furthered a taste for the decorative with which pageant scenes could not compete. Samuel Pepys's amusing description of his visit backstage to the Bridges Street prop room is suggestive[29]. If Pepys in any way expressed the spirit of his age, then his disillusionment at the tawdriness of production furnishings which had appeared so resplendent on stage implies already the acceptance of a theatrical convention that assumed a magical, illusionistic stage. In terms of such a convention, given the close proximity of spectator and spectacle and the harsh light of day, the emblematic decorations of the pageant stages may well have seemed inadequate, crude and naive. Its acceptance, too, furthered a movement in pageant spectacle towards a representation of the actual that undermined pageantry's presentational aesthetic.

In any event the Restoration masters of regular theatre spectacle, like Dryden and Shadwell, never turned their skills to furnishing popular civic show. Nor were they encouraged to do so by the monarch. For reasons personal, political and perhaps economic, the willingness of royalty to occasion or sponsor pageantry was largely spent with the *Aqua Triumphalis*. It was the last grand Stuart public spectacle. It was not, of course, the last of pageantry. For the rest of the century, with occasional intermissions, the Lord Mayor's Shows were paraded in the London streets and on the Thames. Some, particularly those of Thomas Jordan, were lively and entertaining by all accounts. But verbal inadequacy and the corruption of visual elements become increasingly marked. With the gradual *embourgeoisement* of theatrical entertainment, the juxtaposition of the formal and stately with the crude and naive, and the vigorous public celebration of civic and monarchical authority in a context of festive licence, became increasingly less acceptable. But here, as in the matter of royal patronage, we approach those complex political and social impulses which, in addition to formal and preparational factors, furthered the decline of popular pageantry and which lie beyond the scope of this paper. Little in the shows of the early Restoration or later compares with the achievement of the great tradition of English pageantry that runs from Peele through Jonson and Dekker to Middleton and Heywood, where the pageants at their best provided a meaningful fusion of word and image in a spectacle predominantly visual, but at once a popular and, on occasions, an artistically substantial theatre of the streets. John Tatham carried that tradition into the Restoration, but in his Royal Triumphs, and even more in his Lord Mayor's Shows, its dissolution is seen to be well advanced[30].

Notes

1 Tatham considered his contribution to be fairly substantial. He writes in the 1658 pamphlet that as musicians are praised not so much for their song as for their playing so in this Show he has endeavoured to compose a piece 'of perfect Harmony; and from several Discords, to raise a Concord: The Subject I have undertooke (though a body in it self) hath severall dependences like the Tree that gives a being to her many branches'.

2 Particularly important for its observations on pre-Commonwealth pageantry is Glynne Wickham, *Early English Stages*, vols. I and II (London, Routledge & Kegan Paul, 1959 and 1963). The most detailed over-view of earlier pageantry is

David M. Bergeron, *English Civic Pageantry 1558-1642* (London, Arnold, 1971). Some of Tatham's pageants are discussed in R. Withington, *English Pageantry: An Historical Outline* (Cambridge, Mass., 1918-20 2 vols.); and F.W. Fairholt, *Lord Mayor's Pageants* (London, Percy Society, 1843/4).

3   *The Diary of John Evelyn*, ed. E.S. de Beer (Oxford, 1959); *The Diurnal of Thomas Rugg*, ed. W.L. Sachse, Camden Society (London, 1961); *State Papers Venetial* (*SPV*), vol. XXXII.

4   *Diary of Samuel Pepys*, Everyman edn. (London, 1906), vol.I, 418.

5   MS. Corporation of London Record Office (CLRO), *Journals*, XLV, fol. 332 and fol. 422/23.

6   Withington, vol. I, 242 cites a MS. in the CLRO (No. 289) with a detailed breakdown of monies raised and expenses for this entertainment and for the Royal Progress of 1661. The importance of the monarch as lead player not only in royal fêtes but in some Lord Mayor's Shows is suggested in the 1664 speech to Charles II:

This day You Shew as well as See, for You
Are both our *Triumph* and *Spectator* too.

7   *SPV*, vol. XXXII, 29 April and 6 May 1661.

8   J.G. Nichols, *London Pageants* (London, 1837), 79.

9   A notable exception is Thomas Jordan's pageant for 1679. His pageants are generally more lively, humorous and engaging than Tatham's, but are so largely at the expense of the formal unity sought for by earlier pageant devisers. For comment on later pageantry, particularly Settle, and for early eighteenth-century opinion, see Sheila Williams, 'The Lord Mayor's Show in Tudor and Stuart Times', *Guildhall Miscellany*, No. 10, Sept. 1959.

10 The changing relationship between the monarch and his City subjects, the political issues involved in, particularly, the royal marriage, and the place and function of mayoralty in the eyes of the common citizens, are among the highly relevant but complex factors which must be left for treatment elsewhere.

11 John Ogilby, *The Relation of His Majesties Entertainment* (London, 1661). The complex bibliography of this work is discussed by F. Bowers, 'Ogilby's coronation entertainments 1661-89', *PBSA*, 47, 1953. Contemporary published material on the Progress is considerable; see also MS. CLRO, *Journals*, XLV, fol. 101.

12 The fully aquatic nature of this pageant is perhaps the reason Evelyn considered it 'the first solemnity of this nature after 20 yeares', *op. cit.*, 430, and not the 'large Stage or Fabrick ... a Ship, floating, rigg'd and man'd' that greeted the Lord Mayor at Whitehall in *The Royal Oake*, 1660.

13 The pageant is described fully by Withington, 1, p.247*ff*.

14 See MS. 289 in CLRO for payment details to artificers on the Progress. Eric Halfpenny has reproduced from this MS the details of payment, but not sums levied from the Companies, in 'The Citie's Loyalty Display'd (A literary and documentary causerie of Charles II's Coronation "Entertainment")', *Guildhall Miscellany*, No. X, Sept. 1959. See also Tatham's pamphlets, *London's Triumph* 1659, and *The Royal Oake*, 1660. The songs for the pageant were set by the royal musician John Gamble. William Lightfoot is reputed to have excelled in landscapes and perspective views, but little is known of his work. Peter Mills was one of the four surveyors of the City appointed to supervise the rebuilding after the Great Fire. His activity as a City Surveyor as early as 1661 and his connection with pageantry seem to have been overlooked by his biographers.

15 MS. CLRO, *Journals*, XLV, fol. 197-8 and fol. 249.

16 MS. CLRO, *Repertories*, LIII, fol. 166.

17 See HMC, *Dartmouth*, V, 10; and *Ormonde*, New Series III, 23.

18 Including creature comforts: the Clothworkers provided themselves with 'three dozen bottles of Lambeth Ale', quoted in T. Girtin, *The Golden Ram* (London, 1958); the Merchant Tailors laid in wine, but excluded women from their barge: C.M. Clode, *Memorials of the Guild of Merchant Taylors*, 2 vols (London, 1875); a banquet and entertainment was arranged on the day for the Aldermen's Ladies: MS. CLRO, *Repertories*, LIII, fol. 177.

19 The print reproduced here (Plate 1) is from the set of seven in the British Museum: (A set of 7 large plate˥ by D.S.), (London?), 1662. Anne Petrides, *State Barges on the Thames* (London, 1959), reproduced from a 1662 set of seven in the National Maritime Museum. Glynne Wickham *op.cit.* remarked on the importance of this illustration in *Early English Stages, op.cit.*, vol. II, and reproduced it from a Folger copy of Grainger, *Biographical History of England* (London, 1769-74), vol. 12, 30. R.T.D. Sayle, *The Barges of the Merchant Taylors' Company* (1933) noted the likeness between the engraving and Tatham's description.

20   Quoted W.S. Prideux, *Memorials of the Goldsmiths' Company*, 2 vols (London, 1896), vol. II, 131-3.

21   A more cynical view was taken by David O'Neill who remarked to Ormonde that the Queen looked like a prisoner at a Roman triumph. Quoted K. Feiling, *British Foreign Policy 1660-72* (London, Macmillan, 1930).

22   Edward Jerman (German) was the architect responsible for the 1657 Show; those for the 1659 and 1660 Shows are noted above, p. 55.

23   Thomas Heywood, *Londini Sinus Salutis*, 1635. For a discussion of these elements in Heywood's pageants see the three books by D.M. Bergeron, J.G. Nichols and F.W. Fairholt, *op. cit*. Tatham's 'tongs and antique instruments' in the 1661 show led on to Thomas Jordan's 1673 pageant where 'tongs, key, frying pan, grid-iron, and salt-box, made very melodious musick, which the worse it is performed, the better is accepted'.

24   *The Dramatic Works of John Tatham*, ed. J. Maidment and W.H. Logan (Edinburgh, 1879).

25   We have noted the tumbling 'interludes' in the *Aqua Triumphalis*. They were also a feature of the Coronation Progress: Diamond and Nash were paid three pounds for tumbling, CLRO MS 289.

26   The Clothworkers were apparently annoyed at having to pay for this pageant, feeling no doubt that it was not relevant to their celebration: 'a Pageant erected, representing and attending to St. Paul's Church, by order of the said Sir John Robinson without any consent of this company'. Quoted Girtin, *op. cit.*, p. 137. Dispute over the pageants in this Show may account for the disclaimer in the dedicatory epistle and its suggestion that the poet was only carrying out his patron's instructions.

27   Davenant was fully occupied with theatre management. Shirley was amusingly contemptuous of the Shows; his attitude anticipates that of Restoration writers and of Pope and others in the next century: see *Contention for Honour and Riches*, 1633, and *Honoria and Mammon*, 1652.

28   Between 1660 and 1700 *The London Stage* lists only one theatre performance on pageant day, and that at Court: Aphra Behn's *The Rover*, about which there is possible doubt as to the accuracy of the date.

29   *Diary of Samuel Pepys*, vol. II, 19th March, 1665/6.

30 Since this paper went to press our knowledge of Lord Mayor's shows has been extended by L.J. Morrissey's valuable 'Theatrical records of the London Guilds, 1655-1708', *Theatre Notebook*, vol. XXIX, no. 3, 1975. The Guild records point the shift in pageant preparation from competing teams to a regular team and indicate how reduced was the importance of the poet after 1655.

Acknowledgements

The author is grateful to the British Library Board for kind permission to reproduce Plate 1.

BEN ALBACH

A Dutch Actor's Experiences with English Theatre in Amsterdam, May-July 1814

(*translated by* Mrs E. de Wijs-Maher)

Wat zal men zeggen van hetgeen men niet verstaat?

This is how the Dutch actor Johannes Jelgerhuis begins his notes on English performances in Amsterdam, May-July 1814. It means: 'what can one say about what one does not understand?' I will endeavour to give his impressions in the language which was to Jelgerhuis double Dutch[1].

As soon as Napoleon's army of occupation was withdrawn (November 1813) — he writes — communications with England were resumed, after a lapse of twenty years. Within a few months a large contingent of English artists crosses the North Sea: 20 actors and actresses, 60 pantomime players and equestrians with 18 well-trained British horses. They stay in Amsterdam for more than two months. It is a curious situation: an exceptionally long visit of three 'Royal' theatres from London — collaboration between Dutch and English performers which had never occurred since the age of the strolling players; a man of the acting profession describes what he sees, what he himself experiences — it all goes to make this notebook an interesting document.

His remarks proceed from professional experience. For Johannes Jelgerhuis (1770-1836) was not only a well-known actor, but also painter, draughtsman, costume expert; and he was to publish a handbook on the art of gesture[2]. In 1811, he had already written an illustrated account of the performances given by the Comédie Française from Paris to mark Napoleon's visit to Amsterdam. He has great admiration for François-Joseph Talma, yet esteems his fellow-artists Andries Snoek and Mrs Johanna Cornelia Wattier (the Dutch Mrs Siddons) no less[3]. His ideal consists of elegant poses, graceful gestures, natural charm. For him, acting is one unbroken sequence of stately attitudes, for it is French classicism that shapes the taste of connoisseurs. Jelgerhuis has a preference for Racine and Voltaire, plays also in comedy and in domestic drama, but Tragedy alone spells for him True Art[4].

His favourite part is King Lear and of this he writes a detailed description, complete with a self-portrait in his costume, derived, as he says, from Ossian's Fingal[5]. Not, of course, the Lear of that barbarian Shakespeare: a certain Monsieur Ducis has fortunately taken the trouble to refine that irregular and improper tragedy, in conformity with good taste. It's just not done to represent a King as a senile greybeard. The result is that only the title is reminiscent of Shakespeare, and Lear becomes a sort of Philoctetes. Jelgerhuis relates that in Act III Lear appears on stage with lightning flashing alternatively left and right of him, 'which picture delights the audience every time'. Picturesqueness is his prime objective. This is in the Dutch tradition: before Jelgerhuis there were others who combined a talent for drawing with a talent for acting[6].

This man, then, was confronted with English theatre for the first time in his life. On May 1814 the following advertisement appeared in the *Amsterdamsche Courant* under the proud title, 'English theatre in the Amstelstraat':

> English plays and entertainments under the Authority of the Burgomasters. Their Majesties' Servants from the Theatre-Royal of London and Windsor beg leave most respectfully to announce to the Nobility, Gentry and Public in general, this Theatre will positively open on Wednesday next, May 18th 1814, with the celebrated comedy *The Honey-Moon*.

This company, under the direction of Jonas and Penley[7], performed in the German Theatre which was well-patronized by the Jewish community living in the neighbourhood, rich and poor alike. With the traditional Amsterdam fairground just round the corner, this was a genuine popular theatre[8]. The English company put on comedies by Allingham, Colman, Dibdin, Cherry, Mrs Centlivre, Brown, Lillo, Goldsmith, Reynolds and Beaumarchais, as well as two of Kotzebue's domestic dramas currently very popular in Holland[9]. They gave one performance of *Hamlet*. Unfortunately, Jelgerhuis did not see this. It would have been interesting to know his opinion, for he himself had played the King in Ducis' version of the tragedy.

On 31 May this Dutch stage-Lear visited the theatre where 'their Britannic Majesties' Servants' performed a comedy by Andrew Cherry, *The Soldier's Daughter*, and Allingham's farce, *Fortune's Frolics*[10]. Jelgerhuis was delighted with these comedies, reporting:

I saw a comedy which raised many a laugh: several character parts, including a female one, which were all, it seems to me, very well acted indeed.

He did not altogether approve of the voices of the English ladies. These, according to him, 'spoke in a high-pitched, thin tone which I cannot say was very pleasing to the ear'. It is perhaps interesting to note here that Jelgerhuis himself was well-known for his shrill voice and Frisian accent. He remarks on several interesting points: on the high speed of the acting and the rapid delivery of the actors; on their good memorization of the text — he was 'assured that they had no prompter'; on the frequent changes of location; and on the fact that although there are doors in the wings the players always enter in front of the first wing. Another thing he finds typical of the English taste is that the actors enter talking; they can be heard before one sees them. However, it is the movement over the stage which particularly fascinates the Dutch actor. This is something new for Holland.

In his handbook for actors he had given instructions for entering: an actor should always describe a curve, from upstage left to downstage right, from upstage right to downstage left; each actor takes up a position and holds it for a time. When he moves he must do so in curved lines — all according to classical French conventions. 'In observing these rules,' he writes, 'the stage appears larger, whereas by following winding ways it looks small and less spacious, even if it is large.'[11] But now the English actors provided a revelation (see Fig. 4.1). Jelgerhuis writes in his notebook:

Their positioning was most remarkable, spread out over the whole stage, moving past, and in-between one another, in this way indicating natural confusion, an ordered confusion however, although at the same time free of that visible order which is a feature of the French and Dutch theatre, in which most of the actors gather round the prompter, and where they always, with a certain decorum, pass behind each other. Such positioning made asides possible and probable.[12]

This is a great compliment, since deviation from French conventions was for a Dutch actor almost as great a sin as bad manners for an English gentleman. He was especially impressed by the actor who played the Father. 'This actor,' he writes, 'struck me in particular by his postures as well as his speech, all of which excellently portrayed an old man, full of passion.'

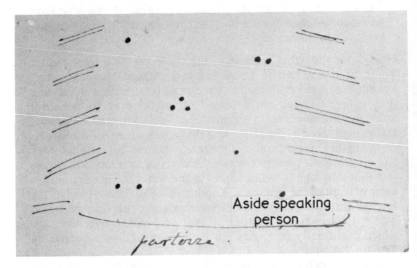

Figure 4.1. Groundplan of Andrew Cherry's Soldier's Daughter

On his second visit to the English Theatre (2 June 1814) Jelgerhuis saw a comedy whose title would infuriate a modern feminist, *The Wonder: a woman keeps a secret*, were it not for the fact that the author was a woman, and as such a rare phenomenon in the world of playwriting: Mrs Susannah Centlivre. The setting is Spain, Jelgerhuis thinks, but according to the text it is Portugal. Again there is much scene-changing which, with open curtain, can be seen by the audience. The ladies' costumes are good; the lady's maids look especially charming in pink and black, and bright blue. Once again the action is lively:

> In great confusion, but observing certain rules as they criss-crossed each other, nevertheless always arriving at the right spot.

(Typically English, in the eyes of a Dutchman.) It is all very entertaining but does not quite fall into the category of popular entertainment, for there were not many spectators at that time in Amsterdam who understood English[13]. But Jelgerhuis is now to acquire personal experience of the genre, and that to a high degree, albeit to his fury and chagrin.

First he goes on tour, studying meanwhile the part he is to act in a new English melodrama of the sort then in vogue, which he hates, but which draws large crowds to the theatre. It is a version of *The Secret Mine*, a melodrama by John Fawcett and Thomas John

Dibdin, translated into the Dutch language by a certain Mr Schmidt[14]. The first performance is to take place on 22 June 1814 in the Schouwburg, the Municipal Theatre of Amsterdam. Numerous artists take part: several well-known Amsterdam actors and actresses; the pantomime player Jan van Well, a celebrated Pierrot, the ballerina Mlle Brulé; the corps de ballet, the orchestra, extras — all these Dutch performers, so states the advertisement, but working in 'collaboration with a score of leading members of the Royal Amphitheatre and Royal Covent Garden Theatre. General direction is in the hands of Mr. William Davis and the show is provided with completely new, specially made decors by the Dutch stage artists W. de Vries and J. Wennink'. This is Astley's famous company[15]. Equestrian melodrama is to be introduced to Amsterdam, following performances of the same show in London less than three weeks before[16]. Jelgerhuis is amazed at what he now sees. He writes:

> On my return from Dordrecht, I found the stage in the theatre altogether strangely decorated. The rear represented an underground mine of red granite with streaks of gold. This gold glittered marvellously. There was a large bridge to enable one to ride on horseback along a raised way, and in the middle, stairs to walk down off it, as will be seen from the accompanying illustration. The whole stage had been affixed so that the horsemen could ride over it. A hundred and fifty yards of cloth had been painted and various alterations made to the stage. (See Fig. 4.2).

The framework at the rear of the stage is intended for the last scene, where the horses climb higher up into the mine, but can be used in other scenes. Three rehearsals are held lasting into the night. All seats have been sold for the première, although the prices of admission are double the usual: but then, it is a very costly show to put on. No less than 3,500 guilders have been spent on wood alone for reconstruction of the stage. So much for Jelgerhuis's comments on the technical side. But now he loses his temper, as he sets about describing the play and its performance. *The Secret Mine*, he says, is one of those 'trivial, monstrous melodramas condemned by people of good taste'. That is bad enough, but the combination of dramatic art with horsemanship, speaking parts with background music, song, dance, pantomime, all in one and the same show ... he is 'ashamed to have to appear in such a monstrosity'. He asks to be discharged, writing a scathing letter to the director[17]. This 'dramatic monster' is an example of what Professor Michael Booth, in his amusing book *English Melodrama*,

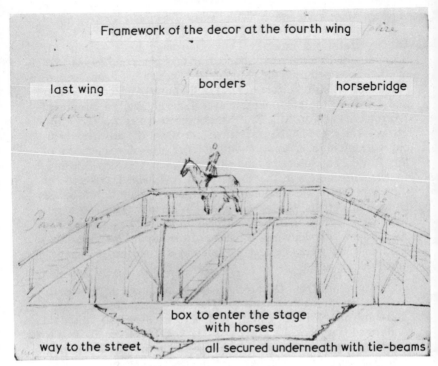

Figure 4.2. *Sketch by Jelgerhuis of the horses' bridge and framework for the decors,* The Secret Mine

calls 'Eastern equestrian melodrama'. It is one of Astley's specialities[18]. The setting is somewhere on the border between Persia and Hindustan. Jelgerhuis draws the decor for the first act: the Governor's garden in front of the palace which looks more Venetian than Persian (see Fig. 4.3). The same two-level construction is used: one of the poles is changed into a pillar as part of the entrance gate. Jelgerhuis himself plays the part of the tyrannical ruler Ismael; a part that must have come easily to him in the circumstances. His notes become more and more aggressive. The story of the play is as follows:

Ismael is the lucky father of the beautiful, poetically named Zaphyra. But as is usually the case with tyrants, he wants more. True, the Persians have overthrown the Hindustani, but the latter have retained a secret mine full of minerals. The melodrama is therefore about the possession of mineral wealth. It sounds highly topical. The treatment of the conflict is, however, rather romantic. Besides his pretty daughter, Ismael has a prisoner, the young Rajah of Hindustan, who knows where the coveted treasure lies. As you will already have guessed, Zaphyra and the Rajah fall ardently in love. Well, he can have her if only he will tell Ismael where he can

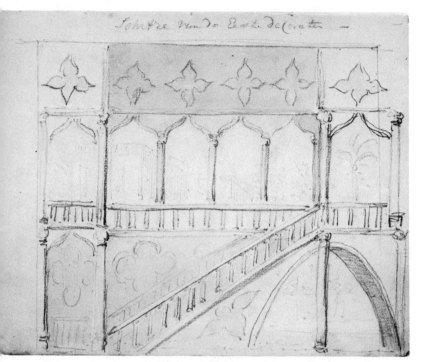

Figure 4.3. Sketch by Jelgerhuis of the palace background of the governor's garden, The Secret Mine, *Act I.*

find the secret mine. At first the Rajah extricates himself from the dilemma by a ruse, and manages to satisfy the Governor with a somewhat lesser treasure. The couple marry, and we witness the wedding feast in the temple — music, ballet and so on. But ... there is a traitor among the Hindustani. Ismael's wrath is unleashed. Zaphyra, who has been let into the secret, manages to keep it — just like Mrs Centlivre's heroine. Now there is a swift sequence of events: imprisonment, liberation attempts, escape. Fierce battle is waged. People run in and out of caves, fires start among rocks and spread into the distance. And there is a real river into which the Rajah jumps, to make good his escape, leaving his bride in the care of a kind horsewoman. At last we see the mine. The scene of battle is before the entrance; the Hindustani offer resistance. Horsemen arrive on the scene. Now Ismael brings a cannon onstage....

In the Amsterdam Theatre Museum, where there is a large collection of Jelgerhuis's drawings, I found a sketch which almost certainly corresponds to the description in his notebooks (see Plate 2A):

The cannon was of wood and contained two flintlock barrels which were ignited with a torch. And the horses on the bridge

Plate 2A. Cannon with horsemen: watercolour sketch by Jelgerhuis

Plate 2B. Watercolour sketch by Jelgerhuis of rear part of mine pit with horsemen inside, The Secret Mine

and in the pit under the stage all made their appearance at a given sign.... The cannon is fired and fighting begins again, finishing with dead horses lying here and there. Fighting between people doing nothing to the point, but moving in utter confusion, pushing one another; — how could it be other than an affront to my good taste, that this met with the approbation of the audience from the very start?

It is clear that Jelgerhuis did not care for horse-play. But was it not asking too much to expect classical French precision in the heat of such a battle? The play continues with the Persian cavalrymen taking the mine. Sawdust swirls into the auditorium. Jelgerhuis made a watercolour of the mine, with the horses standing in the entrance to the caverns (see Plate 2B). A backdrop with openings is let down in front of the framework. It is what Jelgerhuis called 'the mine of red granite with streaks of gold, which glittered marvellously'. At the very end of the play, the rock changes into the Rajah's palace. Persians and Hindustani are reconciled, Ismael has his treasure. Zaphyra and her Rajah fall into each other's arms. As the smoke clears, the audience cheers. It is all very spectacular, like an early Metro-Goldwyn-Mayer show.

Nothing combining so many different theatrical genres had been seen in Holland before. As it happened, Amsterdam was at that time in a festive mood. The Czar of all the Russians, accompanied by the Dutch Court, was paying a visit to the recently liberated, richly decorated capital. The Princess of Orange visited the Municipal Theatre, together with the Crown Prince, the Prussian Successor and several other princes. For the young Prince of Orange, aide de camp to the Duke of Wellington and soon to be one of the heroes of 1815, this Anglo-Dutch horse-show may have been a nice introduction to Waterloo[19]. So everybody was happy, except for Jelgerhuis.

The wrong done to me, the humiliation as an actor of being obliged to take part in an equestrian act, was such an insufferably grievous matter that I should have taken my leave, had not my wife and children held me back.

This, for him, spelt 'the destruction of all culture, the murder of art, prostitution of the stage'. But poor Jelgerhuis was ignorant of what was to come in London: *The Battle of Waterloo, The Invasion of Russia, The Siege of Missolonghi*. Even *Macbeth* and *Richard III* were to be 'equestrianized'.

The Dutch actor consoled himself making sketches, for at least

he was able to appreciate the pictorial qualities of the show. He
writes:

> Sixty soldiers and eighteen horses and the people taking part
> were all in new, most peculiar Persian-style costumes. The
> materials, although not costly, were well-chosen, but heavy in
> weight: steel spangles, gold leather and serge made every costume
> as heavy as lead. The horses, caparisoned with brasses, splendid
> saddles and saddle-cloths, with manes shining like steel, and
> lamps affixed to their heads, everything conspired to amaze. The
> presentation in the mine was especially remarkable: a silent
> tableau, like a painting.

Silent *tableau vivant*, like the traditional dumb show; the Dutch
actor finally feels at home.

Happily for Jelgerhuis, he did not have to take part in Davis's
next show. But he remarked on a waterfall with horses prancing
through it. It was made of whalebones, he says. This was in
Timour the Tartar, a melodrama by Lewis which had already been
presented in London in 1811[20].

For the Dutch actor this first acquaintance with English
showmanship was not an absolute success. The language barrier
was doubtless partly responsible; moreover, a circus such as Astley
and Davis had at their disposal in London was lacking in
Amsterdam. Writing down his feelings of the moment, Jelgerhuis
seems to have completely forgotten his own praise of the English
performances he had seen a month before[21]. Nevertheless it is
clear that the English made a more modern use of space than was
customary on the continent. Natural movement on stage in the
comedies, the split-level construction of a fixed, but variably
adaptable scenery in the cavalry show, the courage to combine
divergent theatrical genres (total theatre in 1814!), beautiful
pageantry — all prove that England was less inhibited by formal
conventions. But Jelgerhuis was too much of a child of his time to
recognize these as signs of the coming Romanticism.

With the end of the generation of great actors in the neo-classical
tradition like Jelgerhuis, the Dutch theatre declined, the stage after
his death (1836) being entirely dominated by musical plays,
harlequinades and French melodramas. Ironically, Jelgerhuis's
best pupil, Anton Peters, was to be very successful in that popular
style: the first romantic actor followed the last tragedian.
Moreover, Peters was the first to play Shakespearean tragedies in
the original version, in the 1850s. But the translations then were
still rather poor. It is only round about 1880 that the gap between

connoisseurs and popular-theatre actors is finally bridged. The inherent vitality of melodramatic acting proved well suited to Shakespearean rôles. Good translations of all Shakespeare's plays started to appear from 1884 (the complete works, by L.A.J. Burgersdijk) and have been produced at intervals up to the present time (i.e. the recent translation of *King Lear* by Mr Evert Straat). However much production styles have changed, the performance of Shakespearean plays has remained pre-eminent in the Netherlands[22]. English dramatic literature occupies an important part in the repertory of the Dutch stage nowadays. The English language is understood everywhere and all overseas players receive a warm welcome by both audiences and colleagues.

Notes

1   Manuscript in the University Library, Amsterdam: 'Iets over het Engelsche toneel waargenoomen in de maanden Meij en Junij 1814. Door J: Jelgerhuis Rz. Hollandsch acteur te Amsterdam.'

2   *Theoretische Lessen over de Gesticulatie en Mimiek, gegeven aan de Kweekelingen van het Fonds ter Opleiding en Onderrigting van Tooneel-Kunstenaars aan den Stads Schouwburg te Amsterdam (1827-1830)* [*Theoretical Lessons on Gesticulation and Facial Expression, given to the pupils of the Foundation for the Training and Instruction of Actors at the Municipal Theatre of Amsterdam*] (Amsterdam, P. Meyer Warnars) Reprinted with English summary by A.M. Hakkert (Amsterdam, 1970).

3   'Schetzende Herinneringen van de Representatiën gegeven in October 1811, door de Fransche Acteurs en Actrices Talma, Duchenois en Bourgoin op het Hollandsche Toneel te Amsterdam. Waargenoomen door J: Jelgerhuis Rzn. Hollandsch Acteur, ter Gelegenheid dat de fransche Keijzer Napoleon Zig in de Stad Amsterdam bevond.' (Manuscript, Theatre Museum, Amsterdam.)

4   Complete list of all the parts played by Jelgerhuis in 'Johannes Jelgerhuis Rzn. acteur-schilder 1770-1836', *Catalogus Nijmegen*, Leiden (Amsterdam, Theatre Museum, 1969/70.)

5   'De toneelspeler J. Jelgerhuis Rz., in zijne voornaamste treurspelrollen, op den Amsterdamschen Schouwburg

vertoond sinds 25 jaren' ('The actor Jelgerhuis in his principal tragic rôles, presented at the Amsterdam Theatre over 25 years') (Amsterdam, Gebroeders Van Arum, 1832). (Contains only an Introduction and *King Lear*.)

6 e.g. Cornelis Troost (1697-1750); Johannes Punt (1711-1779); Marten Corver (1727-1794).

7 The company consisted of the actresses: Watson, R. Penley, Beynon, Lucas, M. Jonas; and the actors: Platt, Salter, Gibbon, Pinley Jr., Stackwood, Burton, Jonas, Etatt, Mountford, J. Jonas, Booth, Franklin (*Amsterdamsche Courant*, 20 May 1814).
According to information kindly given by Miss Sybil Rosenfeld, this travelling company was not of great standing. Around 1815 they included in their circuit Windsor, Henley, Folkestone, Peckham Rye, all in the south of England, and probably also visited Boulogne. It is not at all sure that they had the right to call themselves a Royal Company. (Authentic Memoirs of the Green Room: *Tooneel-aantekeningen, vervat in een omstandige Brief, aan den schrijver van het Leven van Jan Punt*, etc., by M. Corver (Leyden: 1786). These 'Theatre Notes' by the actor-manager-producer Corver — reporting on actors, acting, stage events, audience reactions, dramaturgy, etc. — are the principal source for knowledge of the Dutch theatre in the eighteenth century.

8 The German Theatre (Hoogduitsche Schouwburg) was a private theatre (519 seats), built in 1791 for a German dramatic company under J.H. Dessauer. Operas (Von Weber, Mozart) and German plays were performed here in the original language. In 1852 the name of the theatre was changed to Grand Théâtre (des variétés). The building was demolished in 1951.

9 Repertory of the English Theatre, Amstelstraat, Amsterdam; announcements in the *Amsterdamsche Courant*, 1814:

English Theatre in the Amstelstraat. English Plays and Entertainments under the Authority of the Burgomasters.

18.5   J. Tobin, *The Honey-Moon* (1805)
          J.T. Allingham, *The Weather-Cock* (1805)
21.5   G. Colman Jr., *John Bull, or an Englishman's Fireside* (1803)
          J.G. Millingen, *The Bee Hive* (1811)
23.5   Shakespeare, *Hamlet, Prince of Denmark* (1603)
          J.C. Cross, *The Purse, or The Benevolent Tar* (1794)

25.5	T.J. Dibdin, *Speed the Plough* (1802)
	J. Kenney, *Raising the Wind* (1803)
28.5	T.J. Dibdin, *The Jew* (1798)
	W. Dimond, *The Hunter of the Alps* (1804)
*31.5	A. Cherry, *The Soldier's Daughter* (1804)
	J.T. Allingham, *Fortune's Frolic* (1799)
*2.6	Mrs. S. Centlivre, *The Wonder: A Woman keeps a Secret* (1714)
	G. Colman Jr., *Ways and Means of a Trip to Dover* (1788)
4.6	Kotzebue, *Lovers Vows* (transl.?)
	I. Pocock, *The Miller and his Men* (1813)
6.6	J. Brown, *Barbarossa, or The Captive Queen* (1754)
	I. Pocock, *The Miller and his Men* (1813)
8.6	G. Colman Jr., *The Mountaineers, or Love and Madness* (1793)
	T.J. Dibdin, *The Jew and the Doctor* (1798)
15.6	W. Dimond, *The Peasant Boy* (1811)
	J. Townley, *High Life Below Stairs* (1759)
18.6	Kotzebue, *The Stranger, or Misanthropy and Repentance* (transl.?)
	T.J. Dibdin, *Of Age Tomorrow* (1800)
20.6	J. Boaden, *The Voice of Nature* (1802)
	G. Colman Jr., *The Forty Thieves* (1806)
22.6	G. Lillo, *George Barnwell, or The Merchant of London* (1731)
	G. Colman Jr., *The Forty Thieves* (1806)
25.6	Kotzebue, *The Stranger, or Misanthropy and Repentance* (transl.?)
	T.J. Dibdin, *Of Age Tomorrow* (1800)
27.6	G. Colman Jr., *The Battle of Hexham, or Days of Old* (1798)
	Pantomime: *Don Juan*
1.7	Kemble (?), *Alexander*
	Pantomime: *Don Juan*
2.7	O. Goldsmith, *She Stoops to Conquer, or The Mistake of a Night* (1773)
	G. Colman Jr., *Inkle and Yariko* (1787)
6.7	Beaumarchais, *Follies of a Day, or The Marriage of Figaro* (transl.?)
	G. Colman Jr., *Inkle and Yariko* (1787)
9.7	F. Reynolds, *Laugh When You Can, or The Faithful Black* (1798)

*Performances described by Jelgerhuis. The announced song titles are omitted here. Only for the second performance is the complete cast given. No authors' names are mentioned. The identification can be found in Allardyce Nicoll, *History of English Drama, 1660-1900*, 2nd edn (Cambridge U.P., 1966), vols. III/VI.

10   Allardyce Nicoll, *op. cit.*, vol. II, 305; vol. III, 232; vol. IV, 279.

11   *Theoretische Lessen*, etc., plate 3.

12   This remark seems to contradict the lively groupings of the actors as suggested in the well-known Schouwburg prints of the late eighteenth century. The question arises to what extent these prints are reliable as a document of what was usually seen on the Amsterdam stage.

13   In 1826 a company under Joseph Smithson (with S. Chapman and J.B. Booth) played six Shakespearean tragedies. In 1829 two companies visited the theatre in Amstelstraat, one under W.H. Brien (with Miss Harriet Smithson), one under J.R. Aubry (with Charles Kean as Othello). They all met with a cool reception. Probably these dogged attempts to arouse Dutch interest in the English drama were due to one of the managers of the German Theatre, a certain Mr George Sawyer (documentation Theatre Museum, Amsterdam).

14   John Fawcett (and Thomas J. Dibdin), *De Verborgene groef*, 'groot melodrama in twee bedrijven. Het Engelsch vrij gevolgd door C.F. Schmidt, Amsterdam 1814' (on the title page, erroneously, Farocett). See Allardyce Nicoll, *op. cit.*, vol. IV, 311. For Fawcett, see W. Davenport Adams, *A Dictionary of the Drama* (New York, Burt Franklin, 1904). For full particulars of Astley's production of *The Secret Mine* at Covent Garden, see A.H. Saxon, *Enter Foot and Horse, a History of Hippodrama in England and France* (Newhaven and London, Yale U.P., 1968), 96.

15   The playbills (in the University Library, Amsterdam) mention: 'under the direction of Messrs Ahstley [sic], Davis and Parker; from the 25th of June under Mr. Wm. Davis'. There were thirteen performances of *The Secret Mine*; in an extra presentation for the Dutch Court, the principal scenes from *The Secret Mine* were given after a presentation of *Iphigenia in Tauris* (adaptation by G. De La Touche) by the Amsterdam actors, on 12 July. The Russian Czar saw Ducis' *Hamlet* in Dutch on 4 July.

One of the Dutch actresses, the gifted Mrs Kamphuizen née

Snoek, had to play her part in *The Secret Mine* on horseback, according to Jelgerhuis.

16   The playbill of the Royal Amphitheatre, Astley's, for the 2nd, 3rd and 4th of June 1814, promises performances of *The Secret Mine*, 'by permission of the Theatre Royal, Covent Garden', with the following cast:

> Araxa, Mr. Gomersal; Ismael, Mr. Payne; Assad, Mr. Blanchard; Dimdim, Mr. Herring; Hyder, Mr. Makeen; Abbas, Mr. Foster; Duban, Mr. Decastro; Nasrod, Mr. Wolfe; Sali, Mr. Cardozo; ... Leader of the Hindoo Cavalry, Mr. W. Davis Jun,; ... Zaphyra, Mrs. Makeen; Zobeida, Mrs. Ridgway; Camilla, Miss Adams.

17   Director of the Schouwburg was at that time Andries Snoek, a great actor highly esteemed by Talma. In 1810, for the first time since the foundation of the Schouwburg (1637), actors had taken over the management from the city governors. This situation lasted until 1820.

18   Michael Booth, *English Melodrama* (London, Herbert Jenkins, 1965).

19   The visit of Czar Alexander tó Holland seems to have been for political reasons. A fortnight before his arrival, Princess Charlotte of England had broken off her engagement to the 22-year-old Prince of Orange, heir to the Dutch throne. The Czar came to suggest a marriage between the Prince and his daughter Anna Paulowna. Alexander was received with great enthusiasm at The Hague. The expected royal visit to the Anglo-Dutch performance in Amsterdam did not take place. Only after the Czar's departure did Princess Wilhelmina and her two sons come to see the Dutch and English artists. The future King William II married the Russian princess in 1816.

20   For reactions to that spectacle by Matthew G. 'Monk' Lewis at Covent Garden, see A.H. Saxon, 87-91.

21   Between 17 May and 6 August 1814, 46 performances by English artists were given in Amsterdam: 20 by the so-called Theatre Royal of London and Windsor Players, 26 by the guests from the Theatre Royal Covent Garden, and the Royal Amphitheatre.

22   Jacobus Swart, 'Shakespeare in Dutch Translation', *Delta Review of Arts, Life and Thought in the Netherlands*, Amsterdam, vol. VII, no.2, summer 1964.

Acknowledgements

The author is grateful to the Theatre Museum, Amsterdam, for kind permission to reproduce Plate 2A, and to the University Library, Amsterdam, for permission to reproduce Plate 2B, and Figs. 4.1, 4.2 and 4.3.

KATHLEEN BARKER

*Bristol at Play 1801-53: A Typical Picture of the English provinces?**

In 1801 William Wyatt Dimond, actor-manager of the Bath and Bristol Stock Company, retired from the stage. In 1853 Sarah M'Cready, second wife of William M'Cready the elder, died, and was succeeded as theatre lessee by her son-in-law, James Henry Chute. These two dates are among the most significant in the history of the Bristol Theatre Royal: but why, you may well ask, have I chosen them as terminal points in a paper on popular entertainment?

The answer lies only partly in the truism that it is impossible at this period to draw a hard and fast line between 'legitimate' theatre and other entertainments, either in artists or repertoire; even more, in a provincial city with an established patent theatre, it lies in the influence which developments in each had on the other. What happened to the Theatre Royal affected what happened to other entertainments; any date which is important in the history of the one is likely to have considerable significance for the other. A prime example of this is the fact that the existence of a group of Patent Theatre proprietors, tenacious of their rights to the last letter of the law and beyond, prevented the establishment of any other permanent theatre till as late as 1867 — and even then it was built in Clifton, which legally was outside the city boundary.

It was not, however, within the powers of the most blatant theatrical monopolists to affect the two chartered fairs of Bristol, the St Paul's or Temple Fair held on the Bath side of the River Avon in March, and the St James's Fair held in central Bristol at the beginning of September. Not only did these occasions attract a wide variety of shows and showmen, they created acknowledged 'entertainment areas' more effectively than any Town Planning Act could do, which endured long after the moralists had succeeded in having the Pleasure Fairs abolished, under highly melodramatic circumstances, in 1838.

In 1801, when my story begins, the Theatre Royal in Bristol was partner in the most prosperous and prestigious provincial circuit in

* © Kathleen Barker 1976.

the country, that created by John Palmer and William Keasberry of Bath from 1779 onwards. Keasberry, the Acting Manager, was succeeded in 1786 by William Wyatt Dimond, who was the 'front man' in the concern, Palmer staying in the background to deal with the administration. Dimond's great popularity in Bristol did much to prevent the theatre suffering from the traditional suspicion in which Bristol, the home of hard-headed merchants, held Bath, the exemplum of culture and the *ton*. For if there is one thing guaranteed to damn an artistic enterprise in Bristol, it is allowing its citizens to feel that the management has its interests centred elsewhere, and that Bristol is really only of secondary importance in achieving its aims. So when Dimond retired from acting, and joined Palmer in managing the circuit from Bath, and when, moreover, in 1805 a grand new Theatre Royal was built in that city, it became increasingly obvious that it was in Bath that the power lay. The alienation began, creating attitudes open to exploitation.

It was some time before the theatre managers realized that they were losing ground in Bristol, because there was still a considerable audience to be drawn from troops stationed in the city during the Napoleonic Wars, and apart from shows at the Fairs, there were only occasional circuses and exhibitions of puppets and automata, which generally avoided performances on Monday — the traditional play-night in Bristol. Even so, one can see a tendency in the management to over-react, for example to a London report that they had engaged the boxers Belcher and Gamble at ten guineas a week.

> We presume there is no necessity of contradicting so injurious a report to the inhabitants of the city; but only think it prudent to apprize strangers, and more particularly the Metropolis, in justice to the reputation of the Manager, that it is wholly unfounded, and has arisen, as we imagine, from the circumstance of Belcher and Gamble being at present engaged with a groupe (*sic*) of itinerant Equestrians, &c., who are exhibiting in this city.[1]

Not that the theatre managers were averse from capitalizing on, and even pioneering, non-dramatic entertainments. In the month following that disclaimer, February 1802, they were featuring the Phantasmagoria, a type of magic lantern show in which spectral images were projected by means of multiple sources of light and moving reflecting surfaces, with the effect described by *Felix Farley's Bristol Journal*:

The Spectres seem to emerge from total darkness, at the pleasure of the operator, till they approach within a few paces of the spectator, in whatever part of the Theatre he is placed; nay, so strong is the illusion, that several persons in the gallery were fully persuaded the figures were there also, and actually attempted to grapple with them.[2]

The theatre engagement was repeated in September, but it was not till two years later that a similar show, the Phantasmeidos (the machinery of which was made by a Bristol optician, J. Springer), was shown at the Taylors' Hall in Broad Street during the Temple Fair; the following year Belzoni, 'the Patagonian Sampson' (later, of course, famous as an Egyptian explorer), showed his Phantascope at the Trout Tavern, Cherry Lane, just off St James's Churchyard.

Exclusive to the fairs were the apparently endless supply of freaks, animal and human, alive and dead. The Irish Giant, Patrick O'Brien, who had appeared live at Temple Fair in 1802, died at the Hot Wells in September 1806; the following year a statue of him, 'attired in part of his own wardrobe', was exhibited by his former travelling companion at a house in St Stephen's Avenue. Other regular visitors were stock attractions of the eighteenth century: panoramas, waxworks, travelling museums and mechanical models.

There are disappointingly few traces of live performances — fewer, indeed, than in some decades of the previous century. In September 1806 one Mr Jones followed his panorama with burlettas and dances, and two years later Belzoni had a fit-up in St James's Churchyard featuring a *ballet d'action, The Seven Capes, or, The Pirates of Algiers*, 'for the Display of which, SIGNOR BELZONI has engaged, at a Great Expence, Performers of the first Abilities, from London'[3]. Almost certainly the strollers were there, but they did not indulge in printed advertisements, and misguided local spouters soon found themselves in trouble with the magistrates.

The most prominent and best organized of the visitors were the circuses. The first attempt at a permanent site had been made in the 1790s when Handy and Franklin added an arena to an existing riding school in Limekiln Lane, between the city and the Hot Wells; this enterprise had petered out after a quarrel between the managers, and the circuses of Bannister, Saunders, Adams and Powell — sometimes two troupes at the same time — used temporary amphitheatres in St James's Churchyard or around Nelson Street.

As a rule the performances were limited to equestrian acts, acrobatics, and that perennial favourite, *The Taylor Riding to Brentford*, but occasionally something more ambitious was tried. Saunders, in particular, constructed a fairly elaborate amphitheatre in Nelson Street in January 1803 and stayed for three months, introducing pantomimes such as *Harlequin Statue; or, The Fairies' Gift*, in which

> The scenery, particularly the *Enchanted Garden,* and the *coral grot*, with emblematical figures, are finely executed: the dresses are neatly and handsomely fancied, and the characters were ably supported.

A month later, an advertisement of *Cupid's Present* described

> the Theatre, by means of new and singularly constructed Scenery and Machinery, arranged in different gradations apparently moving by Magic Power, forming the *Stage* into *a Representation of Cupid's Triumph.* [4]

No doubt the machinery creaked and jerked; but this sounds something more than the usual fair-time fit-up.

However, it was not from the circus proprietors that the first direct challenge to the Theatre Royal arose, but from the lively commercialism of one Walter Jenkins, a broker, who had taken the sadly unsuccessful Assembly Rooms off Prince's Street, and having during 1811 refurbished and rearranged them so that they might serve as dining hall, concert room or theatre, looked round to see what honest penny he could turn with them. The New Theatre, Prince's Street, as Jenkins provocatively rechristened the building, would hold 600 in the Boxes and Gallery and 900 in the Pit — not far off the capacity of the Royal — and its first theatrical clients were Charles Incledon and Charles Mathews the elder in their entertainment, *The Travellers*, for which they wisely obtained the Mayor's licence in November 1811. In January 1812 Masquerade Balls were advertised, then cancelled; 'ENTERTAINMENTS entirely new' were promised, and turned out to be acrobatic and rope displays by Wilson and Sieur Harnn Michalets Sanches, who had appeared with Bannister's Circus back in 1806, and for whom the building was now renamed the Regency Theatre.

Confrontation with the Royal, however, did not take place till after August 1812, when Lawler, who had been with Elliston at the Surrey, opened the Regency as a burletta house during the Royal's summer closure.

The Entertainments that are to be produced, will combine Grandeur, Interest, and Comic Effect; but never departing from the strictest line of decorum. The more juvenile part of society will find in them that entertainment which they could not derive from the regular Drama, intended for the gratification of the mature and expanded mind; yet they will be sufficiently rational to agreeably amuse the adult, and occasionally be made the humble instrument of celebrating the glorious victories of our army and navy.[5]

The manager's first notion of juvenile entertainment was a piece alarmingly called *The Monk and the Murderer, or, Blood will have Blood!* but the accent was on lighter fare, and Lawler and his successor, Clarke from Exeter, seem to have scored a considerable success. They even managed to lure away from the Theatre Royal Stock Company Bristol's favourite clown, Bob Gomery.

Perhaps this was the last straw for the theatre managers; at any rate, despite the fact that the Regency deliberately avoided theatre nights as far as possible, Charlton, the Stock Company's Acting Manager, put it to the Theatre Royal proprietors that the performances were 'extremely injurious to their interests' (not to mention illegal), and between them they arranged an 'information' which put John Betterton, Mrs Glover's brother, into gaol on the eve of his Benefit. This action not surprisingly only succeeded in rousing considerable sympathy — and a bumper Benefit — for Betterton and long-lasting animus against the Theatre Royal.

It was very foolish of the proprietors to allow themselves to be stampeded in this way, for the Regency was really a rather tatty concern, riven with feuds and only spasmodically effective. A patriotic piece 'on the late Glorious Atchievement (*sic*) of Earl Wellington' was currently advertised but never performed; and the equestrian statue built for a serious pantomime of *Don Juan* proved, when it came to the point, to be too big to go through the prop-room doorway, a débâcle which had to be tactfully explained away by Betterton[6].

Internal squabbles, rather than the vindictiveness of the Theatre Royal management, finally closed the Regency in March 1813. In August, West and Woolford's Company performed hippodramas at the Royal, leaving Bristol just before Adams arrived, with a troop including the young Ducrow, for the September Fair. Then in mid-November Adams advertised that he had taken the Regency, and intended 'to open it IN A FEW DAYS, with a Grand Display of _ HORSEMANSHIP, BURLETTA, and PANTOMIME

PERFORMANCES, and a variety of other AMUSEMENTS'[7] —
but the proposal seems to have come to nothing.

Certainly the petty tyranny of the theatre proprietors contributed
to the discernible drop in popularity encountered by the Company,
which cannot be entirely attributed to economic considerations,
important though they undoubtedly were. The Bath Company's
lease of the Royal ran out in the summer of 1817, and after some
not very creditable manoeuvring, the theatre was let to John Boles
Watson, Jr., of the Cheltenham and Gloucester theatres — a shifty
near-bankrupt, whose season collapsed in May 1818. By that time
the prestige and popular esteem the Theatre Royal had enjoyed
over fifty years had been almost totally dissipated.

General conditions, however, were not such as to tempt effective
rivals, though Clara Fisher and her company of Lilliputians
occupied the Assembly Rooms briefly with extracts from *Jane
Shore* and *Richard III* — that apparently irresistible lure to infant
prodigies of both sexes. Otherwise it was the mixture as before:
circuses managed by West and Woolford, Adams and Powell; solo
entertainments by Mrs Beverly, Incledon, and Charles Mathews;
Mr Gyngell's French Company (whatever that was); and a rash of
boxing matches.

It was possibly the latter which led William M'Cready the elder,
who took over management of the Royal in 1819 at the age of
sixty-four, to address the citizens of Bristol in these terms:

> It is yet problematical, whether in Bristol the Stage shall preserve
> its legitimate appropriation to the representation of our divine
> Shakespeare's works, and to the exercise of our first actors'
> talents, — or whether it shall be converted into an arena for the
> display of Pugilistic Contests, and the low senseless mummeries,
> by which (falling into the hands of inexperienced and grasping
> adventurers) it must eventually be disgraced and polluted.[8]

Managerial prospectuses have much in common with election
manifestoes, particularly when it comes to carrying them out;
M'Cready had to survive commercially somehow, and to do this he
was happily willing in practice to follow the divine Shakespeare's
works by *Tom and Jerry*, complete with pugilistic contests, and
engage any attraction from a puppet show to an opera company.
At Fair times and at Christmas the entertainments in the way of
acrobats, jugglers, pantomimists and dioramic effects rivalled the
travelling showmen; horses, dogs, cats, and even more miscellan-
eous fauna (live and manufactured) were to be seen, not only in
booths and inn-rooms, but on the Theatre Royal stage. An 1822

pantomime had 'a Stupendous SERPENT or BOA-CONSTRICTOR pursuing a BUTTERFLY, producing an effect hitherto unknown in this country', while a week later there were *'Two Stupendous SERPENTS*, or, BOA-CONSTRICTORS, each pursuing a BUTTERFLY, In opposite directions, producing A BRILLIANT EFFECT, *NEVER ATTEMPTED BY ANY OTHER ARTIST.'*[9] The previous year M'Cready had staged a 'Historical Melo-Dramatic Entertainment' called *The Egyptian Tomb*, displaying a full-scale reproduction of Belzoni's discovery. Against this, what chance had the showman's Egyptian Mummy, 'entirely unwrapped as far as Propriety will permit', or even the copy of Belzoni's own exhibition, brought to the Great Room in Wine Street in 1825.

If M'Cready showed himself unconcerned about distinctions between the legitimate and the popular, his competitors for their part were rapidly losing any particular respect for the position of the theatre. There was no longer any attempt to avoid playnights, which in any case were now four or five a week for at least six months of the year; and while the project to turn the Assembly Rooms into a theatre had proved abortive, it had certainly brought the Rooms back as a popular booking by entertainers, at the expense of the Merchant Taylors' Hall in Broad Street. The Great Room at 50 Wine Street provided another regular site, and in the mid-1820s a building opposite the Drawbridge was fitted up as a tiny theatre-cum-exhibition room known, rather flatteringly, as the Gallery of Arts; it was used for such various purposes as Bettes' Fantoccini, panoramas and performances of one of the innumerable Infant Roscii, Master Burton.

It was in this decade that circus proprietors began to work towards having a permanent building in the city. Perhaps encouraged by his success in hippodramas at the Theatre Royal, Ducrow adapted a riding school in Portwall Lane for a month's season, out of fair-time, in late 1825. Ryan, who had taken over Adams's troupe, fitted up his own Olympic Circus in Panting's timber-yard in Lower Montague Street, alongside St James's Churchyard, in August 1826, and stayed till November, despite the competition of Ducrow at the Theatre Royal. In August 1827 Ryan was back constructing a new and better arena on the same site:

> This extensive BUILDING, being 100 feet in length, by nearly 60 feet in width, will be Brilliantly Illuminated with Gas, superbly and tastefully ornamented by one of the first Artists in Bristol. Containing Front Boxes — Side Boxes — good Pit — and a spacious Gallery, which have been judiciously laid out, that

every class of persons will find themselves safe and secure, without a possibility of being interrupted from one place to the other. Also, an entrance being separate to each place, the higher and better Orders need no alarm in visiting this Fashionable Place of Amusement, where the Performances will be found chaste and highly finished.[10]

For five years all told, up to and including 1830, Ryan used this site during the September Fair, advertising larger and better-lit buildings every year.

The blurring of distinctions between the fare offered by the Theatre Royal and other sources of entertainment, and the strengthened independence of non-theatrical entrepreneurs, apparent during old M'Cready's management, grew greater after his death in 1829 and during the ensuing four years' chaos, which destroyed almost all the goodwill he had been at such pains to re-establish during his ten years at the helm. Finally his widow, Sarah M'Cready, was allowed to take the theatre lease in 1834, but with not much more than sentimental sympathy to support her. She faced circumstances in every way depressing: recurrent outbreaks of cholera, a recession in trade, the running-down of the theatre environs accelerated by the Bristol Riots, the general upheaval in the provincial theatre and uncertainty in that of the metropolis. In 1849 the Rackhay, a festering slum at the back of the theatre, was swept by cholera, and its inhabitants looked out of their windows onto a newly reopened graveyard to see their neighbours' bodies being brought out for interment; Mrs M'Cready dared not open the theatre for six months.

William M'Cready had finally made his way by his unquenchable, Micawber-like ebullience; Sarah could only cling on grimly and survive by concentrated application and a quite illogical courage. It is infinitely to her credit that in twenty of the most difficult years in provincial theatre history she kept going indomitably, paid her rent and her actors even though it emptied her own purse, and preserved a continuity of management which was invaluable when at last the tide began to turn.

But her lack of personal resources left her much more vulnerable to competition, especially from the circuses, than any of her predecessors. In December 1832 Ducrow had obtained a licence for a new 'National Olympic Arena', erected in North Street to the design of his tame architect Atkins, which was used by Ryan in 1833 and in subsequent years. The nearby Full Moon Inn provided useful stabling facilities and accommodation for artists; and the site, as the *Bristol Gazette* shrewdly observed, 'though out of the noise of the Fair itself, is sufficiently near to prevent visitors having to travel out of their way'[11]. The permanent building Ryan finally erected on this site in 1837, and which nearly bankrupted him, remained till almost the end of the century, latterly as a Salvation Army citadel. Besides this Arena, Price and Powell put up a New Circus Royal with the front entrance in Milk Street and the Gallery door in Barr Street, and in the spring of 1842 both circuses were in full swing. This had such a depressing effect on theatre attendances that Mrs M'Cready had to close her season a month early.

Moreover, as the general movement towards a free stage grew, so entertainers of all kinds enlarged their scope and took more risks with the material they included in their shows. Again, it was the circuses which sailed nearest to the wind; though they left full-length hippodramas to engagements at the Theatre Royal, in their arenas they progressed from costumed processions and short burlettas to mimed spectacles such as *The Idiot Witness; or, The Queen's Page of the Sixteenth Century*, in the course of which 'various interesting situations and effects occur, particularly the grand and impressive Equestrian Tableaux of Queen Elizabeth's Court at Greenwich'[12]. In the same programme Powell had 'a Grand Equestrian Scene, representing the Shakespearean Characters of SIR JOHN FALSTAFF, SHYLOCK, and RICHARD III' — though I find it difficult to envisage Shylock's role in this particular act. By 1840 Ryan was so blatant in his inclusion of dramatic material that the Theatre Royal Proprietors had to take a very threatening line with his local manager, Usher (the former Clown of the Coburg), and he shut up shop for that season; but the long-term effects were negligible.

Ryan's Circus — as it continued to be called long after Ryan's only connection with it was limited to a charitable Benefit given by other visiting proprietors — was used also for a multiplicity of entertainments from Masquerades to Cornish Wrestling, but primarily it provided a focal point for the touring equestrian companies of Ducrow, Batty, Cornwall, Hughes and Cooke, and also played host to some eminent foreign troupes: Tourniaire's, Franconi's and Macarte's in particular. Tenting circuses used the adjacent Moon Fields or occasionally ventured into the expanding village of Clifton, where at the top of Park Street the Horticultural Gardens housed at various times Macarte and Bell, Van Amburgh, and even a peculiar venture into pantomime and *poses plastiques* run by Mr and Mrs R. Power, late of the Theatre Royal, Bristol.

During Mrs M'Cready's management the Pleasure Fairs, which

had been under attack for many years, were finally abolished. The proximate cause of the moralists' success was the sensational murder of Mrs Mary Lewis, mother-in-law of Samuel Charles Bartlett, a strolling player, in 1836. Bartlett, leading man of Ingleton's Sans Pareil Company, was accused of shooting her for a pitifully small bequest which might have enabled him to set up in management independently. The accounts of the inquest and trial contain fascinating glimpses of the life in these travelling shows. Here is some of the evidence given by 16-year-old Henry Lovell, whom Bartlett had sent to get ammunition for his pistol:

> There was a rival show of a similar kind erected close beside Ingleton's; on Mr. Ingleton's front stage you could converse with a person standing on Mr. Middleton's front stage.... There is a great deal of noise made at these shows by drums, trumpets, shouting, and firing off fire-arms. Noise is one of the means made use of to draw attention to the performers; when the public hear a drum beating at one place, and a louder noise at another, they sometimes go to the loudest of them.

Lovell went on to describe the construction of the booth:

> The outer stage is separated from the inner by a green baize; the pit and gallery are between the outer and inner stage. An actor going from the outer to the inner stage passes down by the pit and gallery; from the outer to the inner stage, is, I think about as far as to the wall of the court (twenty yards).[13]

The evidence against Bartlett was entirely circumstantial but overwhelming. By macabre coincidence, at the moment the Judge was pronouncing sentence of death, Bartlett's wife was giving birth to a still-born child. If this were not enough, in the next Fair the strollers actually gave a dramatized version of 'the lamentable tragedy of Lippet's lane, or the inhuman murder of his mother-in-law by Bartlett'[14]. No wonder there was a wave of revulsion against the Pleasure Fairs and the moralists were able to get them suppressed in 1838.

But this suppression proved no help to the 'legitimate' theatre. Quite apart from the inevitable indiscriminate backlash of the lurid scandal, it meant that showmen and entertainers had now no particular reason to concentrate their visits within specific periods; any time of year was now as good as another.

In addition, a new local competitor began to arise in the 1840's, the tavern music hall. Its heyday in Bristol was not till the next decade, but already in January 1845 James Doughty was advertising the success of his Cider House in Broad Street, and his engagement of 'Mr. J. Freer, the great nondescript Singer, from the Glasgow and London Concerts'. The Concert Room was open from 7 to 11 p.m. and 'no females or boys' were to be admitted[15].

Doughty is one of the most intriguing characters in the history of Bristol entertainment. In 1838 we find him as a minor actor on the Theatre Royal stage, alongside the young Dion Boucicault; he reappears as Clown in circus after circus in Bristol; in November 1854 he introduced the youthful Louisa Herbert, later of the St James's Theatre, to the local stage; and his act with performing dogs was incorporated in a Theatre Royal pantomime of 1862. This act was seen in Brighton forty-five years later by Sybil Thorndike and Lewis Casson during the days of their engagement, when Doughty must have been about eighty-five; he died in 1913 somewhere in his nineties, working almost to the last.

His was the most successful Concert Room of the period, and gave a start to the Great Mackney, for one. However, it was not long before the London Oyster Rooms in High Street, and the Post Office Tavern and the Beaufort Rooms, both in Broad Street, were following suit. This area, a honeycomb of courts and passages bordering some of the most notorious rookeries of Bristol in St James's Back and the Pithay, became a centre of gaffs and concert-halls in the next decade. The *Bristol Times* described a visit to a typical 'coal hole' in Broad Street:

> We went down a court and up a ricketty pair of stairs into an oblong room, with a wing on the left, as you entered. The place was fitted up with forms with backs, and stands on the top of the backs for glasses, &c. It was crowded with men and women, girls and boys — some of the latter did not appear to be more than 14 or 15 years old. All seemed quite 'at home,' and a couple that sat just before us were entwined in each other's arms, whilst the *inamorata* listened, with no great appearance of bashfulness, to the roughly-told tale of her *inamorato*'s love. At the upper end of the room was a small and primitive stage, with a curtain of paint and canvas in the front, and green baize on the right; the former pulled up like a window blind, and the latter was pulled along like a bed-curtain. On the left-hand side of the stage, which, being close to the wall, needed no curtain, was a grand piano, played by a man with a very shiny hat on; he was accompanied by another individual with his hat off....[16]

To meet the requirements of rather more respectable forms of entertainment, more public halls were being built at this period, the most important being the Victoria Rooms, opened in 1842 to serve the polite and moneyed Clifton area. This speedily attracted most of the good concert artists, and many one-man entertainers, actors giving play-readings, and even some theatrical companies like Dickens' Amateur Company of the Guild of Literature and Art, who had reckoned that their prices would be too much for the Theatre Royal's usual audience. As the seats at the Victoria Rooms were priced at about three times the level of those at the Royal, they were probably right.

There has been a tendency to see the wave of readings, lecture recitals and the like as offering respectable alternatives to the theatre. I find this an unacceptable theory, if only because the same artists are quite as likely to turn up on the boards of the Theatre Royal as those of the Victoria Rooms, the Broadmead Rooms, the Royal Albert Rooms in College Green, or the Athenaeum in Corn Street; often they went from one to another, and only once have I found an artist making specific appeal to those reluctant to be seen in a theatre. The appetite for novelty and. popular entertainment of all kinds was growing so fast that no one building could possibly have contained it, even had its management wished to abandon its monopoly of the 'legitimate drama'. That so many of these entertainers were actually engaged at the Theatre Royal, and that so many popular elements entered into or modified its repertoire, are just two indications that in a growing city there was a sizeable clientele for whom all the managements were competing.

This uneasy, and, from the Theatre Royal's point of view, ultimately destructive state of affairs continued throughout Mrs M'Cready's lesseeship. As she grew older she became less and less able to do more than keep the place going from one penny-pinching week to the next; she had neither resources nor energy to do more — though the wonder is that she was able to do even that. In her last years she had her resourceful and enterprising son-in-law, James Henry Chute, as lieutenant, and when she died in the spring of 1853, and Chute took over the lease, there was something like a revolution in the repertoire and whole aim of the Theatre Royal. Chute intended to make his theatre once more 'a Temple of Drama' which would gain support from the educated (and better off) citizens, and in the process he firmly and deliberately cut away the accretions of popular entertainment, launching into a series of prestige reproductions of Charles Kean's successes, and elaborately-mounted Christmas entertainments, burlesques and sensation dramas, as opportunity offered. As a consequence he could afford to ignore the growing number of music halls; let the circuses have the animal acts, the ropedancers and the acrobats, and never mind if they mounted an equestrian version of *Uncle Tom's Cabin* or a rival pantomime on the *Valentine and Orson* legend at the same time as the Royal itself.

The process of stratification of entertainment now became overt, reversing the movement which may be claimed to have started when Dimond retired to Bath. Before 1801 no real rivalry existed between 'legitimate theatre' and 'popular entertainment'; after 1853 the theatre deliberately rejected competition; but in between we have a fascinating period of developing interaction which may well have been typical of the larger English provincial towns.

Notes

1   *Bonnor & Middleton's Bristol Journal*, 9 January 1802.
2   A full description of the content and technique of these shows can be found in J.E. Varey's articles on Robertson's Phantasmagoria in Madrid, *Theatre Notebook* 9, 4, 89-95 and 11, 3, 82-91.
3   *BMBJ*, 13 September 1806, and *Bristol Gazette*, 1 September 1808.
4   *BMBJ*, 26 February and 19 March 1803.
5   *Felix Farley's Bristol Journal*, 15 August 1812.
6   *Bristol Mercury*, 7 December 1812. For local reaction, see particularly *Bristol Mirror*, 23 January 1813.
7   *FFBJ*, 13 November 1818.
8   *Prospectus* of 6 March 1819.
9   Theatre Royal playbills, 22 and 29 January 1822.
10 *BG*, 23 August 1827.
11 *Ibid.*, 5 September 1833.
12 *BMy*, 19 October 1839.
13 *Ibid.*, 9 April 1837. This paper gives an almost verbatim report of the trial.
14 *BG*, 7 September 1837. Lord George Sanger in *Seventy Years a Showman* (London, McGibbon & Kee, 1966), 50-2, has a garbled account of the affair; his remarks on the popular reaction against 'the play-actors who killed the poor old woman' are interesting.
15 *BMy*, 11 January 1845.
16 *Bristol Times*, 3 February 1855.

SYBIL ROSENFELD

Muster Richardson
— 'The Great Showman'

John Richardson, more familiarly known as Muster Richardson, was born in 1766 on the lowest rung of the social ladder, in the workhouse at Marlow[1]. He never seems to have resented his early experiences as he chose to be buried in the town. After doing some menial jobs there, he left to make his fortune in London where his first employment was at cow-house in Islington at 1s a day. In 1782, when he was about 16, he made his first appearance on the stage with Mrs Penley, who was performing at a club room in the Paviour's Arms tavern in Shadwell with a cast of two men and two women who shared the proceeds of 5s a night; among the pieces were *Chrononhotonthologos* and *Midas*. The little company was then engaged by Timothy Moore who was playing at Brompton near Chatham. Richardson described to Pierce Egan[2] how they travelled 'with our wardrobes on our backs, some with bundles, and others with scenes under their arms, going to the Gravesend boat'. Again they played in the club room of a tavern, but this time with success. After a while Richardson quit the stage and opened a broker's shop in London. By 1796 he had saved enough money to rent the Harlequin tavern near Drury Lane stage door which was frequented by theatre people. From among his customers he got together a company and opened his first show at Bartholomew Fair in 1798[3]. He engaged two Drury Lane scene painters, the younger Thomas Greenwood and Thomas Banks, for his scenery and a dressmaker named Davis to 'decorate' his company. The band was selected from itinerant musicians in the streets, to wit three blind Scotsmen who were noted clarionet players. In the same tradition as Hogarth depicted in his Southwark Fair, Richardson built a platform over a gingerbread stall outside a window on the first floor of a tavern. Almost incredibly he is said to have performed twenty-one times a day and to have done excellent business in spite of the fact that the crowds abused the pieces and Richardson himself did not think much of them.

From Bartholomew Fair he took his company to Edmonton Fair, the last one of the season. Following his success at both, he had caravans built during the winter so that he could extend his circuit. The next summer, after visiting Windsor and Stepney Fairs, Richardson opened a booth at the famous Stourbridge Fair near Cambridge, and here he met with disaster. He was taken into custody for refusing to pay his rent for the ground but was rescued by a gift of five guineas from Brunton, lessee of the Norwich Theatre. Not only were his audiences trifling but he lost all but three of his horses in a flood and his two waggons were in pawn in the pub yard. With the three remaining horses and his caravan he got his company back to London, partly owing to the exertions of the clown Jefferies and a musician who made enough money by busking on the road to feed both actors and animals. Richardson took a theatre in Waltham Abbey where he earned only 9s 6d until a bespeak by the magistrates filled the house and enabled him to pay off his debts. He next set up a booth at the opening of the Paddington Canal, from the profits of which he was able to retire for the winter. During this vacation Richardson made a round of the private theatres, and from Minton's in Queen Anne Street he engaged William Oxberry who was with the company for two seasons. Among fairs visited in 1800 was that at Twickenham, where Richardson decided to play an extra night after the end of the Fair though presumably he had not got a licence for this. Copeland and Russell, whose company was at Richmond, threatened to apply to the magistrate to have the whole troupe taken into custody. The threat was delivered when they were enjoying a treat at Twickenham Ait, consuming as many eel pies and as much ale as they could. Richardson immediately went to see Mrs Jordan, who was living nearby, and she not only told him to proceed with his performance but arranged to make up a party to attend[4].

Richardson's next port of call was St Albans Fair, where he always met with encouragement from both inhabitants and corporation and was allowed by the magistrates three performing days after the Fair in perpetuity. From this time onward Richardson met with increasing success. He visited in his time sixty fairs[5] covering the London suburbs, Surrey, Berkshire, Bucks. (including his birthplace Marlow), Bristol, Hants., Kent, Suffolk, Essex, Norfolk, Cambridgeshire and Hunts. At the end of his circuit, which opened at Greenwich at Easter and closed at Bartholomew Fair in September, the company was dismissed, the waggons stowed away, the dresses packed in the wardrobe and the music collected on a shelf[6].

In 1826, after nearly thirty years of this itinerant life, Richardson decided to give up and to auction his properties. The auction was held at his cottage in Southwark on October 31 by George Robins, and the catalogue[7] is of great interest in showing how much material he had accumulated for his show. But as only £2000 was bid, Richardson bought in the goods and continued for another ten years. The fairs were, however, declining and just before his death the showman complained at Deptford Fair about the reduction of prices he was forced to make; he had never before charged less than 6d but was obliged to accept coppers in order to compete with opponents who charged only 1d[8]. A nomad by temperament, he preferred to live in a caravan, and it was only three days before his death that he was persuaded to move into his cottage. There he died at the age of seventy on 14 November 1836. He was buried in Marlow, as he requested, in the same vault as his beloved Spotted Boy — of whom more later.

In his will[9] he described himself as a gentleman. In a codicil he stated that he suffered from a nervous affliction and so was unable to sign his name. According to Egan[10] he left less than £10,000. The statements that he bequeathed legacies of £500 to the actor Johnson and £1000 to Cartlich, another actor, are not confirmed by the will[11]. He provided annuities for his nephews and a niece but left his cottage, household goods and residual estate in trust for Charles and Elizabeth Reed, who had been musicians in his company and had resided with him. His horses, waggons and theatrical properties were to be sold by his executors for the benefit of the Reeds and their children. The codicil records the death of Charles Reed and transfers the trust to his widow who was then Richardson's housekeeper. The only other theatrical bequest was £100 to Samuel Lewis, an occasional performer in the company, but this was cut out in the codicil owing to his repeated misconduct.

The only known portrait of Richardson depicts him attired as a gentleman in a top hat. He has a shrewd and humorous countenance and is said to have had dark piercing eyes and a healthy sunburnt visage. At the fairs he wore a blue coat, velveteen inexpressibles but dingy worsted stockings[12]. Like the managers Tate Wilkinson and Jemmy Whitely he was a theatrical eccentric. He spoke with a broad accent but his manners were agreeable, simple and unaffected except when he was irritated[13]. He was hard working and abstemious, had a pretty wit and could be relied upon to extricate himself from awkward situations. Thus, when the equestrian Cooke trampelled his horses on Richardson's parade he retaliated by letting off firecrackers and so frightening off the intruders. Many anecdotes are told of his self-effacing charity.

Frost avers that he paid the ground rent of poorer showmen when their receipts, owing to bad weather or other mishaps, were insufficient to cover their debts, and never asked for repayment. When a subscription was raised for the sufferers from a fire at St Albans 'a plain-looking man, in a rusty black coat, red waistcoat, corduroy inexpressibles, and worsted stockings, entered the committee room, and gave in his subscription — £100', no mean sum. When asked his name he proudly replied 'Richardson, the penny showman'[14]. He was good to his employees, encouraged shy players on the parade, always rewarded merit and gave visiting actors free entrance to his show.

We must now examine the various facets of this show: the theatre, the actors, the plays and the scenery and wardrobe.

The fair theatres of the early nineteenth century differed from the old booths; they were no longer wooden huts with a small balcony for the parade. The parade itself had developed into a large stage framed by poles and curtains and had become a much more important feature of the whole. As for the theatre, it seems likely that the hundred enclosing shutters, 8 ft high by 5 ft wide, mentioned in the auction catalogue were clamped together to form side walls above which rose a canvas top in the shape of a tent; Clark Russell remembered the rain dripping through it. Richardson must have been one of the first showmen to use this travelling type of theatre.

There are several pictures of the exterior which, though basically similar, all show variations. He seems to have reconstructed it about 1807 as playbills refer to his 'New Theatre', and all the illustrations date from after this. The best known is Rowlandson and Pugin's engraving of Bartholomew Fair for *The Microcosm of London*, 1808, which gives a corner view of the booth with two queues lining up, one in front and one at the side, so that there must have been two separate entrances. Three flights of steps, two in front and one at the side, lead up to the parade on which a trumpeter, a clown, a pantaloon and a dancer are standing. The other well-known engraving, also of Bartholomew Fair, is by Theodore Lane for Egan's *Life of an Actor*, 1825. In this the platform is on two levels with three flights of steps to the lower one and a central flight to a larger, upper one, the parade taking place on both. Two five-piece bands are placed on each side of the upper platform. Rowlandson's unfinished drawing of Greenwich Fair in the British Museum illustrates a much smaller booth and suggests that Richardson may not always have used all his platforms. This is borne out by the auction catalogue which refers to several booths and makes the point 'that the business is never limited but can often be extended to several situations at the same period'. The theatre was, therefore, to some extent expandable as, for instance, when some particular show was exhibited. Thus the Pie Powder Court Book records that at Bartholomew Fair in 1811 Richardson paid for two exhibitions, one small, the charge being 12s instead of the usual 8s. The Greenwich drawing depicts only a crude ladder in front up which a buxom woman is being helped by a clown. On one side is a woman's three-part band consisting of a drum, tambourine and violin, and on the other acrobats are performing. Rowlandson made an etching of the parade in 1816 in a slightly altered version and W. Jones painted a water colour from the etching in 1826[15]. This last shows an orchestral box in which the band consists of a male violin, flute and clarionet with a woman playing the triangle outside.

All these were published during Richardson's life time, but the most detailed engraving of the booth dates from 1838, two years after his death, and commemorates the Fair in Hyde Park in celebration of Queen Victoria's coronation (see Plate 3)[16]. The booth, which was the most conspicuous in the Fair, had two wings and a parade with many figures, some dancing, a man beating a gong and two bands in opposite boxes. The lighting consists of six lamps on poles in front and two hanging behind as well as illuminated letters V and R over olive branches. The spectators are of a much genteeler type than usually shown.

Hone [17], who visited Bartholomew Fair in 1825, has recorded that the platform was 100 ft wide and 30 ft high. The back was lined with green baize and festooned with fringed crimson curtains, except at two points where the money-takers sat in boxes fitted up with Gothic shrine work. The platform was gay with banners, and a large number of these — blue satin, English, Scottish, French, Chinese and Turkish with poles and ornamental tops — are listed in the auction catalogue. This frontal alone is said to have cost £600 and the whole theatre to have been 'so well constructed in all its parts that it can be erected without the smallest difficulty in a few hours'[18]. Among the items in the auction catalogue are 30 scaffolding poles 30 ft high; 20 strong platforms almost new, 2 ins thick; 1000 yds of green baize and about 500 yds of crimson and scarlet morine with deep fringes which, as we have seen, were used as backing for the platform. Panels at the rear, bearing lifelike figures of knights in suits of armour, emphasized the Gothic atmosphere and are visible in both the Lane and Hyde Park engravings.

There were usually two bands, and the auction catalogue lists

Plate 3. Richardson's Travelling Theatre at the Fair
in Hyde Park, 1838

two portable orchestras for six musicians, two long drums, a pair of kettle drums and two small hand organs by Beloda. In addition there were trumpeters with gay banners. The bands were garbed in scarlet costumes, similar to those of the beefeaters, or sometimes in a type of Asiatic dress. They passed continuously from the parade outside to the theatre within.

When darkness fell the booth was illuminated by 1500 variegated lamps, a number confirmed by the auction catalogue. There were also hanging chandeliers and lamps on stands.

Whilst the bands played, members of the company paraded, danced and sang. Clowns, harlequins, punches, pantaloons and big heads jostled knights in armour, tragedians in doublet and hose with plumed hats and mythological gods, and dancers mingled with fashionable ladies to entice the crowds into the performances. A vivid description sets the scene:

> the space in front of his theatre was always the most crowded part of the fair, and whilst the performances were going on inside, a sufficient number were 'pulled in' by the exertions of a couple of clowns in grin and grimace; a melancholy Hokee-Pokee, King of the Cannibal Islands in a Robinson Crusoe sort of costume; an unexceptionable dandy, who would have passed muster in Bond-street, and the numerous assortment of dons and damsels, countrymen and chambermaids, Tartar chiefs and *tarter* dancing-girls, sailors and their Black-eyed Susans, bare-legged Scotchmen and bare-bosomed fairies &c. who occasionally mingled together in a mazy dance, to the inspiring sounds of the band, part of whom, we regret to say, figure in the vestments of bishops, while part were in a sort of Asiatic dress, to half fill the booth when the doors were opened[19].

In addition a barker whipped in audiences through a speaking trumpet: 'Just going to begin — now's your only time'; and in his walk-up speech he would run down the rival attractions of wild beast shows and appeal to men of sense with mention of Roscius and Shakespeare[20]. Only one character never appeared on the parade — the ghost; he was the pièce de resistance within. Yet the parade show could be more exciting than that in the theatre[21]. Novelties were introduced, such as *poses plastiques* in 1833 when a well-formed young man, dressed as a statue, displayed a series of Greek attitudes as a gladiator, listening slave &c. whilst a range of twelve musical bells was added to the band[22].

The theatre was long and narrow (100 ft long by 30 ft wide), and when the audience descended into it they found rows of timber benches leading down to the elevated stage which had a painted proscenium with royal arms above and a green curtain. The orchestra was lined with crimson cloth and accommodated five violin players in military costume; between it and the stage was a large space which, when all other seats had been occupied, was packed with groundlings to the discomfiture of the lower ranks of seat holders. The theatre is said to have held nearly 1000[23]; a figure that might be thought exaggerated but is supported by the auction catalogue which lists 100 seat boards 1½ inches thick and 20 to 30 ft long with 40 brackets to support them of thick solid timber. There is no illustration of Richardson's actual theatre but Robert Cruickshank[24] engraved a Bartholomew Fair booth interior which shows a typical melodrama with a white-robed ghost wreathed in smoke, a monk, a man with helmet and dagger and a heroine in plumes against a setting of moonlit Gothic ruins. There are two stage doors with boxes above which do not look practicable; spectators are seated in the pit and others standing at the side. Richardson prided himself that his entrance fee was 6d but it is doubtful whether this gallery ticket entitled you to do more than stand. The gallery could not have been a separate balcony since the auditorium could only slope down on the far side of the platform to the height of that platform (i.e. 30 ft) and this would preclude any other seats than sloping rows of benches. Perhaps the best seats at the back were reserved as boxes. The prices advertised on playbills were boxes 2s, pit 1s and gallery 6d, and entrance tickets for all three feature acrobats. The charges were high for a short show when compared with those of a full-length performance in a provincial theatre where they were boxes 3s, pit 2s and gallery 1s. The higher prices would go to show that the booth attracted some better-off patrons, a few of whom are seen in the prints mingling with the rougher elements.

With his horse-drawn caravans and waggons Richardson moved his theatre, scenery, props and actors from fair to fair. By 1826 he possessed six large caravans, some with 6-inch wheels and some with 9; nine flat-top caravans about 40 ft in length, with 6-inch wheels, and 6 wind-up jacks for the waggons.

Turning now to the programmes: the usual one consisted of a short play, nearly always a melodrama, a pantomime sometimes ending with a panorama, and a comic song between play and pantomime. The melodramas were an innovation in the fairs which had hitherto presented ballad operas and pantomimes or drolls, based on legends and chapbooks, interlarded with comic interludes. The melodramas, though unsophisticated, were more coherent; folk drama had taken over in abbreviated form the type of romantic melodrama popular at the patent theatres. A count of available playbills, with additional information from other sources, gives a total of 44 plays, 20 pantomimes and 9 panoramas. The play was changed every day but a popular pantomime was presented with different plays. The length of performances has been variously estimated at half an hour, twenty minutes and about quarter of an hour[25]. The length of the performance may have varied according to the number of spectators waiting for admittance. Richardson used a device that when sufficient people had paid, a messenger was dispatched into the theatre to call out for John Audley — which was a signal to sound the gong and end the performance quickly. The show was repeated every hour to allow time for the parade and the changeover of audiences. As thirteen to fourteen shows were given a day, they would work out at just under the hour, provided opening times were midday to midnight.

Speed and concentration were essential, and if dramas were sliced out of plays such as *Virginius* or *The Grecian Daughter* they were brought rapidly to the climax. Thus the former was 'brought at once to the grand incident that attaches to his name, and with a bold contempt for the unities, he kills his daughter without any of the intermediate rigmarole with Appius'[26]. But most of the plays were specially written melodramas cobbled together by hacks. Medieval settings were popular, as in *Agnes of Bavaria, or Spectre of the Danube*, which was advertised as founded on an incident in 1435; *The Crusaders, or Champions of the Cross*, featuring Richard Coeur de Lion; *De Montford Castle, or the Midnight Assassination* and *The Fatal Prediction, or the Cell of Mystery*, both portraying the manners and customs of feudal times. Scott's novels were responsible for several adaptations and Scottish settings such as *Castles of Athlin and Dunbaine, or the Spectre of the North; Donald and Rosaline, or the Spectre of the Rocks; Gowrie Castle* taken from Robertson's *History of Scotland; Warlock of the Glen* (from Scott's *Black Dwarf*) and *Marmion*. At least two pieces had a Chinese setting: *Children of the Desert*, 'a Chinese melodrama', and *The Orphan of China, or The Court of Peking*, which may have had some connection with Francklin's tragedy. Classical settings were those of *The Grecian Daughter*, presumably hacked out of Murphy, *Virginius*, and *The Roman Wife, or a Father's Vengeance*.

Monks, murderers and outlaws abound and ghosts were essential, appearing in white sheets with white satin slippers and red hearts to claim retribution. If the author had omitted a spectre it was necessary to import one. There is an amusing story that, when one piece was going badly and the audience was becoming restive, Richardson sent for the popular tragedian, Cartlich, to restore good humour by improvizing. The actor protested that he had just been killed in full view of the audience: "Has he", subjoined the manager in a tone of exaltation, "then the piece is saved — on with his ghost"[27]. Richardson gave it as his opinion 'that to give any *treasury* a good *turn*, there is nothing like the UNITIES for producing *effect*, and *blunt* into the bargain — a *gong* — BLUE or RED FIRE — and a BLEEDING GHOST'[28].

Other attractions were processions and ceremonies: a marriage in *Donald and Rosaline*, a funeral in *Gowrie Castle*, an execution in *The Fatal Prediction*, and the taking of the veil in *The Hall of Death*.

When a version of *Blue Beard* was presented at Bartholomew Fair in splendid style, the booth was besieged, but the greatest houses were brought by the burletta *Tom and Jerry* — concocted by Kelly for £5[29]. Comedies were the exception, though a version of *Paul Pry Just Dropt In* written expressly for Richardson was presented about 1826-7. Among properties in the auction catalogue are those for *Der Freischutz*, completed by Godby, and the spectacle of *The Coronation* by Kelly. The pantomimes followed the usual pattern except that they were short, consisting of comic business and three mechanical tricks. *The Paris Diligence, or Harlequin's Journey* may serve as an example. It opened in an inn yard:

> The Paris Diligence just ready to start; Bales of Goods packing; the Passengers arrive, are anxious to commence their Tour, which by the Magic of Harlequin and Tricks of Clown is attended with much Confusion, but is arranged in order by the Goddess of Reason.

The second scene is a room in the inn:

> where Pantaloon and Lover both get and lose their Dinner by the Power of the Magic Sword, and it closes with the flight of Harlequin and Colombine, and a scene of bother about a Calve's Head.

In scene iii, a picturesque view, there is the usual vain race after the fugitives in which 'Pantaloon [is] knocked up, the Lover knocked down, and the Clown with his hands full of Business'. Scene iv transports us to a seaport with a lighthouse where the runaways are pursued and nearly taken but find a new method of building a ship and leave Pantaloon, Lover and Clown at a stand. In the last scene of a street in Paris, Harlequin is seized but, by the interposition of the Goddess of Reason, the parties are reconciled and the show concluded with a panorama of Paris. Pantomime changes and tricks by Garland, Kelly, Sation and Godby were among the props at the auction.

The panoramas were of scenes abroad and at home, including Amsterdam, Lake Como, Gibraltar, Montevideo, Niagara and St Helena as well as of Glamorganshire, London and a naval review in which a pillar emblematic of British victories arose from the ocean. Panoramas were not obligatory but several were repeated in different programmes. Richardson cashed in on the popularity of the form but it is likely that they were no more than painted cloths and were not of the revolving kind seen in the theatres from 1820.

There are a few playbills which record a different type of programme, and unlike the other bills these are dated[30]. Two are for Brook Green: 5 May 1819, *Point of Honour* (Charles Kemble) and a farce, *The Sleeping Draught* (S. Penley); 4 May 1820, *The Earl of Warwick, Edward and Nancy*, and Bickerstaff's farce *The Sultan*. Prices were the usual provincial theatre ones — boxes 3s, pit 2s and gallery 1s — and the doors opened at 6 p.m. for 7 p.m. Similarly at Wandsworth, 8 July 1819, *The Earl of Warwick* was followed by a farce, *Fortune's Fool*, and on 10 July, the last of the three nights, *Where to Find a Friend* (Leigh) was followed by *The Sultan*, but there is no mention of boxes. These were full evening's entertainments, and were undoubtedly performances given by special permission of the magistrates after the fairs were over.

We now have to consider the players, of whom there were as many as seventy. According to Frost, Richardson preferred to recruit actors from those who had learned a trade, as they were more dependable than those who had been strollers from childhood. This was not altogether true for, as early as 1799, Tom Jefferies, a clown from Astley's, his wife (a singer from the Royal Circus) and Miss Sims from Astley's, were engaged. Certainly several of his players went on to make their names elsewhere. For example, William Oxberry went to Covent Garden in 1807; Saville Faucit was later manager at Margate; Abraham Slader and Rose became well known at Astley's; Vaughan played at Drury Lane and then went to America with G.F. Cooke. None of these names appears on the playbills which probably date from a later time. It is claimed that the pantaloon, Jemmy Barnes, was in the company [31] and there exists an IOU for £10, signed J. Barnes and dated 29 May 1834[32], but this may be the Joseph Barnes, a bank clerk, to whom Richardson made a bequest in his will. Another of his actors, John Cartlich, who had the great advantage of a booming voice which could be heard all over the fairground, became famous as Mazeppa at Astley's and retired to a pub named Mazeppa at Horsley Down[33]. The interchange of players with Astley's is understandable as the circus produced the same kind of short pieces. Other members of the company were the dancers of African Sal and Dusty Bob of whom we have a print.

But the most famous of all Richardson's trainees was Edmund Kean (then Carey). There can be no doubt that as a child he was for a while in the company, for Richardson told Egan this, giving specific details which, however, have caused confusion. He said that Mrs Carey applied to him for an engagement in 1799 with her two sons, Henry and Edmund, and a daughter who remained with him during the summer. *Tom Thumb* was got up to show off the talents of the boys, Edmund being cast as Tom and Mrs Carey as Queen Dollalolla. At Windsor the show opened with this piece and *The Magic Oak*, after which Edmund received a royal command to recite passages from plays at the Castle. If Edmund was born in 1789[34], and this is not altogether certain, he was then about ten years old. The difficulty lies in the fact that Mrs Carey is not known to have had other children. Some playbills list Mrs Carey, others Mr and Mrs H. Carey, but the only one with any indication of date, 1807 in ms., records H. Carey as Pantaloon with no mention of Edmund. Presumably the family left after 1799 but Henry Carey and his wife returned about 1806. In that year Richardson gained permission to perform whole pieces for two nights after Battersea Fair. Edmund Carey, who by then had had experience in Jerrold's company, applied for a job and, being short of actors, Richardson gladly engaged him. On the first night he acted Young Norval in *Douglas* and on the second Motley in *The Castle Spectre* at 5s a night. It seems likely that Mr and Mrs H. Carey stayed on in the company when Edmund joined Mrs Baker's in September.

Richardson also engaged occasional performers. Of these the best known was the Spotted Boy, a freak from the Caribbean, who was introduced between pieces and brought in a fortune. According to the Pie Powder Court Book a spotted child was first shown at Bartholomew Fair in 1806 and appeared again in 1808-9 under one Stacey, but in 1810 Richardson partnered Stacey in exhibiting him[35]. His real name was George Alexander and his skin was a patchwork of brown and white, his hair mixed black and white and his countenance interesting, his limbs admirably proportioned, his ideas quick and penetrating and his infantine simplicity captivating. Richardson was devoted to him and was grief-stricken when he died young. As we have seen, he arranged for them to be buried in the same vault and was always reduced to tears when he gazed on his portrait[36]. Another engagement was that of Signora Josephine Giradelli during Portsmouth mart. She was a Venetian 'fire proof female' who claimed to have performed before royalty on the continent and in the London Theatres Royal about 1816. Among her feats were passing a red-hot iron over her hair, tongue, arms and legs; holding her arms in flames; washing her hands in boiling lead and then pouring it into her mouth. She performed every two hours from 2 to 6 p.m. Tyrolesian peasants on stilts 4 ft high were another attraction between melodrama and pantomime.

Regular performers were paid punctually every week on a drumhead and were discharged by being asked to leave their names with the stage manager, who also functioned as wardrobe keeper and scene shifter.

The showman prided himself on his scenery and wardrobe and sometimes advertised on his playbills that he had 'a splendid collection of scenery unrivalled in any Theatre', painted and designed by first-rank artists. As we have seen, Greenwood the younger and Thomas Banks, two young scene painters at Drury Lane, were employed by him early in their careers. Pierce Egan also mentions the Grieves[37], but there is no supporting evidence for this. The auction catalogue adds Andrews senior, who was working at Sadler's Wells. On opening his new theatre about 1807, Richardson advertised twenty new scenes by first London artists. A good many of these were stock and served many melodramas in which settings were frequently repeated. On the available playbills we find a cavern used seven times; a hall and a chapel (on one occasion illuminated), five; a castle exterior and prison cell (one Chinese), four; a convent (one with an altar) and a view of mountains (one with a tomb), three; a Gothic chamber (one with a sliding panel), twice. Among others mentioned once are the following landscapes: Cotswold fields, street, exterior of a cave, grove and cottage, cut wood, rocks, and distant abbey, as well as the following interior scenes: castle chamber, front apartment, study, abbey. Specific places include a Chinese palace, a distant view of a Chinese town with bridge and pagoda, sea view of Africa, a wood with African huts (presumably for a piece *Africans*), and a Danube bridge. Scenery for pantomimes include a cottage, view of St Alban's, ruined abbey, inn yard and room and picturesque view (these last three served in *The Paris Diligence*).

Scene changes were frequent, as many as seven in *The*

Wandering Outlaw. The auction catalogue records about seventy drops, 10 ft 6 in high and 14 ft wide, including street scenes, back and cut woods, moonlight, prisons, castle interior and exterior, palaces, landscapes, waterfalls, mountains, a chamber, interior of a church with transparent windows and three sets of wings with three changes to each, six stage doors and a great number of set pieces to match the scenes. The theatre, then, was reasonably well equipped though, with three wing changes to seventy drops, the same wings, as usual at the time, must have served with many back-cloths. Among the properties were basket-work giants, dwarfs and dragons, six stage guns along with fighting and dress swords, Turkish scimitars and daggers, all very necessary for the melodramas. The only criticism of the scenes comes from the *Era Almanack*[38], which considered them well painted but too delicate for their purpose.

Richardson took great pains with his wardrobe and the dresses specially made for him were of excellent quality[39], so that in many instances they were adjudged superior to those of the patent theatres[40]. They had to be of good material to stand up to daylight. The auction catalogue provides us with many details. It lists the following sets: 25 Chinese dresses with caps, fans and shoes; 20 Indian dresses with headdresses, bows and arrows; 20 Turkish dresses richly trimmed; 20 Roman dresses with burnished helmets and breastplates, and 30 Scottish dresses, some richly trimmed. There were French, Spanish, German and Dutch costumes, dresses for skeletons, crimson robes and cushions for *The Coronation*, and old men's modern suits; 6 satyrs' and furies' dresses, 4 harlequins' and 6 clowns', these last four items with masks; countrymen's smock frocks, watchmen's and officers' coats, heralds, black and grey pilgrims' cloaks, and Peruvian and Roman shifts, 4 richly-trimmed nondescript dresses with expensive wigs and masks. Single costumes were for Wolsey, Paul Pry, Sir Giles Overreach and Il Bondicani, a richly-trimmed high priest's dress with a mitre and an Indian Priest's dress.

Accessories included shields, spears and battleaxes, flesh-coloured stocking pantaloons and bodies, character stockings, stage boots, shoes and sandals and good character wigs. After Richardson's death 334 lots were sold at auction[41]. Among the effects and costumes were a trick bottle and box and trick sword, a coffin and pall, tomb of Capulet, old oak chest with a skeleton, two spangled women's dresses, one white clown's, five chintz dresses, three magicians' and five musicians' dresses, a demon's dress spangled and ornamented with a gilt mask and mace, an executioner's dress and cap and an admiral's coat and hat trimmed with gold lace, as well as costumes for a lion, bear, monkey and cat with two masks and eight fans. A large scene waggon fetched only £14 and a carriage for scenery only £8. It is evident that the wardrobe and props were extensive and varied and that efforts were made to distinguish national costumes.

After Richardson died the theatre was taken over by John Johnson and Nelson Lee but continued to operate as Richardson's Theatre. Both had at some time been with Richardson, and Lee had had a varied career as actor and manager at Sadler's Wells[42], conjuror at Vauxhall and Harlequin at the Surrey. Both became proprietors of the City of London Theatre in 1848[43] but they carried on Richardson's until 1852 in spite of the gradual decline and closing of the fairs. A catalogue[44] of the final sale by Lloyd on 15 March 1853, at Richardson's cottage, is evidence of how the show had deteriorated since the great showman's days. Instead of 70 there were only 16 drop scenes and only three pairs of wings painted on both sides. A new item was changeable flaps for the pantomime. Covered vans and parade waggons, a stage front and an orchestra were among items sold piecemeal.

In the thirty-nine years that Richardson entertained the populace at the fairs he provided a theatre and gave performances of a standard above those of his competitors. So he rose by degrees to be 'the most renowned of dramatic caterers for those classes who are prone to enjoy the unadulterated drama'[45] until he obtained 'a managerial supremacy that must be not a little enviable even in the eyes of Mr. Elliston himself'[46].

Notes

1   Main contemporary accounts are: Pierce Egan, *Life of an Actor* (London, 1825), 206-18, expanded in his *Pilgrims of the Thames in Search of the National* (London, 1838), 81-119; W. Hone, *Every-Day Book* (London, 1830), I, 1182; W. Jerdan, 'Biographical Sketch of Richardson the Showman', *Bentley's Miscellany*, I, February 1837, 178-86; obituary, *Gentleman's Magazine*, 7 March 1837, 326-7.

2   *Pilgrims.*

3   The date is usually given as 1796 but Richardson's name does not figure among the showmen in the Pie Powder Court Book

of Bartholomew Fair (Guildhall Library, ms.95) until two years later. From 1793 a gingerbread stall was under the name of Richardson and may have been his as he mentions having a booth above one.

4   Egan, *Life of an Actor*.
5   Full list given in the auction catalogue of 1826 (see note 7 below): Greenwich (2), Brook Green, Stepney, Bow, Wandsworth, Ealing Green, Fairlop, Brentford, Staines, Chertsey, Ham Common, Kingston, Hounslow, Uxbridge, Iver, Reading, Henley, Marlow, Wycombe, Oxford and the Forest Meeting, Ascot Heath Races, Cotton Hill nr Guildford, Windsor, Bristol, Portsmouth, Postdown, Mornhill Fair nr Winchester, Dover, Stroud nr Chatham, Maidstone, Ashford, Dartford, Bromley, Mitcham, Charlton, Ipswich, Harwich, Colchester, Tiptree Heath, Chelmsford, Newmarket, Prittlewell, Brentwood, Romford, Hoddesdon, Wadesmill, Edmonton, Enfield, Waltham Abbey, North Hall, Harley Bush, Stebbing, Beckington Common, Lynn, Wisbech, Sandwich, Camberwell, Bartholomew Fair, Peterborough, St Albans.
6   Egan, *Pilgrims*.
7   Guildhall Library, Gr. 3.3.1.
8   Egan, *Pilgrims*.
9   PRO Prob. 11, vol.1871, 36.
10 *Pilgrims*; an article by John Oxenford, *Era Almanack* (1896), gives the figure as £20,000 but is not to be relied on.
11 *Pilgrims*.
12 V&A, Enthoven Collection, unidentified cutting in Richardson file.
13 Thos. Frost, *The Old Showmen* (London, 1874), 217-18.
14 W. Clark Russell, *Representative Actors* (London, 1872), 286, quoting *Records of a Stage Veteran*.
15 Etching in *Rowlandson's World in Miniature* (London, 1816); water colour, 1826, in Salford Art Gallery.
16 Original drawing in Guildhall Library, 3.3.1; engraving after S.C. Wilson.
17 *Op. cit.*
18 P. Egan, *The Show Folks* (London, 1831), n.9.
19 Guildhall Library ms. 1514, cutting dated in ms. 11 September 1830.
20 G. Raymond, *Memoirs of Robert Wm. Elliston* (London, 1844), 111; Egan, *Pilgrims*.
21 *Era Almanack*, 82.

22   Guildhall Library broadsheet, *Bartholomew Fair, 1833*.
23   Jerdan, *op. cit.*
24   P. Egan, *The Finish to the Adventures of Tom, Jerry and Logic* (London, 1869), opp. p.113.
25   Frost, *op. cit.*; Enthoven cutting; Jerdan, *op. cit.*, 181.
26   *The Interpreter. The Itinerant Drama* (1834), Guildhall Gr. 3.3.1.
27   *Ibid.*
28   Egan, *Show Folks*, 21.
29   Egan, *Pilgrims*.
30   Guildhall playbills under Wandsworth.
31   Clark Russell, *op. cit.*, quoting Mark Lemon.
32   Guildhall ms. 1514.
33   *Gentleman's Magazine, op. cit.*
34   Giles Playfair, *Kean* (London, Reinhardt & Evans, 1950), x, Playbill, March 1801, gives his age as eleven.
35   Presumably a spotted Indian shown in 1798 and a spotted boy in 1832 shown by Anders were different freaks.
36   Jerdan, *op. cit.*
37   *Pilgrims, op. cit.*
38   *Op. cit.*
39   Frost, *op. cit.*
40   Egan, *Finish to the Adventures*, 114.
41   Jerdan, *op. cit.* I have been unable to trace the sale catalogue.
42   *Pilgrims, op. cit.*
43   R. Mander and J. Mitchenson, *Lost Theatres of London* (London, Hart-Davis, 1958), 38.
44   Guildhall ms. 1514.
45   Jerdan, *op. cit.*
46   Hone, *op. cit.*, 1196.

Acknowledgements

The author is grateful to the British Library Board for permission to reproduce Plate 3.

DENIS GONTARD

An Example of 'Popular' Itinerant Theatre: Gémier's National Travelling Theatre (1911-1912)

To put a theatre on the road, on a cart, under a canvas circus, has always been a sort of dream for every company manager. Without coming back as far as Thespis' cart or Molière, one can say that almost each company manager has, at least once in his life, thought of using an ambulant theatre because this meant the possibility of enlarging the audience of a company from a town to a whole country.

At the end of the nineteenth and at the beginning of the twentieth century, with the development — all over Europe, but chiefly in France — of Socialism, the idea of 'bringing the theatre to the people' — as they said — was in the air. Years before Firmin Gémier — French actor, director and theatre manager — put the idea into practice, a French journalist and poet Catulle Mendès imagined a theatre which would not be stuck on one place but which would go almost everywhere in France, including villages which had no playhouses in which to perform. In 1899, Catulle Mendès thought of a theatre which 'would move and would multiply itself' and asked a Parisian architect — Lucien Hubaine — to draw 'the plans of a collapsible and portable theatre'[1]. Two years later, the same Mendès presents his project to the Ministry of Education where a commission had just been created in the frame of the Secretary of State for the Fine Arts. And in 1905, Mendès wrote in a Paris magazine:

> There is not, in one place, a big enough, enthusiastic — or even curious — public to maintain a low-priced theatre all the year round; but there is enough public everywhere to receive it brilliantly.... Consequently, all difficulties coming from the necessity of having a great public disappear, move back and — literally — vanish since the theatre is no longer implanted some-where, but moves.[2]

Catulle Mendès' idea of a travelling theatre was very attractive, but it needed help from the state to be realized. Since no subsidy was given to its promoter, the idea of such a theatre was abandoned in 1906.

So, the French government took no further interest in a project which can be considered vital for the prospects of theatre in our country.

In 1910, the same proposition to build a travelling theatre in France was presented in Paris. But this time the promoter was a young Parisian barrister — J. Paul-Boncour, soon to be deputy, then minister, and finally, Prime Minister. Paul-Boncour had followed, with the greatest interest, all the different attempts at popular theatre at the end of the nineteenth and during the first years of the twentieth century. He knew that another poet, dramatist and journalist — Maurice Pottecher — had founded in 1895, in a tiny village in the Vosges, Bussang, 'The Theatre of the People'. He had taken note of the dozen attempts to implant 'popular' theatres in and around Paris: the 'Civil Theatre' of Louis Lumet, the 'Theatre of the People' of Henri Dargel, the 'Popular Theatre' of Belleville, the 'Theatre of the People' of Henri Beaulieu, etc ...[3] Thus he could, in his Report to the Fine Arts in 1910, make an accurate, though severe, statement on the situation of the theatre in France:

> One can say that, apart from a few big towns like Lyons, Rouen, Marseilles, etc., which have regular companies and playhouses whose efforts are not always appreciated enough, apart from spas and holiday places which welcome good quality companies and even our members of the Comédie-Francaise all the rest of the provinces are deprived of theatre.[4]

To repair this lack, Paul-Boncour proposed the creation of a travelling theatre. He pointed out in the same report the necessity of creating such a theatre:

> We must use a more efficient system and, among all those which have been proposed to you, I do not know a simpler and better one than the one which consists, not of drawing the people to the central districts or theatres, where they are not used to going, but of going to people at home, in the districts of the outskirts and of the suburbs.[5]

But, one again, the Chamber of Deputies and the government did not pay sufficient attention to the project, which was not subsidized and was hence abandoned.

Firmin Gémier, whose direction of the Théâtre Antoine, in Paris, was going smoothly, thus allowing him time to spend on other projects, understood the situation of the theatre in France fairly well. The many tours he had done gave him an accurate impression of the theatrical emptiness of the French provinces. He also knew, by experience, all the difficulties of tours: badly equipped theatres, lack of time in each visited town, difficulties of transportation by rail, tyranny of provincial playhouse managers, etc.

All this gave him the idea of realizing an old plan of his: the creation of a travelling theatre which would visit provincial towns, but also villages and country places which did not possess a theatre. He asked, in the newspaper *Comoedia*:

> Is there not, at the very origin of our art, a kind of need of a nomadic life that our epoch, intellectually absorbed by capitals and big cities, seems strangely not to have appreciated? And true theatre, logical theatre, imbued with a millennial tradition, is it not, consequently, a travelling theatre, a theatre which anticipates the crowd's wishes and calls it loudly in to the performance, as our first buffoons did many years ago, those who were, on the roads, the first actors, our primitives?[6]

Gémier, who had known J. Paul-Boncour for many years as a friend of the theatre, found in the young deputy a firm supporter of his cause (although Boncour did not get money from the government for his own project!) and, at the beginning of 1911, he started making plans for his travelling theatre.

We will now begin by analysing the creation of Firmin Gémier's itinerant theatre in 1911, its development during the two seasons 1911 and 1912, and its end during the autumn of 1912. Then we will deal with the problem of whether Gémier's Théâtre National Ambulant was a 'popular' theatre or not.

To free himself from all the difficulties mentioned above, Gémier decided to build his own travelling theatre which, with its own company and scenery from the Théâtre Antoine, would wander from one rural town to another and, in a canvas theatre, present the masterpieces of the drama. He asked two young engineers — Henri and Jacques Febvre-Moreau — to start work on the plans of a collapsible canvas building (see Fig. 7.1) which could be erected and dismantled quickly and — to be modern! — would be hauled by steam traction engines (see Plate 4A): the so-called locomobiles. The two engineers started work on the first plans of the theatre in January 1911, and the theatre was completed in June.

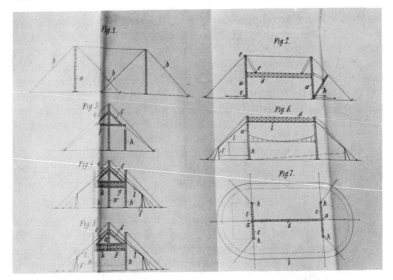

Figure 7.1. Process of erecting Gémier's canvas theatre

Gémier asked his scenery maker from the Théâtre Antoine — Émile Bertin — to alter some of the existing scenery to fit the stage of the travelling theatre, and to build new scenery for the creation of new plays.

Then began what we can call the adventure of Gémier's National Travelling Theatre (*Théâtre National Ambulant*). All the materials for the playhouse itself and for the actors and scenery required thirty-six heavy wagons hauled by eight huge tractors. The latter were built at the engineering shops of Aveline and Porter in Rochester (Kent), and sent by sea to Bordeaux, probably on a cognac ship coming back empty. Then, from Bordeaux, the tractors travelled by train to Paris where they arrived in time for the inauguration of the theatre in June.

The theatre itself, which could hold 1600 people, was the central element of the whole (see Plate 4B). Around the playhouse and the stage — 21 ft wide — were the wings, the dressing-rooms for the artistes, the wagons devoted to the administration. All the wagons were very big and extremely luxurious. The administration wagon was divided into three sitting-rooms: one to be used as an office, one for Gémier himself and one for his wife Andrée Mégard, who was a member of the company. Gémier advertised so successfully that a car manufacturer — Felber and Sons — offered to build, for the director of the travelling theatre, a private car with two benches

Plate 4A. Four traction engines of Gémier's travelling theatre

Plate 4B. Interior of Gémier's travelling theatre

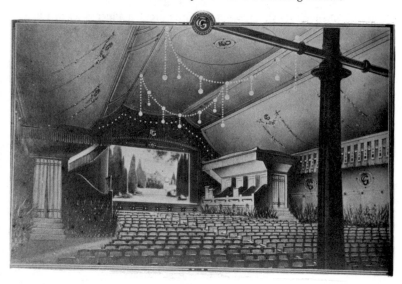

of four seats each, bow windows, etc.! All this, because Gémier said that he wanted his new theatre as near a replica of the Théâtre Antoine in Paris as was possible.

During the first season of 1911, the whole of the French press was full of articles about the first 'theatre on motor-cars'. Everyone was anxious to see the eight tractors, the thirty-six wagons, the 'playhouse' with private boxes 'fashioned out of two cars, each of which contains four gorgeously upholstered compartments'[7].

The opening performance, announced in all French national papers, was given on Friday, 7 July 1911, in Paris, on the Esplanade des Invalides, before three ministers and a very large crowd. The company presented *The Swallow Submarine* — a new play by Moreux and Pérard, two contemporary writers — and the sixth and seventh parts of an adaptation of Tolstoy's *Anna Karenina*. On the following days the programme included Balzac's *La Rabouilleuse*, Beaumarchais' *The Barber of Séville* and Molière's *Dépit amoureux* (in two acts). The success of these first performances of the travelling theatre was so great that Gémier had to lengthen his stay in Paris. At last, on the morning of Friday, 21 July, the convoy of the theatre started in the direction of Versailles where a performance was planned for the same night.

But on that first trip the tractors presented difficulties on the road, the canvas theatre took too long to be erected and the performance had to be postponed until the next day, when Gémier's travelling theatre obtained as great a success as in Paris. Success again, and full audiences, for each performance in Versailles and during the whole of that first tour in the North of France: in Lille, Armentières, Calais, Boulogne, Berck and Amiens. There were technical difficulties, however, which slowed down the theatre here and there: at Boulogne, one tractor was out of order, another one hit a house and, above all, country bridges were not resistant enough for the heavy weight of some tractors and their wagons! But, in spite of all the inconveniences and loss of money which they involved, in spite of delays from town to town, the *Théâtre National Ambulant*, thanks to the firm will of its director and to the great success it found at each stop, completed its first and very encouraging tour to Compiègne, Creil, Chantilly, Pontoise, Argenteuil and Saint-Germain-en Laye, on 1 October 1911.

Thus, in less than three months, the National Travelling Theatre visited thirteen provincial towns, gave fifty performances, dealt with all kinds of difficulties. It collected 192,604 francs[8] which, for the time, was a great amount of money, especially if one bears in mind that, in order to enable everyone to attend performances, Gémier made the prices of admission extremely low — 0.50, 1 and 1.50 francs. At the same time in the Paris theatres, rates of admission ranged from 1.50 to 15 francs in ordinary playhouses (and went from 0.50 to 6 francs even in a very 'popular' place of entertainment like the Théâtre de la République, which was devoted to melodrama). This meant that, during its first tour in France, Gémier's National Travelling Theatre must have been full all the time.

At the end of that first three-month tour, Gémier's attempt to decentralize theatre in France proved to be a great success. It was also proof that a quality repertoire — Molière, Beaumarchais, Balzac, Tolstoy — could attract as many spectators as second-rate contemporary cheap plays.

During the autumn of 1911, Gémier, with the experience of a first tour behind him, made plans to develop his travelling theatre more systematically in 1912. Not only did he plan a longer summer tour in Normandy, in the North and East of France, including Belgium and Luxembourg, but he also wanted to organize a winter tour with some important alterations in the rolling stock and implements he had used for the first season. Tractors — too heavy, too slow and too often out of order — were abandoned for the train. Part of the iron framework of the canvas theatre was replaced by timber, which was much lighter. And, finally, repertoire was altered in order not to show the same plays to the same audiences: Molière's *Tartuffe*, Daudet's *Arlésienne* and Lucien Néptoy's (contemporary dramatist) *The Little Ones*, all from Gémier's Théâtre Antoine repertoire, were to be presented in 1912.

That second and last tour [9], which started at the end of May 1912 and ended at the end of September, was as great a success as the first. Everywhere there were crowded and cheerful audiences, demands for extra performances and real participation on the part of the public[10]. The success of the National Travelling Theatre proved the merits of such an enterprise. But does this indisputable success provide sufficient reason to speak of 'popular' theatre?

As a matter of fact, Gémier's main intention when he created his National Travelling Theatre was to offer to the French provinces a first quality classic and modern repertoire — to bring a huge potential public back to good theatre. And in so doing, he no doubt bore in mind the possibility of bringing back a 'popular' public. But we must point out that he did not call his canvas theatre the

Popular Travelling Theatre — as, nine years later, he called one of his other institutions (National Popular Theatre) — but the National Travelling Theatre. In so doing, according to Paul Blanchart, Gémier

> meant to reach the whole of the country, including little towns without playhouses, the whole of France visited in three or four tours during three or four months, from June to September. He [Gémier] asserted, at the same time, his ambition to create a classic and modern repertoire of an authentic national value, a repertoire which could, one day, enrich itself with works raised up by that direct contact between drama and popular audiences 'newer' than the Parisian public [...] altogether more receptive and less *blasé*. [11]

We therefore think, with Paul Blanchart, that although the quest for a 'popular' public was in Gémier's mind, this quest was not his primary intention. Visiting the whole of the country, bringing good plays to publics who were deprived of theatre, creating a repertoire of undeniable value: these were his first targets. There is no doubt that in doing this Gémier *also* aimed at creating an authentic 'popular' theatre. But we believe he was much too smart to put the search for a 'popular' theatre in first place. To us, the notion of 'popular' theatre is in itself so difficult to pull apart, to grasp and then to define, that only beginners attempt to do so. Not an old fox like Gémier!

If we may say so, we believe that the simple fact of mentioning the word 'popular' can, as in legends of the ancient times, make popularity disappear. And, to give contemporary illustrations of what we mean here, Jean Vilar's *Théâtre National Populaire* is better known as TNP than under its full title. In a similar way, Roger Planchon told us in 1969 about his *Théâtre de la Cité* of Lyons-Villeurbanne:

> I have never called the Théâtre de la Cité 'popular' because I think that I know what is popular public. ... People who work in factories cannot see a theatre performance, cannot decode it.[12]

In a very recent interview with *Le Monde*, Planchon, five years later, sticks to the same point. In answer to the question 'What is, for you, popular theatre?' he replies:

> Like everyone else, I can only write this word between inverted commas. As I have said many times, workmen go into theatres only to build them.[13]

In conclusion, we would suggest that the point of knowing whether Gémier's National Travelling Theatre was indeed 'popular' or not is not the main question. What is of more importance, in our opinion, is the fact that in 1911, in a France deprived of practically any decent theatre life outside Paris, Gémier, with no help from the state, succeeded in creating a travelling theatre which brought to the provinces first rate dramatic productions; that these performances were given in a playhouse which was as refined and as comfortable as Gémier's own theatre in Paris; and, above all, that during these seven months on tour, the travelling theatre was full each night. Filled up with workers of the coal country in the North of France and their families, but also with middle class, upper middle class and, why not, bourgeois people. All of them — from the coal miner to the factory doctor — united in the pleasure of attending a good theatre performance, do, in a certain way, answer the question: was Gémier's National Travelling Theatre 'popular'?

Notes

1   CF. Paul Blanchart, *Firmin Gémier* (Paris, L'Arche, 1954), 128.

2   Catulle Mendès, 'The Popular Travelling Theatre', *Je Sais Tout* magazine, Paris, 15 September 1905. .

3   For further details, see my *Décentralisation Théâtrale en France* (Paris, SEDES, 1973), 21ff.

4   J. Paul-Boncour, *Report to the Commission of Fine Arts* (Chamber of Deputies, 1910), 177-8.

5   J. Paul-Boncour, 171.

6   Firmin Gémier, *Comoedia*, 19 February 1911.

7   Frank Norton, 'A theatre on motor-cars', *The World's Work*, May 1912.

8   Figures given by Paul Blanchart in his *Firmin Gémier*, 138.

9   At the end of 1912 Gémier had other projects in mind: performances at the Paris *Cirque d'hiver*, foundation of the *Théâtre National Populaire*, etc., and therefore did not want to extend the experience of the National Travelling Theatre.

10 'When I find a municipal band and its choir, I play *The Arlésienne* and it is, then, always an extraordinary night which fills the theatre to the maximum and brightens our

performances.' Gémier, quoted by Paul Blanchart, 141-2.
11   Paul Blanchart, 125.
12   From an interview I had with Roger Planchon on 20 January
     1969; cf. my *Décentralisation Théâtrale en France*, 12.
13   Yvonne Baby, 'Roger Planchon's territory', *Le Monde*, 2 May
     1974.

WILLIAM BRASMER

The Wild West Exhibition and the Drama of Civilization

At this time in American history it is difficult to view the Wild West Exhibition with any attitude less than derision. To de-mythologize the Wild West Exhibition's popularity, to debunk the legends which it propagated, to revise the biography of its progenitor — that intuitive performer but rather inept showman, Buffalo Bill Cody — may be too temperate a position. The social upheavals of our time suggest that a point of view must be taken about this form of nineteenth-century entertainment; we are told that reparations should be paid to the American Indian whose lands were stolen and whose animals were destroyed by those who were glorified in the Wild West Exhibition.

Truly it is difficult today to view the Wild West Exhibition with detachment. Social historians of American entertainment no longer document the Wild West Exhibition as a fascinating episode in showmanship. Nor can it be treated as an embodiment of Frederick Jackson Turner's 'frontier hypothesis' — that keystone of late nineteenth-century American historiography which explained the development of the American civilization as deriving not from European forces but from the uniqueness of the environment of the New World and the existence of free land for settlement. Thus, for many persons, the Wild West Exhibition and the continuation in the Hollywood western of the myths it first popularized, with its stereotype of the American Indian and its blatant disregard for his life and property, is viewed as cultural genocide 'by subverting the Native American's various ethnic identities and retaining him as a racial scapegoat'[1].

We are trapped today by a sense of guilt towards whole tribal nations. Ashamed of the cheap dramatization in show terms of the slaughter of Indians and animals, we view the Wild West Exhibition as an aberration — an entertainment form of our grandfathers' era. And yet our own times may be like our grandfathers'. Certainly the beliefs and the practices of the latter years of the nineteenth century are dominant in contemporary American society: white supremacy, rugged individualism, nostalgia for a lost wilderness in a crushing period of urbanization, the struggle between the cultures of the eastern and western seaboards, and the constant search for American uniqueness. Whatever our feelings about social injustice today, we should be able to view the activities of the nineteenth century and see in them who and what we are. As silly and degrading as the Wild West Exhibition may seem, therefore, a clear picture of its origins and its nature can lead us to understand our own popular entertainments. Moreover, the Wild West Exhibition presents to us a form of entertainment in which pictorial realism, the aesthetic of the nineteenth-century stage, reached its most complete realization.

At the very peak of its development in 1886 and before it became a part of the circus, the Wild West Exhibition was not just a glimpse of reality; it was reality itself, pictured with all of the true artifacts of western life from tepees to Deadwood Stage Coaches, a life in which the real heroes (Pawnee Bill, Texas Jack, and W.F. Cody) and the villains (Sitting Bull, Indian Horse, and Rocking Bear) were played by their real live selves. The Wild West Exhibition[2] does become interesting for us as it draws together all of the conventions of the nineteenth-century pictorial realistic stage, primarily in the spectacular use of these conventions in *The Drama of Civilization*, produced by Nate Salsbury and Buffalo Bill from a scenario by Steele MacKaye, with scenery designed by Matthew Sommerville Morgan, and performed at Madison Square Garden in New York in 1886. No other theatrical production so exploited the aesthetic principles of pictorial realism in the late nineteenth century. After the original production in New York and its subsequent presentation in England and Europe, the style of pictorial realism was to find further manifestation only in the motion picture.

Wild West enthusiasts date the origins of the show from 1882 when W.F. Cody planned North Platte, Nebraska's 'Old Glory Blow-Out', a Fourth of July celebration of cowboy rodeo acts climaxed by a buffalo hunt in which Cody demonstrated his prowess as a killer of this noble animal. Exactly when Cody envisioned this outdoor spectacle it is impossible to know; however, the antecedents for such a show had been developing many years previous to Cody's Independence Day celebration. Bronco-busting and range roundups had been performed many years earlier. An exhibit called 'Cowboy-Fun' had been given at Deer Trail, Colorado, on 4 July 1869, and wild steers were ridden in the Fourth of July celebrations at Cheyenne, Wyoming, in 1872[3]. P.T. Barnum had staged a buffalo hunt in 1843 in

Brooklyn, New York, and Wild Bill Hickok in 1870 had taken buffalo to Niagara Falls, New York, to exhibit.

Earlier even than the exhibition of cowboy skills was the exhibition of Indians. As early as 1827 at Peale's Museum in New York a group of Iroquois Indians were presented; they demonstrated how 'they lay in ambush and the manner of scalping an enemy' [4] and performed other Indian activities like the war whoop and tribal dances. George Caitlin, the eminent artist of Indian life, opened an 'Indian Gallery' at Clinton Hall in Philadelphia on 25 September 1837 where he exhibited and lectured on the pictures he had made in the Far West and the Indian curios he had collected. In 1840 he repeated his exhibit in London but added persons in a *tableau vivant* to demonstrate the Indian dances and other customs. (These scenes were performed by out-of-work Londoners; only later fourteen stranded Ioway Indians were substituted.) Barnum had first exhibited Indians at his American Museum in 1841 and by 1843 their performances had become the main drawing card and had raised Barnum's ire. 'The lazy devils', Barnum wrote in a letter, 'want to be lying down nearly all the time and it looks so bad for them to be lying about the Museum, I have them stretched out in the work shop all day'[5].

It may have been the Indian agent John B. Clum who organized the first full Indian show. Clum was agent for the Apaches on a reservation in Arizona Territory and in 1876 he took some Indians to the east coast to experience its cultural benefits, paying for the travel by exhibiting the Indians at stops along the way. Their first performance was at the Olympic Theatre in St Louis on 8 September 1876. A playbill of the event provides us with this information:

FIRST TABLEAU
The Indians in Full Costume

SECOND TABLEAUX
An Indian Encampment
The Surprise! The Fight! Thrilling Hand-to-Hand Combat
Taking of the Scalp!   Triumph of the Whites!

THIRD TABLEAU
An Indian Council of War

FOURTH TABLEAU
Indian Woman Mourning the Death of Her Husband

FIFTH TABLEAUX

Grand War Dance   Preparing for the War-Path

PART SECOND — FIRST TABLEAU

Indian Telegraphic System

SECOND TABLEAUX

Whites Encamped   The Indians Attack
Capture of the Hunter   Taking of the Scalp
Securing the Prisoner to the Stake   Indian Scalp Dance
His Torture

THIRD TABLEAUX

Indian Police Regulations   Arresting a Renegade

FINAL TABLEAUX

The Indians at Home, and at Peace
Squaws engaged in Domestic Labor   Social Games
The whole concluding with a Social Dance.[6]

The true interest in the Indian was not fed just by the few exhibitions of red-skinned savages, before Buffalo Bill Cody and others exploited his presence in the Wild West Exhibition. Rather it was given substance by the many plays, novels, and cheap pieces of popular literature printed in the nineteenth century. From 1800 to 1900 some 88 plays centred on Indian life. A few of the plays are distinctive, but most remain known only by title as just thirty are extant. In the beginning the Indian was usually delineated as an 'exotic' — the Indian squaw portrayed as a stock, stage heroine caught between the demands of tribal duty and affection for the white settler, or the noble Indian chieftain, fiery with fellow warriors, honourable when confronting white settlers, and given to loud laments over the destruction of his land and people. By 1840 the Indian was shown as a barbarous savage pitted against the gun-fighting frontiersman who saved beseiged settlers and stalked the despoiler of white womanhood. It was this Indian character who found his way into the cheap yellow-back novels which proliferated from the house of Beadle and Adams.

The first yellow-back Beadles appeared in June 1860, and were soon established with a crude woodcut of an Indian in battle dress on the front cover. Over 300 were published in this series before a second series of Beadle's Pocket Novels appeared in 1869. From that point the cheap literature multiplied into the New Dime Novels, Frank Starr's Ten Cent American Novels, Beadle's Pocket

Library, Beadle and Adams' Twenty Cent Novels and many more. In most series at least half of the stories were concerned with life and problems in the unsettled lands across the western shores of the Mississippi and a large portion of these contained the bloodcurdling adventures of frontiersmen and cowboys and the treacherous activities of Indians. These novels, which circulated primarily in the East, presented a lively but melodramatic and untruthful picture of the West — a picture which the Wild West Exhibition was to copy even as some of the writers of these novels helped to propagate the Wild West Exhibition itself.

If the origins of the Wild West Exhibition can be found in entertainments other than W.F. Cody's 'Old Glory Blow-Out', the initial popularity of the Wild West Exhibition during its first seasons, 1883-5, was prompted in part by a change in America's leisure pursuits. Wishing to escape the debilitating effects of the Civil War and being gradually freed from the doom of work by the Industrial Revolution, the American learned to play in the latter years of the nineteenth century. Not just in the home, clustered around the recently acquired parlour organ, but outside the home Americans sought leisure entertainment in the growing multiplicity of forms which showmen and theatre entrepreneurs set before them. The more affluent flocked to newly built summer resorts like Saratoga Springs to enjoy the walks and band concerts and to indulge in the craze for the sport of croquet. For the less affluent, cheap excursions on the expanding railroad systems provided delight. Most small towns towards the end of the century had a Town Hall or Opera House where touring companies or a standard stock company played. For instance, during the season of 1887-8 Edwin Booth, with Laurence Barrett as co-star, played on tour a repertoire of seven Shakespeare plays for 258 performances in 72 different towns, 48 being one-night stands[7]. For those who could not find complete pleasure in the pictorial splendour of the theatre with its multiple painted scenery, giant panoramas toured from city to city and drew thousands, especially if they depicted battle scenes of the War Between the States or Roman History, or presented dissolving views of the Overland Road to California or of a trip down the Mississippi River.

The emergence of Buffalo Bill as a popular hero derives from the legends in his autobiography, *The Life of Hon. William F. Cody* (1879), and the fictitious exploits devised by E.C.Z. Judson (Ned Buntline), a hack writer of serial literature. It was Buntline who, having failed to storm eastern literary circles with the publication of the *Western Library Journal and Monthly Review* in Cincinnati in 1844, turned to popularizing a rather unknown frontier scout, Buffalo Bill Cody. Buntline sensed in Cody's scouting ventures with the Fifth Cavalry a personage, if not of heroic proportions, at least capable of becoming a dime novel hero. On 23 December 1869, in the *New York Weekly*, the first instalment of Ned Buntline's serial *Buffalo Bill, the King of Border Men* appeared. Buntline had found his hero, but whether he invented the nickname of 'Buffalo Bill' for Cody matters little. We do know, however, that Henry Gordon Bennett, owner and editor of the *New York Herald*, spent $500 to pay for Cody's trip to New York in February 1872. The reasons for such an expenditure are unknown, but Bennett must have sensed Cody's news value, especially after the publicity Cody gained in 1872 for scouting the three-day western buffalo hunt provided for the amusement of Grand Duke Alexis on his visit to America. During Cody's stay in New York he attended the Bowery Theatre, accompanied by Ned Buntline, and watched a hack melodrama about his supposed exploits — Fred G. Maeder's adaptation of Buntline's serialized story, *Buffalo Bill, the King of Border Men*.

After his return west in the summer of 1872 Buntline beseiged Cody with suggestions to go on the stage. Whether Cody was short of cash or whether he was prompted by the applause he heard on appearing in the Bowery Theatre audience, we don't know; however, Cody did travel to Chicago in late winter to join Buntline in a unique theatrical adventure. There, on 16 December at Nixon's Amphitheatre, Cody appeared on stage in *The Scouts of the Prairie; or, Red Deviltry As It Is*, a hastily put together play by Buntline in which he drew on episodes from his dime novels and dramatized exploits of frontier scouts, treacherous Indians, and renegade whites with such nefarious names as Mormon Ben, Sly Mike, and Phelem O'Laugherty. Not able to learn or understand his part, Cody improvised his lines on stage while Buntline, Texas Jack, and an Italian cancan dancer in the role of Dove Eye, the Indian Maid, followed suit.

Although a text of the play no longer exists, its plot can be reconstructed from the numerous press reports in Chicago newspapers. The *Chicago Daily Tribune* provides a terse summary of the action:

> ... numerous bloody conflicts, wherein persons who, a minute before, were twenty miles away, are telegraphed back, and get there just in time; the beautiful Indian maiden with an Italian accent and a weakness for scouts; the lovely white girl held in

captivity by the aborigines; the poetical trapper and his felicitous homilies on the beauty of nature and the superiority of water to rotgut as a beverage; the cambric-clad Pawnees ... the inexplicable inebriate who manages to keep drunk for several days without a drop of anything; the prairie fire, the fight for life, the vengeance wreaked on the murderous redskins and the grand tableau at the close — all this put together furnish rare entertainment for the toiling masses who patronize the show.[8]

The Scouts of the Prairie lasted six days in Chicago and then toured to seven Eastern cities before it opened at the Bowery on 31 March 1873. For the next eleven seasons Cody appeared in at least twelve border dramas — each devised to display his personality and to capitalize on his authenticity as frontier scout and Indian fighter. Only two of the plays remain today, but their titles reflect their blood and thunder nature — *Red Hand; or, Buffalo Bill's First Scalp* (1877), *Knight of the Plains; or, Buffalo Bill's Best Trail* (1878), *Buffalo Bill at Bay; or, Pearl of the Prairie* (1878). Whatever success Cody had during his trouping with border dramas was modest: he grossed about twice the daily expenditure, approximately $150. It is not wrong to think that Cody was envious of P.T. Barnum, whose five ring circus was attracting thousands to the Hippodrome in New York with such spectacular extravaganzas as 'The Fall of Babylon' and 'Montezuma and the Conquest of Mexico' and netted an average of one half million dollars a year[9].

Despite the lack of real success with these border dramas, the years spent in acting in them aided Cody in testing a formula which he was to duplicate year after year in the Wild West Exhibition. This formula becomes apparent from the descriptions of the plots of the border dramas which appeared in countless newspaper reviews; and, although the formula varied depending on the skills of the frontier performers available, it was a simple melodramatic one, stressing the pictorial realism of each event in the play. The formula was simply:

a) An opening scene in which most of the characters are introduced
b) Individual scenes which display the skills of individual frontiersmen or cowboys
c) Scenes of Indian life and the customs on the frontier
d) A battle, chase or escape scene
e) The exploits of Buffalo Bill
f) A final scene of a natural disaster or of Indian treachery which is concluded with the triumph of the white man

If Cody discovered the formula, it was Nate Salsbury who made it work. Nate, who had served in the Union Army, took up amateur theatricals after the War and eventually organized his own touring stock company, 'The Troubadors'. After the 'Old Glory Blow-Out' in 1883, Salsbury joined Cody and remained as general manager season after season.

The Wild West Exhibition reached its greatest development in just four short years, 1883-7, from its beginnings in the 'Old Glory Blow-Out' in Nebraska to its culminating production of Steele MacKaye's *The Drama of Civilization* at Madison Square Garden in 1887. The subsequent grand tours of England and Europe by Cody and his outfit merely enlarged the legends of Buffalo Bill, and hoards of sophisticated Europeans accepted Cody's pictures of the adventuresome West, in which frontier settlers battled marauding Indians, cowboys slaughtered buffalo, and Westerners were sure shots with rifles (see Plate 5). During these grand tours heads of states sheepishly deigned to ride around the central arena in the opening scene, the American flag was flaunted in front of royal families, and the 'performing' Indians were photographed — solemn and imperturbable — against the architectural splendours of the Old World or in a gondola on the Grand Canal in Venice. These tours established in European minds the simplistic notion that American culture was epitomized by the wild and woolly West. In turn Cody capitalized on the adulation and success he won in Europe in his subsequent tours of America and during the 1893 World's Columbian Exposition in Chicago, where he probably played to one quarter of the twenty-seven million persons who attended that great fair.

But it is *The Drama of Civilization* which remains unique, for Cody's exhibition would have floundered by 1887 if three additional talents had not come together to infuse into the mélange of cowboy tricks and displays of frontier prowess a sense of historical pageantry. Never fully documented by circus or Wild West historians, *The Drama of Civilization* remains the only true achievement of the Wild West show.

It was not Cody but Nate Salsbury, the general manager for the Wild West Exhibition, who dreamed of an extravaganza which would outline the history of the Far West. The dream came to mind in the summer of 1886 when Cody's outdoor exhibition was playing at Erastina, Staten Island, New York. Here, because of the closeness of a large metropolitan audience, the availability of excursion boats for transportation, and the general aura of an amusement park which the exhibition had, thousands were in

Plate 5. Late nineteenth century poster of Buffalo Bill's
Wild West exhibition

attendance on a good summer's day. Cody basked in his popularity, spent much of his time drinking and spinning tall tales with his cronies, but had no idea of what to do with his show next. Among the many prominent visitors to Cody's encampment that summer was Steele MacKaye, a theatrical genius of diverse talents — teacher of the Delsarte acting system[10], inventor of theatrical machinery, manager of the innovative Madison Square Theatre, and late of the lecture stage where he had delivered a commentary to eight large murals of Civil War battles painted by Matthew Sommerville Morgan. It was MacKaye who helped Salsbury envision the outdoor Wild West Exhibition as an indoor historical drama to be entitled *The Drama of Civilization*.

Salsbury was wise to listen to MacKaye's plans, for MacKaye was more imbued with the concepts of pictorial romantic staging than any other nineteenth-century theatre artist, even David Belasco or Henry Irving. As a playwright MacKaye may have been a melodramatic hack, substituting theatrical effects for dramatic development and relying on stage machinery to provide a montage of deftly edited scenes: MacKaye's plays, like *Through the Dark* (1879) and *Anarchy; or, Paul Kauvar* (1887), are unreadable today except for the tantalizing stage directions. As a theatrical inventor, however, MacKaye ranks second to none. His patents for trick stage devices contributed the essential solutions for many staging, sound, and lighting problems. Moreover, his plans for the Spectatorium to be built for the Columbian Exposition in Chicago in 1893 — a gigantic theatre to seat 8,000 with a mammoth stage encircling half of the audience and fitted with twelve miles of railroad tracks for the shifting of scenery and a complex lighting system with a 'luxaueator' for the projection of optical illusions — has continued to inspire theatre technicians.

MacKaye's choice of Matt Morgan to paint the scenery was equally wise, although Morgan had accomplished little in the American theatre, confining his efforts first to political cartoons for *Frank Leslie's Illustrated Weekly*, then heading the design department of the Strobridge Lithography Company, Cincinnati, and eventually in the seventies painting cycloramas, panoramas and large allegorical pictures which were often displayed in theatres. However, before immigrating from England to America Morgan had been a scene painter at the Princess's Theatre during Charles Kean's important management 1851-9, designed sets and costumes for the Christmas pantomimes of Gilbert a'Beckett and Henry J. Byron at Covent Garden in the early sixties, and drawn extensively for English periodicals, primarily *Fun, Tomahawk*, and

Britannia. Gleeson White in *English Illustration*[11] may find his work not worthy of serious consideration, but when one exhumes Morgan's woodcut illustrations from the *Half-Penny Journal, Boy's Own Magazine* and other cheap periodicals, they display an audacity and largeness of scope suitable only to the expansiveness of the Wild West Exhibition.

Three talents thus coalesced — Salsbury's organizational ability, MacKaye's penchant for mechanical stage trickery and his ability to direct large productions, and Morgan's facile brush which could cover large areas of space. MacKaye, having persuaded Salsbury of the worth of the project and engaged Morgan to design the sets, then set about writing a scenario which was to display his latest stage inventions and present the Wild West in a historic order, adding certain other pictorial elements he thought necessary. These dramatic elements MacKaye outlined in a letter to Salsbury:

1. The aboriginal savage in his garb of skins, and with the weapons used before the white man appeared
2. The emigrant trains
3. Prairie fire
4. Stampede of wild cattle
5. Life of mining camp
6. Life of fort
7. A realistic presentation of the formation and bursting of a cyclone in the mountains.[12]

MacKaye believed that this scenario he had submitted effectively organized the story of the pioneer against the awful elements of nature as well as the pioneer's conflict with the animals of the plains. Salsbury, the pragmatic showman, approved but provided wise counsel in a letter of 7 September to MacKaye:

> Your scenario is a Corker, if you can carry it out. Let me impress upon you that, in dealing with the Wild West actors, you must try to get broad effects without burdening their minds too much. For, as sure as fate, they will weary of the job if limits are too narrow.... At this distance, it is quite impossible for me to know just how you intend to put your ideas in force. But it seems to me that success will depend on the simplicity of action and the grandeur of mounting.[13]

And on 5 November, after a flurry of letters concerning problems with the scenery, Salsbury thought again of the scenario and its main protagonist and wrote to MacKaye:

...A word as to Cody. You will find him petulant and impulsive, but with good, crude ideas about what can be evolved from the material. He will want to introduce (by my suggestion) the whole outfit to the audience, before the actual show begins. I think it will have a convincing effect on the people, and put them in a mood to accept without criticism the rest of the show.[14]

To house their epic pageant MacKaye and Salsbury chose what was known in 1886 as Madison Square Garden. Located between Fourth and Madison Avenues and Twenty-First and Twenty-Seventh Streets, the building is not to be confused with the ornate baroque structure designed by McKim, Mead and White and erected in the early 1890s. The 'Old Garden' MacKaye utilized was a crude brick wall enclosure with a rickety roof which had been erected to encircle a vacant lot where Barnum had often pitched his tent. Inside this ramshackle structure horse shows and chicken shows had taken shelter over the years, and the building was commonly spoken of as the 'Madison Square Beer Garden'. MacKaye employed carpenters to build a stage at one end of the horse track arena and construct a grid of support beams on the roof to carry the weight of the panorama drops and to hold the winches which moved them. A trench was dug across Twenty-Seventh Street to install a steam line from a railroad car shop, the steam being used to power four six-foot exhaust fans which would whip truckloads of dry leaves around the arena for the prairie cyclone effect.

Within the expanse of space of the Garden Morgan's work had to be monumental and MacKaye ordered four semicircular moveable panoramic drops measuring 40 ft high by 150 ft long. The scope of Morgan's task, compounded by the fact that all of the reconstruction and painting of the Garden had to be accomplished around a horse show then in progress, is given the right amount of puffing in his press release before *The Drama of Civilization* opened:

At the Madison Square Garden, Mr. Matt Morgan is painting a picture half a mile long and fifty feet high. Mr. Morgan puts in mountains whole, and the chief criticism made by finical art critics is, that his valleys are larger than the original. — The artist swung in a chair-scaffold, yesterday, away up in the roof of the Garden. At this dizzy height, he was painting the top of a California redwood tree. He limned a crow on one of the topmost boughs at such an airy pinnacle that the bird took fright, and almost fell into the middle distance. Then Mr.

Morgan caught a rope, swung down the tree a little, painted a knot hole, and put a chipmunk in it. Then he swung up again into the air and covered the top of Pike's Peak with eternal whitewash. After that he turned to painting a cyclone — so natural, that he had to hold his hat on with one hand, while he employed a brush with the other.[15]

The cost of mounting the production, including MacKaye's fee for rehearsing troops of soldiers and Indians, is somewhat in doubt. The *New York Times* of 31 October 1886 reports that $60,000 was spent; but MacKaye, on 7 December 1886 in a letter apologizing to Salsbury for the overrun of expenses, provides Salsbury with the figures for the original estimate for carpentry and painting — $6,552[16]. The exact figure, therefore, is not known, but certainly it must have been several times the $8,500 Salsbury had budgeted.

The exact nature of the performance of *The Drama of Civilization* is best described in a full review of the first performance in the *New York Times* of 25 November 1886[17]:

BUFFALO BILL IN DRAMA
FOUR WILD WEST EPOCHS AT
MADISON SQUARE GARDEN

Patriotic playgoers crowded Madison Square Garden last evening to applaud the first performance of Mr. Steele Mackaye's last great drama, which was acted with great spirit and power by Buffalo Bill, several dozen cowboys, cowgirls, and genuine greasers, besides a hundred and fifty Indians of various tribes in full fig and feather.

Mr. Mackaye's drama is divided into four 'epochs,' named on the bills as follows: 1. The Primeval Forest. 2. The Prairie. 3. The Cattle Ranch. 4. The Mining Camp. The first epoch is supposed to be that preceding the discovery of America. The primeval forest is shown — a really beautiful scene, by the way, and with happy moonlight effects. It is the hour preceding dawn. A bear lazily shuffles to the spring, gazes curiously around and disappears. Two timid deer peer from behind the trees, then come forth, followed by a herd of elk. As they are gathered by the spring, several Indians steal upon them and a shower of arrows is fired. The sun rises. A band of Sioux and a band of Cheyennes meet. The great chiefs, Blooming-Thunder and Hole-in-the-Ground, hold a pow-wow and make peace. The war dance follows, interrupted by the onslaught of a band of Pawnees under the fierce sachem No-Bugs-on-Me, and a rough-and-tumble massacre closes the scene.

The second act shows the prairie. A dozen live buffalo are at the water hole. Suddenly Buffalo Bill's wild yell shrills through the silence, and the cheerful pop of the Winchester stimulates the herd in its mad flight to safety. The emigrant train comes on; the prairie schooners and their oxen, burros, and mules; the going into camp; the supper and preparations for night; a natural and interesting picture. Darkness comes. All are sleeping. Suddenly a distant glow on the horizon, brightening and widening — nearer and nearer till the prairie is a sea of rushing fire — then the wild yell of alarm — the fighting of fire with fire — the stampede — deer, buffalo, mustangs, Indians, and emigrants — all fleeing together — a stirring scene.

The third epoch — but why epoch? — is the cattle ranch. Illustrating the cowboy in his glory, riding the bucking mustang and lassoing the bounding and bumptious steer. Suddenly comes the curdling whoop of the Comanches and Kiowas, led by Seven-Fleas, Son-of-a-Gun, Loaded-for-Bear, Busted-Flush, Peach-Blow-Spittoon, Two-Buckets-of-Red-Paint, and other famous chiefs, who go into the hair-raising business with a painstaking enthusiasm which fanned the audience to an uproar. Just at the most exciting point of the massacre a troop of cowboys arrive and the noble red men are sent to the happy hunting grounds in a body.

The fourth 'epoch' is devoted to the incidents of a mining camp — presumably in Colorado. There is considerable fun, according to the frontier notion of fun, including a duel to the death with revolvers. The lightninglike arrival and departure of the pony express and some rather tame rifle shooting are among the incidents. The Deadwood stage appears. The horses are quickly changed, and it rolls away. The scene changes. A dark and dangerous canyon is shown. Passing here the stage is 'jumped' by a band of road agents, who go through mail, express, and passengers with that cheerful skill and celerity for which the Western road agent is famous. The scene shifts back to the mining camp. Thunder is crashing and lightning flashing, and one absurd sentinel, supposed to be a United States cavalryman, is patrolling the line of tents. Suddenly comes a roar, the tents sway and then are leveled, several dummies are whirled wildly in midair, and the curtain drops upon what is supposed to be the terrific destruction of the camp by a cyclone.

Taken as a whole the show is excellent. The scenery is more than good, the incidents of frontier life are realistic, the dances and ceremonies of the Indians are spirited and effective, and the pictures presented upon the vast stage, or, rather, in the vast scene, are full of interest and beauty. The most prominent drawback to enjoyment is afforded by the 'orator,' who prepares each scene with a pompous and insufferably long and unnecessary description of what is to be. The orator should be boiled down or lassoed. He speaks well, but there is too much of him. The pantomimes describe themselves, and need no assistance.

During the first 'epoch' a moose thought it would be funny to wander out of the primeval forest and take a stroll around the Garden within the tanbark inclosure. For 10 minutes he wandered and gazed, and, so to speak, took in the town. When the curtain fell Stick-in-the-Mud, Jumping Polecat, or some other of the great chiefs in full war paint, came running in pursuit. Assembled New York drew a long breath and watched the onslaught of the famous warrior on the denizen of the primeval. With a blood-curdling yell the fierce sachem rushed upon his prey. Just as he was within striking distance the moose turned his head — flip! flap! scrabble! — it was beautiful to see the way the simple-hearted child of the forest got over the railing out of the way of that moose, and in shelter behind three dudes. The moose wasn't angry. He gazed after the flying chief more in sorrow than in wrath, then continued his stroll, pausing every now and then in front of a box to allow some lady to pet him, and despite the fact that he was afterward 'shoo'ed' to his cage by a desperate cowboy, remained the hero of the evening.

Before the production opened newspaper advertisements gave it large space. For instance, the *New York Herald Tribune* emblazoned:

MADISON SQUARE GARDEN
Adam Forepaugh   Sole Lessee
OPENING POSTPONED TILL
WEDNESDAY EVENING, NOVEMBER 24
Nightly thereafter, with matinees
TUESDAYS, THURSDAYS, AND SATURDAYS
BUFFALO BILL'S
BUFFALO BILL'S
WILD WEST
WILD WEST
WILD WEST
(W.F. Cody and Nate Salsbury, proprietors and managers)
Grandly famous and altogether new
A PERFECT BLAZE OF NOVELTY

Inauguration of the most stupendous and in every respect
grandest, most unique, thrilling, sensational, perfect
and superbly artistic and realistic exhibition
ever seen or attempted in the metropolis
of America
A Grand Drama of Civilization by STEELE MACKAYE
Gorgeous Scenery by MATT MORGAN
Mechanical Devices by NELSE WALDRON
ADMISSION, 50c, CHILDREN UNDER 9, 25c
WEDNESDAY, NOVEMBER 24
MONSTER FREE PARADE[18]

The action in *The Drama of Civilization* was not confined to the
stage, but took place in the horseshoe shaped arena in front of the
stage; and between each of the four episodes trick riding, feats of
marksmanship by Cody, Annie Oakley and others were displayed.
The whole performance must have resembled an equestrian drama
at Astley's, moving from stage to arena, although MacKaye's
extravaganza had in addition a menagerie of animals rented from
the circus proprietor, Adam Forepaugh, and the action was backed
up with the dissolving panoramic views of Matt Morgan, an effect
which MacKaye heralded as the first use of a moving cyclorama in
any theatre. During the first performances MacKaye's 'blaze of
novelty' had problems with scene shifts. However, the mechanical
difficulties were worked out by Christmas time and the entertainment ran without pauses between the 'epochs'. A free souvenir
plaque of Cody and the addition of a final *tableau vivant* of
'Custer's Last Stand' helped to swell crowds until the final
performance on Washington's Birthday, 22 February 1887. This
history of the Far West envisioned by Salsbury and MacKaye had
been a success, but new fields had to be conquered. What better
place than London during the celebrations for the Golden Jubilee
of Queen Victoria! The *S.S. Nebraska* was chartered for the voyage
to England and 97 Indians, some 200 animals including 18 buffalo,
and a host of cowboy and frontier personalities embarked on 31
March.

Salsbury had chosen to set up the Wild West Exhibition next to
an American trade fair housed at Earl's Court off the Brompton
Road. A large outdoor circular arena was built near the halls
housing the trade fair. Pictures in the *London Illustrated News*
show the arena having a track about one-third of a mile in
circumference, one half of which is backed with tent pavilions for
the audience grandstand seating. The rest of the arena had a

backing of small hills and painted forest scenery[19]. None of this had the scope of Matt Morgan's over-sized cycloramas for *The Drama of Civilization*, although the encampment of the personnel around the arena in 35 tents including 15 Indian tepees added a picturesque quality which was lacking in the scenic embellishments.

After several preview performances for notables, Cody opened his show on 9 May 1887. For his first English appearance he scrapped much of MacKaye's scenario and returned to the formula which he had first developed for his exhibition: pony express races, attacks on emigrant trains and Deadwood stage coaches, trick shooting, bronco-busting, buffalo roundups, and a final battle scene — 'Custer's Last Stand'[20].

Too much has been made of the fashionable craze which the Wild West Exhibition and Cody excited during the London performances: the command performances, the visits of royalty, the lionizing of Cody in press and salon — all of it reads today like an adventure out of a yellow-back novel. The Cody legend was greatly magnified during the London engagement and Cody's show had the right Western hoop-la to attract thousands, but it had neither the historical sweep nor the pictorial grandeur of *The Drama of Civilization*.

Salsbury planned a tour to other English cities. First was Birmingham, where the show was tepidly received. A decision was made to move indoors and to revive some of the pictorial material in MacKaye's scenario and it was announced that for the Manchester showing a covered arena was to be connected to the 8,000 seat grandstand at the Salford Race Track. This arena and seating area was heated by steam against the winter chill and lighted with the electrical equipment from the American trade fair in London. According to the programme for the opening perform-ance at Manchester on 17 December 1887, $40,000 worth of scenery was supplied by Matt Morgan, seven panoramas each 200 ft long and 30 ft high and worked on drums. Whether these panoramas were the original sets from *The Drama of Civilization* or were painted new in Manchester from Morgan's drawings it is impossible to say, but they do represent Morgan's last work on the English stage and perhaps the last work of a scene painter trained in the atelier of the Grieves. Their $40,000 cost does seem excessive compared to the estimate for the original sets for *The Drama of Civilization*.

As in the Madison Square Garden showing, an orator provided a semblance of a historical narration to link the seven different eposides, all of which were profusely described in the *Manchester Guardian* of 19 December 1887:

The first episode shows the primeval forest of America before its discovery by the white man. It is night, and the boles of great trees are dimly seen in the moonlight. With the gradual coming of day animals begin to stir. A bear and a herd of elk wander across the glade, followed by a couple of Indians, evidently seeking elk steak for breakfast. Sunlight streaming through the trees discovers two bands of Indians approaching from opposite directions, and in a conversation between their respective chiefs ... we have an illustration of what can be done with sign language. An Indian courier rushes in to announce, in the same unspoken tongue, the approach of a hostile band, and the scene closes with a sharp skirmish which strews the glade with dead bodies. The Indians fight with a fine glow of fierceness, but their war whoop will be voted a fraud by readers of Fenimore Cooper. The next two episodes, which are given in the form of tableaux, represent the landing of the Pilgrim Fathers and an incident in which the Princess Pocahontas saves the life of Captain John Smith. Both pictures are composed with much skill. Next we see an Indian tribe on the march, with women, children, and baggage.... 'Red Shirt,' a savage of noble bearing, and with a really important face, rides at the head of the tribe. Camping ground is fixed upon, and while the women set up the tents the braves run races and engage in other manly pastimes — setting up tents is not, we believe, regarded as a manly pastime. While this is going on scouts come in with news of the approach of a hostile tribe. The tents are struck in a moment, the women, children, and baggage disappear, and the warriors begin the war dance to put themselves in trim for the expected fray. The scene closes, however, before the hostile tribe put in an appearance. The wooded Atlantic coast in which these events occur changes now to the bare, rolling prairie. We see it under a scorching sun, and the scene gives the effect of immense distance.... A band of buffaloes scampers across, with Buffalo Bill in pursuit.... An emigrant train of several waggons appears, and the emigrants make preparations to camp for the night. But an attack of Indians has first to be beaten off. The onset, made by a large party on horseback, is sudden and fierce, and a good deal of powder has to be burnt before the emigrants can light their camp fire and settle down in peace. Evening comes on, and in the moonlight there are some sports, the best feature of which is the Virginia horseback reel, an extremely pretty thing.... In the meantime our emigrants get to sleep, and darkness and silence fall on the prairie. Afar on the horizon appears a red streak of fire. It rapidly advances, and finally the flames burst out close to the camp. Not a boy in Manchester but knows how to deal with an emergency of this kind. But the emigrants have not time to fire the prairie in front of them, and only the fall of the curtain saves them from certain death.

The element of fun, in which the entertainment is otherwise not rich, is introduced at this stage in the shape of bucking horses. These are wild prairie mustangs spoiled in the breaking, and now vicious enough to resist all ordinary attempts to mount them. And in this, more perhaps than in anything else, do the cowboys show their skill in handling horses. Numerous are the varieties of vice in these animals, and the audience seemed greatly entertained with the struggles between horse and man. The amusement furnished by the bucking horses suggested the reflection that while up to this point the scenes had been pictur-esque and of absorbing interest there had been nothing to make laughter. The orator intimated that if anybody in Manchester would bring down a refractory horse the cowboys would have great pleasure in riding it. And one can believe it, in view of a kind of wild joy they seemed to take in mastering their own animals.

After a further display of trick shooting three other episodes were given, the *Guardian* reported. The first pictured the 'lazy life on a cattle ranch' with an attack by Indians. Then 'Custer's Last Stand' was displayed, which the orator described as 'the reddest page of savage history'. And for the final scene there was the attack on the Deadwood stagecoach plus a natural holocaust, supplied by the Blackman Air Propellor Company, which swept everything away.

The reviewer for the *Manchester Guardian* correctly understood the aesthetic of the Wild West Exhibition:

> It is the conjunction of scenery ... with people who have lived the phases of life it represents that gives its peculiar interest and value to the 'Wild West' Show. We are told that everything about it is real. The emigrant waggons the audience sees crossing the prairie have ... been there. So with the Deadwood stagecoach, and about the buffaloes, the Indians, and the cowboys there is of course no doubt. In short the show is realism as close as it can be managed.

With cold weather in mid-January, audiences for the Wild West Exhibition in Manchester diminished and the performers became demoralized. Ed Goodman, Cody's nephew, wrote from Manchester to his parents reporting that Cody had bronchitis and the houses for the show had become very small. After laying plans for a return London engagement to recoup the increasing financial losses, Salsbury left Manchester for America to plot a summer season at home. The London engagement did not materialize. Cody and his troupe went to Hull on 4 May and gave a single performance, utilizing two football fields, before sailing for home on the sixth of May.

Over the next years Cody sustained his rôle as a popular Western hero on the newspaper publicity gleaned from the English command performances and the London and Manchester engagements. Repeated tours to Europe in the mid-nineties refurbished the Cody legend and Cody's intervention in the truce negotiations of the Sioux War of 1890-1 gained him notoriety and allowed him to exhibit some survivors of the massacre of Wounded Knee as freaks rather than as proud natives seeking redress for wrongs.

In 1894 James Bailey, the indomitable circus proprietor who controlled both Barnum's Circus and Forepaugh and Sells Brothers Circuses, took over as general manager of Cody's Wild West Exhibition. Bailey forced Cody to forgo long stands and take to the road. Cody was reduced to barnstorming. Although Bailey devised efficient railroad transportation for the show, the size of Cody's Wild West Exhibition was modest in comparison to the major circuses on the road; the Ringling Brothers Circus in 1893, for instance, carried no less than 70,000 square feet of canvas in the tent tops alone while Cody transported less than 5,000[21]. Moreover Cody never trouped with more than 600 persons while the major circuses travelled with thousands. Season after season Cody persisted, presenting the same format of Western cowboy acts that he had devised in the early 1880s, occasionally adding for novelty a crack drill team or Mexican Gauchos. A clear and rather pitiful picture of the difficulties of touring and attracting audiences is recorded in a diary of the 1896 season kept by M.B. Bailey, superintendent of electric lights for the Exhibition: the accidents to performers, the cancelled performances due to weather, and the impossible show lots located too far from public transportation are endlessly documented as the Exhibition moved from Pennsylvania to Ohio and through Illinois to North Dakota[22].

The Wild West Exhibition declined in popularity as the nineteenth century waned. Showmen other than Cody devised their own Wild West shows, but these lasted only a few years and were absorbed into the 'after-show' or 'extra concert attraction' of the circus. And Miller Brothers Ranch Real Wild West, organized in 1907 and operating under several titles until 1949, had little of the romantic atmosphere of frontier life as portrayed in the Wild West Exhibition, as the Miller Brothers show concentrated on rodeo acts and displays of horsemanship. Despite the claims of the practitioners that the Wild West Exhibition was a unique popular entertainment form, the history of the Exhibition was exceedingly short, beginning in 1883 and reaching its peak of development in *The Drama of Civilization* in 1887.

Today the Wild West Exhibition appears to have been an aberration, a display of frontier prowess and butchery. The excitement an audience displayed at the sight of a staged buffalo hunt in the Wild West Exhibition must seem now to have been a fraudulent response. How can one glory in the destruction of this imposing animal which in the 1850s numbered forty million and by 1890 had been decimated to less than 1,000[23]? Haunted as we are by the destruction of whole Indian nations, we must view with shame and disgust the thrill an audience sensed when Indians entered an arena with a whoop only to be blasted in a blaze of rifle fire. Even the reality of the Wild West Exhibition, so sought by Cody, Salsbury, and MacKaye in the style of production they developed, was never a true reality, for the Wild West Exhibition eliminated human speech. Never on stage or in the arena did the protagonists of the Wild West Show speak to each other. Without dialogue there was no development of character. Without debate there was little understanding between persons of different heritage. Without language there could be no enlightenment in the audience.

The Wild West Exhibition was essentially a pageant in dumbshow; the history it presented was pictured in terms of the realism of the stage melodrama. We may recollect with interest the panoramas the performers presented, but we can never rightfully know about the events they pictured until we hear such voices as Ten Bears, the Commanche chieftain, speaking to us from the past:

> I was born upon the prairie, where the wind blew free, and there was nothing to break the light of the sun. I was born where there were no enclosures, and where everything drew a free breath. I want to die there, and not within walls. I know every stream and every wood between the Rio Grande and the Arkansas. I have hunted and lived over that country. I lived like my fathers before me, and like them, I lived happily.[24]

Notes

Manuscripts and documents on William F. Cody and the Wild West Exhibition are housed in several libraries in America. The Circus World Museum, Baraboo, Wisconsin, contains an extensive collection of lithographic materials, programmes, and couriers. The Western History Section of the Denver Public Library has scrapbooks, newspaper clippings, route cards, photographs, and correspondence of Cody and Salsbury. Additional correspondence of Salsbury can be found in the Collection of American Literature at Yale University; and the Library of the Performing Arts, New York, holds other Salsbury items. The Buffalo Bill Historical Center at Cody, Wyoming, has a few manuscripts and documents and much Cody memorabilia. The Garst Museum, Greenville, Ohio, contains Annie Oakley memorabilia. The state historical society libraries of Nebraska, Kansas, Illinois, and Ohio also house interesting items.

Any study of the Wild West Exhibition and William F. Cody must begin with Don Russell's work, *The Lives and Legends of Buffalo Bill* (Norman, University of Oklahoma Press, 1960), which has a definitive bibliography. This study dispels many of the legends about Buffalo Bill and presents a documented sequence of the events in his life, although it is laudatory in tone and often romantically views its subject through the eyes of a 'western buff'. A recent work by Russell, *The Wild West* (Fort Worth, Amon Carter Museum of Western Art, 1970), is a splendid monograph published in relation to an exhibit held in Forth Worth of pictorial materials on the Wild West Exhibition.

Biographies abound on persons associated with Cody. Walter Havighurst, *Annie Oakley of the Wild West* (New York, Macmillan, 1954), and Jay Monaghan, *The Great Rascal: The Exploits of the Amazing Ned Buntline* (New York, Little, Brown & Company, 1951), should be consulted. And the works on the American Indian, other Western legendary heroes, and the role of the Western frontier in the development of American cultural patterns in the nineteenth century are too numerous to mention. Unfortunately there are no studies on Nate Salsbury and Matt Morgan, nor has there been significant appraisal of the importance of the production of *The Drama of Civilization* as the major expression of the Wild West Exhibition.

1   Ralph and Natasha Friar, *The Only Good Indian ... The Hollywood Gospel* (New York, Drama Book Specialists, 1972), 2.

2   Although the Wild West Exhibition is often called a 'show', Cody and most Wild West showmen preferred the word 'Exhibition'.

3   Don Russell, *The Lives and Legends of Buffalo Bill* (Norman, University of Oklahoma Press, 1960), 292-3.

4   *New York Post*, 30 October 1827, quoted in Brooks McNamarra, 'The Indian Medicine Show', *Educational Theatre Journal*, Vol. XXIII, No. 4 (December 1971), 436.

5   The letters from P.T. Barnum to Moses Kimball, the manager of the Boston Museum, have recently been used by Neil Harris, *Humbug: The Art of P.T. Barnum* (Boston, Little, Brown & Company, 1973), 53.

6   Pat Ryan, 'Wild Apaches in the Effete East: A Theatrical Adventure of John P. Clum', *Theatre Survey*, Vol. 6, No. 2 (November, 1965), 152.

7   Philip C. Lewis, *Trouping: How the Show Came to Town* (New York, Harper & Row, 1973), 140-5.

8   *Daily Tribune*, 18 December 1872, quoted in William Coleman, 'Buffalo Bill Takes the Stage', *Players*, Vol. 47, No. 2 (December 1972), 85.

9   Russell, 259-60, provides some income figures for Cody's seasons, and Harris, 245-9, utilizes Barnum's ledger books for the first time and estimates his yearly receipts.

10 François Delsarte (1811-71), French teacher of vocal expression, who formulated exact rules of gesture and movement to portray dramatic emotions. MacKaye studied with disciples of Delsarte and was the first to bring Delsarte's principles to America where they became the basis for instruction at MacKaye's drama school, founded in 1884 at the Lyceum Theatre, New York.

11 Gleeson White, *English Illustration, 'The Sixties', 1855-1870* (London, Constable, 1897; reprint edn: Bath, Kingsmead, 1970), pp.57, 76, 80, 92.

12 Percy MacKaye, *Epoch, The Life of Steele MacKaye* (New York, Boni & Liveright, 1927), Vol. II, 77.

13 *Ibid.*, 76.

14 *Ibid.*, 81.

15 *Ibid.*, 83.

16 *Ibid.*; Appendix, liv. MacKaye's letter to Salsbury presents a detailed estimate of the costs and is interesting as it provides

figures on a stage labour and materials. For instance, the chief carpenter, Waldron, received just $40 weekly while Morgan was paid $250 weekly for his painting.

17   p. 5, col. 2.

18   *New York Herald Tribune*, 21 November 1886, 7.

19   Ed Goodman, Cody's nephew, wrote to his parents from London, 22 April 1887, and estimated the grandstand seating as 50,000, which is highly improbable. Stella Adelyne Foote, *Letters from Buffalo Bill* (Billings, Foote Publishing Co., 1954), 30.

20   The stand of General George Custer at the Battle of the Little Big Horn on 25 June 1876 against a small handful of Indians has been depicted more than any other battle scene in American history: a total of 848 pictures according to Don Russell, *Custer's Last* (Fort Worth, Amon Carter Museum of Western Art, 1968). Numerous artists have portrayed the final death scene of Custer and lithographs of the event have circulated by the thousands, especially when used as advertisements for the Anheuser-Busch Brewing Association. Russell traces the history of the many illustrations, but he does not mention the depiction of the battle on stage or in the Wild West Exhibition.

21   Charles Philip Fox, *A Ticket to the Circus* (New York, Bramhall House, 1969), 89, provides full measurements on the tents carried by Ringling Brothers Circus.

22   Bailey's diary appears in the Appendix to Dexter Fellows, *This Way to the Big Show* (New York, Viking Press, 1936), 343-52.

23   David Dary, 'The Buffalo in Kansas', *Kansas Historical Quarterly*, Vol. XXXIX, No. 3 (Autumn 1973), 338.

24   W.C. Vanderwerth, *Indian Oratory* (New York, Ballantine Books, 1972), 132.

Acknowledgements

The author is grateful to the Library of Congress, Washington D.C., for the use of Plate 5.

WILLIAM GREEN

Strippers and Coochers — the Quintessence of American Burlesque

The essence of the American burlesque show is that it is a leg show. For over one hundred years, from the 1860s until very recently, the shape of the leg, the curve of the torso has kept burlesque in the forefront of American popular theatre and has differentiated it from other types of light entertainment. Questions of morality aside, the resiliency of the genre is related to the inventiveness of theatrical managers in displaying more and more of the female dancer in very specialised routines with less and less clothing. In this respect the structure of the show has gone through an evolution — the chorines and soloists moving from subsidiary positions to stage centre and almost into the laps of the audience. Crises in the economic life history of burlesque have been averted again and again by tearing away another veil, inventing another gyration to woo new audiences.

Actually, the development of burlesque in the United States may be divided into approximately three periods: 1750-1868, the age of traditional burlesque; 1868-1922, the era during which the modern burlesque show evolved; and 1922-present, the period of nudity, smut, and decline.

Undraped women on stage, of course, are not — and never were — the exclusive province of American theatre. But by a strange series of coincidences and clever exploitation of those coincidences by theatre managers of the late nineteenth century, the semi-clad woman (by the standards of the day) became the catalyst for creating a new and native American theatrical form out of elements from the minstrel shows, variety shows, vaudeville and the old traditional burlesques with their Aristophanic roots[1].

The female in tights first appeared on the American stage at the Thalia Theatre in New York in 1827 in the person of a Mlle Hutin. But it was not until 1861 when Adah Isaacs Menken, in a production adapted from Byron's *Mazeppa*, came on stage so attired on horseback that a rage for the tights-clad performer set in [2]. These were solo acts.

Imagine the effect on the audiences when *The Black Crook* opened at Niblo's Garden on Broadway in September 1866 with an entire chorus wearing tights. This mass display of ladies' legs on stage happened by accident. In order to help the members of a foreign ballet troupe stranded in New York earn a little money, the managers hired them to 'put on a parade in tights and ballet skirts' as part of what was otherwise a dull drama. The Amazon parade caught the imagination of the theatre-goers, and *The Black Crook* played to full houses. In fact, it was kept alive through revivals for twenty-five years despite opposition of the press and clergy.

So the leg shows had entered. And by May 1869, fourteen out of New York's sixteen theatres were featuring 'naked drama'. This prompted Olive Logan, a successful actress of the day, who in 1868 had turned from acting to writing, to attack what she termed the nude women on the New York stage singing vulgar songs 'capable of indecent constructions, accompanied by the wink, the wriggle, the grimace, which are not peculiar to virtuous women, whatever else they are'[3].

From a chorus line the tights parade went to an entire production when Lydia Thompson and the 'British Blondes' arrived from England in September 1868. This all-female troupe opened in New York in a type of traditional burlesque drawn from Greek mythology entitled *Ixion, ex-King of Thessaly*. While reactions to the production varied, the daring costumes shocked the spectators. 'Those of the first and second rows, as well as the principals, wore over their covered legs a semblance of skirts, a foot in length, of thinnest mull with countless flounces', reports Bernard Sobel[4]. Adverse criticism notwithstanding, the fame of the 'British Blondes' spread rapidly. The company enjoyed a long and successful career in the United States. Undoubtedly Miss Thompson and her troupe never intended to transform traditional burlesque, but they did firmly establish the appearance of the tights-clad female chorus line.

Aristophanic influences, *The Black Crook*, 'British Blondes' — these all represent key samplings of the foreign element which contributed to the development of American burlesque. Some students of the genre consider them too remote, even too refined, to be given much weight in the study of the subject. American burlesque, as the label is used today, connotes a tawdry, male-oriented type of entertainment with loads of blue comedy and bare flesh, interspersed with song and dance.

Probably the individual most responsible for taking burlesque in this direction and giving it its own indigenous form is Michael B. Leavitt. Leavitt has credited Lydia Thompson with introducing the type of production which served as a model for his own shows. However, Leavitt, who had been a burlesque pioneer as early as 1842, also borrowed ideas from minstrel shows, variety, and the extravaganzas. What emerged was a show with a tripartite structure in which the first part featured musical numbers and comedy; the second — known as the olio — presented specialty acts; and the third consisted of an afterpiece and grand finale. One of Leavitt's original contributions in adapting the minstrel show format was the substitution of women in segments formerly performed by men. Girls, however, never appeared in the olio.

The Rentz-Santley shows — as Leavitt's company was known — placed the emphasis on dancing. Although the females performed in tights, there was no nudity, no provocative dancing, and only occasional *double entendres* in the dialogue. Playing continuously to capacity houses, the Rentz-Santley shows lasted about ten years. But the technical divisions Leavitt had conceived persisted for many more, and provided the basic format for modern burlesque shows.

By the 1870s American burlesque had its own structure and its own focus in the predominance of the female performer. Another necessary ingredient in giving it its indigenous character came from the honky tonk. This was a nineteenth-century drinking establishment first found in the San Francisco area catering to a rough clientele such as miners and sailors. The honky tonks sold drinks, women, and entertainment. They were in effect low-class night clubs. The entertainment consisted of variety numbers, comic routines, dramatic sketches, and afterpieces — the very types of material which blended into the Leavitt-constructed shows. The entertainers, in facing primarily uncouth audiences, had to depend on their wits and their own routines much more than when playing in regular theatres. Audience interplay was more spontaneous. Not only did the honky tonks supply talent to the burlesque world — although burlesque performers of the era tried to deny this — but they created an entirely new type of audience, one attuned to earthy, non-intellectual theatre. This was an audience where Victorian prudery was not a factor. This was an audience which accepted the salacious. This was an audience which was ready to attend the more formal burlesque shows as they flowered in the latter portion of the nineteenth century.

Actually, two trends can now be discerned in American burlesque. One, following the Leavitt tradition, was woman-centred but clean. The shows featured light entertainment, straddling the line between vaudeville and variety. Stars such as May Howard and Rose Sydell came to the fore. Among representative troupes successfully touring the country may be counted the Ada Richmond Burlesquers, Ada Kennedy's African Blonde Minstrels, the Victoria Loftus Troupe of British Blondes, and Mary Fiske's English Blondes. The Miner family, leading theatre owners of the day, booked these burlesque shows into their houses and actively sponsored burlesque productions. The chief elements in all these productions were dancing by the chorus and comedy sketches.

Against the clean burlesque productions, and eventually overshadowing them, was the world of dirty burlesque. Sam T. Jack, an alumnus of the Leavitt company, became notorious for the shows he presented at his theatres in New York and Chicago. 'Jack's famous living pictures', relates Bernard Sobel, 'were often, as likely not, merely exhibitions in the nude'[5]. Little Egypt, who thrilled so many people at the 1893 Chicago World's Fair with her 'umbilical gyrations', first performed at Jack's Chicago house.

The dirty burlesque movement picked up adherents through two off-beat types of shows: the 'turkey-shows' and the 'behind-the-tent' shows[6]. The 'turkey shows', dating from the 1880s, got their name from burlesque shows that opened around Thanksgiving and ran through the holidays. Filled with holiday gaiety, people were more liberal with their purses and more inclined to take in a show. As a result, the entertainers earned extra money for the purchase of their own turkeys. The 'turkey show' degenerated into a type of one-night operation in which a producer gathered some out-of-work performers and put together a makeshift production. The 'behind-the-tent' shows roamed the rural areas. They operated on the same principle as the 'turkey shows': small companies playing one-night stands with shabby sets and costumes and with plenty of smut. Since the 'behind-the-tent' shows often had to compete with country fairs and carnivals with their time-honoured backroom sex displays, the 'behind-the-tent' companies could get pretty rough in their comic material and dance routines.

During the Gay Nineties — a slump period of burlesque — the technical structure of the shows underwent some modifications. Immediately after the olio an 'Extra Added Attraction' was given — usually a wrestling match, a prize fight, or a hootchee cootchee dance. Then came the afterpiece in which the entire company performed a travesty of a Broadway show or of some public event. And the show closed with the Amazon parade. It is possible that the added attraction was placed in the show to aid the box office during the business decline. What is important in the change is that with the appearance of the solo cooch dancer, the act from which the striptease was to evolve appeared.

Between the chorus girls in tights and the solo cooch dancers, the national characteristic of burlesque was established by 1900. True, comedy became king in the golden age of American burlesque, the years 1900-1914, but comedy without the girls was unthinkable if a show were to survive. Sime Silverman, founder and editor of *Variety*, stated in the issue of 11 December 1909, 'Were there no women in burlesque, how many men would attend? The answer is the basic principle of the burlesque business'[7]. The following year Dan Dody, ensemble and stage director for the Columbia Circuit — the major burlesque booking organization of the period — observed, 'Girls are the answer to the burlesque show of today' [8]. And Sidney Wire of *Billboard* (the rival theatrical publication to *Variety*) commented in the issue of 22 March 1913 that 'ninety percent of the burlesque audiences go to burlesque theatres to see the girls'[9].

Much has been written about the comedy of burlesque's golden age. Such comedians as Billy Watson, Bozo Snyder, 'Sliding Billy' Watson, George Bickel, Tom Howard, Alexander Carr, Ted Healy, Al Shean of Gallagher and Shean, Vinnie Henshaw, Al Reeves, Frank Bush, and Willie Howard deserve recognition for the major rôle they played in the history of burlesque. And their routines, known as 'bits', are important for the new direction they gave to the comedian's art. Instead of interrelated scenes, the 'bits' were short sketches performed *commedia dell' arte* style. With a single theme, a title, and the punch line of the skit, the comedian improvised his material. How bawdy the 'bit' was depended upon the local mores of the community. These burlesque 'bits' later became the black-out sketches of the revues[10].

So with due respect to the comedian as the central performer of the burlesque show until bumped by the striptease about 1930, let us return to the girls. There were the chorus girls and the soloists. Oh, the chorus girls of the golden age: tights-clad, hefty creatures, ranging in weight from one hundred and seventy-five to two hundred and fifty pounds in many shows! Imagine the high kicking of Billy Watson's 'Beef Trust' — as his troupe was known.

Coochers is the term applied to the solo dancers. It derives from *hootchee cootchee*, a descriptive label traced to Little Egypt's belly dancing at the 1893 Chicago World's Fair. Little Egypt (the stage name for Catherine Devine[11] was probably the first American female entertainer to appear before a large public with a portion of her torso exposed — her stomach — and to delight her audiences with the muscular gyrations she performed with that stomach. The origin of her dance — 'the ancient harem dance of bondage' — need not concern us here. What is significant is that Little Egypt gave Americans bare flesh in motion and catchy, sensual terminology for describing body undulations.

Cooch dancers used such exotic labels as 'Salome' dancers in the period 1900-1908, and 'Venus' dancers for a number of years after[12]. They also came to be called soubrettes, a more refined term. The line between a coocher and a soubrette is often hard to define, especially since soubrettes depended on cooch movements in their dance routines[13]. These movements, most simply defined, are physical gyrations and undulations frankly calculated to suggest sexual intercourse. Soubrettes did not remove clothing as a rule. But they did depend on the coy and coquettish qualities associated with the traditional soubrette of the theatre from whom they got their name.

To a great extent, the degree of cooch dancing depended upon whether the performer was in a clean or a dirty burlesque company. The distinction between the two types of companies has already been alluded to. With the organization of the travelling companies into wheels in the early years of the twentieth century, the managers, in the face of keen competition, varied in their attitudes as to how clean, or family-like, their shows should be. The powerful Columbia Circuit championed clean shows. The Empire and Mutual Circuits, in contrast, tended toward dirty shows — more provocative dancing, more bare flesh, more smutty comedy.

Clean shows faced a serious problem with the type of entertainment they offered. On the one hand, the attempt to keep a comparatively high moral tone led to dull and repetitive presentations. On the other, attempts at novelty in the routines brought the shows close to either musical comedy or vaudeville. The noted comedian Joe Cook summed the problem up neatly when he described clean burlesque as 'the swellest entertain you could find. It was a mixture at a lower price, of most of the good qualities of musical comedy plus the good qualities of vaudeville. The standard comedians were very clever'[14]. But what identity did a clean burlesque show have to keep it burlesque? The ultimate answer, as the 1920s revealed, was 'None'. And dirty burlesque won out completely by 1925 when the Columbia Circuit capitulated and went over to dirty burlesque. The same struggle was taking place among the stock companies, especially in New York which had become the centre for burlesque stock shortly after the First World War.

In the battle between clean and dirty burlesque, the producers could exploit only one resource: the girls. Individual comedians and their routines could distinguish a particular company and attract devotees to the shows, but in considering the profession as a whole, burlesque comedy was limited in its potential for development. Dirtier dialogue, more risqué situations, phallic props? These devices were simply variations on the same theme. Besides, the best comic talent had attracted the attention of Broadway. Al Jolson, Jack Pearl, Jack Haley and Jimmie Savo, for example, were lured to the Great White Way. With them went their routines and 'bits'.

But the girls and their dancing could bring something new to burlesque. And the Minsky Brothers in New York — Billy, Abe, Herbert and Morton — were quick to sense this. Starting at the National Winter Garden on Houston Street in the late 1910s, Billy and Abe considerably revamped the shows. (Herbert and Morton joined them a few years later.) They brought in top variety talent, interspersing their speciality performers throughout the show instead of restricting them to the olio. And they broke with the tradition of the 'Beef Trust' style chorus girl, substituting the Minsky girl. She was a pretty, lithe, scantily clad, brassiereless dancer who undulated her entire body when she moved. Over her body she wore a filmy union suit which left little to the imagination, especially when she was engaged in the breast jiggling which was one of the early innovations of a Minsky show[15].

In order to give the patrons a more intimate view of the chorines and soubrettes, the Minskys installed a runway in the National Winter Garden. The runway soon became a stock architectural feature of a burlesque house. Indeed, some theatres had three, one centre for the general audience and two for the box patrons[16]. Only the soubrettes and chorines played on 'Varicose Alley', as the runway was nicknamed, with the main stage the province of the comedians, singers, and variety artists. The proximity to the audience on the runway encouraged a more provocative type of dance routine. Carrie Finnell, for example, performed the first 'Tassel Dance' on a Minsky runway. Rowland Barber delightfully describes this dance as one in which 'tassels attached to the breasts were made to whirl at will, singly and together, by articulation of the mammary muscles'[17]. In 1934, such ramps were banned in New York, and they soon fell into disuse elsewhere.

In spite of the innovations of the Minskys — and Billy deserves the credit for most of them — burlesque in the 1920s suffered a decline in popularity. The reasons were varied. Key among them was a change in women's fashions which resulted in shorter skirt lengths. In the days of long skirts the sight of a female leg, although encased in tights, was considered most shocking. The sight of a Millie De Leon actually baring one leg while performing in Philadelphia in 1915 set the audience to groaning and howling[18]. However, when fashion decreed that it was perfectly proper for milady to reveal her gams, burlesque lost a great deal of its wicked reputation.

Then the growth of cheaper forms of entertainment such as the radio and motion pictures helped knock out a large segment of the burlesque audience — a segment which had attended the shows, among other reasons, because burlesque offered the most reasonable form of entertainment. The rise of rail rates had a serious effect on the travelling shows; and the increased pay scales of stage hands helped raise producers' budgets — which, in most instances, were shoestring anyway.

Not even bare bosoms could lure back sufficient customers. For by 1922, exposure of the bare leg had extended to exposure of the upper torso, with, in the protocol of the burlesque world, the soubrette allowed to reveal more than the chorine. In fact, just as Broadway had enticed burlesque's comedians in this decade, it now went in for nudity in the revues of Ziegfeld, George White, and Earl Carrol, stealing away this new attraction of burlesque.

Against this combination of forces, burlesque began to stagnate. The same types of shows were played week after week. Poor imitations of Broadway song and dance routines filled the productions. The chorus girls, a scarcity on the market at best, were both uninspired and uninspiring as they went through their numbers in sloppy fashion. Moreover, they were not particularly attractive.

Just at this crucial lowpoint in its history, burlesque bounced back with the introduction of the striptease. Though the origin of this 'ritual' is somewhat obscure, it swept burlesque back into big business in the 1930s. Female performers had removed clothing in the course of their acts in earlier eras. But the modern striptease involves more than a removal of clothes.

It is a solo number performed by a new type of speciality dancer, one who drove the soubrette from the burlesque stage. Harold Minsky (a younger member of the family) credits 'Curls' Mason with the first recorded modern striptease in 1921[19]. The term itself, according to Rowland Barber, was invented by two Minsky press agents, Mike Goldreyer and George Alabama Florida[20]. While youth and prettiness are prerequisites for a stripper, these qualities in themselves could not produce the stars of the profession. Herbert Minsky points out that the girls 'have to be taught rhythm in a manner synchronous with music. They are taught to strip and unclothe by specialists in the atmosphere and lighting of the stage'[21].

The modern striptease is an erotic dance, with a definite technique to it. The steps in stripping are known

> in succession as the Flash or entrance; the Parade or march across the stage, in full costume; the Tease or increasing removal of wearing apparel ... and the climactic Strip or denuding down to the G-string, followed by a speedy retreat into the obscuring draperies.[22]

Surviving from cooch dancing in the stripper's routine are such essential bodily movements as the fishtail — the hip-wiggling part — and the bumps — the forward and backward movement of the abdomen. Although there may be an art to performing a good striptease, the dance itself is sensual and primitive, calculated to arouse the libido of the audiences. A stripper who can maximize the quantity of bumps and grinds she can do during the chorus of a popular song is known in the profession as working 'hot'.

Basically a mechanical dance, the striptease depends upon the ability of the stripper to inject novelty and personality into her performance. Among the most talented of the strippers who have succeeded in capturing their audiences through their personalities as well as their bodies have been Ann Corio and Hinda Wassau — pioneer strippers in that they made the transition from soubrette to stripper[23]; Gypsy Rose Lee — probably the most sophisticated and literary of all; and Margie Hart, Georgia Sothern and Winnie Garrett.

Burlesque reached the epitome of its evolution in the striptease. Under the stresses of competition, the burlesque producers gave the striptease more and more prominence in the shows until an act which had once been an encore became the mainstay of the medium. The teasing element decreased, with the strip element accompanied by 'hot' dancing taking over.

This led to an ever-intensifying battle between the forces of decency in a community and the burlesque producers, to police raids, and to law suits. Even the Minsky family — which had continued to expand its activities at a rapid rate, eventually invading Broadway in 1931 — was not immune. The family only relinquished its position in the burlesque industry when, in 1942, the court ruled that burlesque shows were 'offensive to public morals and decency', and banned such performances from the New York theatrical scene.

In the last thirty years burlesque has continued to sputter in other parts of the United States. Little talent is found in the few shows remaining. The routines of the chorus girls have a sameness about them; the strippers' acts are more or less identical; the comedians do not use original material. The better comics have long since taken their acts into other entertainment media, primarily night clubs and television variety shows. The star strippers also deserted the shows for night clubs and strip clubs where their acts now are called 'Art' and a beer at the bar costs ninety cents and up. The Burlesque Artists Association had its charter revoked in 1957 by its parent union for failing to organize its performers properly and for not adequately protecting its members.

One by one the old burlesque houses have closed in Boston, San Francisco, Pittsburgh, and other metropolitan centres, victims of morality drives, real estate ventures, or urban renewal projects — for these theatres had been built in prime city locations.

And as more tolerant attitudes towards nudity and loosening sexual morality have spread in recent years — accepting on a small scale what would not have been tolerated in a full-fledged production — new forms of frankly sexual entertainment have come to the fore. Go-go dancers, silicone injections, and topless and bottomless bars provide audiences with erotic thrills with no pretence of theatrical art.

Burlesque, in contrast, was (and maybe still is) a part of the world of the theatre. Its audiences have been nationwide. Primarily male, and somewhat uncouth, they patronized live theatre at prices they could afford. In the best sense of theatre, they were an active, not passive, audience. They participated fully in what they saw and heard on stage, responding in lively fashion to the comic 'bits' and other acts in the earlier days of burlesque as well as to the girls. The performers, in return, especially the best of the coochers, soubrettes, and strippers, encouraged audience participation, even deliberately drawing members of the audience into their acts.

Producers found ways to increase that participation by bringing the girls directly to the audience via the runways. When the runways were abandoned, the artistes fell back on the very illusionistic nature of the theatre — tricking the audiences into believing they were seeing a completely undraped female before the stripper was ready to let them glimpse her nearly nude body.

Burlesque brought happiness to audience and performer alike. It momentarily raised with laughter and shouts the spirits of many individuals normally living lives of quiet desperation, yet timid about attending more formal presentations of plays. It provided jobs for entertainers, stagehands, and other theatre personnel, sometimes bringing them handsome fortunes, sometimes, as with Gypsy Rose Lee, fame as well as fortune. With all its strengths and weaknesses, burlesque has made its mark on American popular theatre.

Notes

1 I allude to such works as *The Beggar's Opera*, which opened in New York in 1750, Sheridan's *The Critic*, and Poole's travesty on *Hamlet*.

2 Bernard Sobel, *Burleycue* (New York, Farrar & Rinehart, 1931), 5. This work is invaluable for a study of American burlesque. For other general studies, see also William Green, 'A Survey of the Development of Burlesque in America', Thesis, Columbia University, 1950; and Irving Zeidman, *The American Burlesque Show* (New York, Hawthorn Books, 1967).

3 Quoted in Walter Prichard Eaton, *The Actor's Heritage* (Boston, The Atlantic Monthly Press, 1924), 277-8.

4 *Burleycue*, 13.

5 *Ibid.*, 52. Zeidman notes that the first burlesque company to use tableau settings and 'living pictures' was the Ida Siddons Burlesque and Novelty Company in 1883 (p.39).

6 Zeidman, 38-9.

7 Quoted in *ibid.*, 11.

8 Quoted in *ibid.*, 60.

9 Quoted in *ibid.*, 11.

10 For a discussion of the origin and development of the 'bit', see Ralph G. Allen, 'Our Native Theatre: Honky-Tonk, Minstrel Shows, Burlesque', *The American Theatre: A Sum of its Parts* (New York, London, and Toronto, Samuel French, Inc., 1971), 273-313.

11 Zeidman, 61.

12 *Ibid.*, 60-1.

13 See *ibid.*, 118-19, for a discussion of the talents of the cooch dancers.

14 Quoted in Sobel, 158.

15 Rowland Barber, *The Night They Raided Minsky's* (New

York, Simon & Schuster, 1960), 169.

16 Zeidman, 115.

17 *The Night They Raided Minsky's*, 200. Miss Finnell must have been a spectacular performer, for Irving Zeidman describes another routine of hers when she was on the Mutual Wheel in which she popped 'up her breasts to the tune of "Pop Goes the Weasel," singly and in unison, by purely muscular action, with no strings attached' (p.115).

18 Zeidman, 15-16.

19 Harold Minsky, 'Striptease Goes West", *See*, 9, no. 2 (March 1950), 16.

20 Barber, 340.

21 'Minskys See Peril to American "Art" ', *New York Times*, 25 February 1937, 10.

22 Bernard Sobel, 'Take 'Em Off!', *Saturday Review of Literature*, 28 (18 August 1945), 23.

23 Zeidman, 119-20.

PETER ARNOTT

Aristophanes and Popular Comedy: An Analysis of The Frogs

As the study of popular theatre tends to concern itself with non-literary or subliterary forms, it may seem curious that I have chosen to present, in this connection, the detailed scrutiny of a literary text. I do so in the conviction that, in Aristophanes, traditional scholarly and editorial analysis has often failed to provide a satisfactory solution to crucial problems; and that such problems may well respond to a more pragmatic type of analysis based on modes of performance rather than on literary genres. The Aristophanic *vis comica* is hard to define, harder to translate, and harder still to reproduce on the modern stage. Nevertheless, if we can say anything with conviction about Aristophanes, it is this: that his work was firmly grounded in a tradition of popular farce that he acknowledges, implicitly or explicitly, in virtually every page that he writes. It has been my good fortune to be involved in the production and performance of Aristophanes perhaps more often than most; and I hope, in this paper, by using one controversial scene as a test case, to show how the examination of traditional comic devices, which are essentially those of the popular theatre, may illuminate the interpretation of a passage which has defied conventional exegesis.

The year 405 BC was not a happy one for Athens. The war with Sparta was nearly lost; racked by internal dissension and driven into desperate courses by mismanagement, the city seemed to delight in inflicting on itself the wounds it was unable to inflict on others. Yet one event at least helped to lighten the beginning of this dismal year. At the Festival of the Lenaea, Aristophanes presented his comedy *The Frogs*. It was, unlike some of his earlier plays, a complete and immediate success, and was rewarded with the unique tribute of a repeat performance. In our own time, though less popular on the stage, it has won distinction of a different and less satisfactory sort. Perhaps no comedy, out of the eleven by Aristophanes which have survived, has been more keenly scrutinised for hidden meanings and recondite allusion; perhaps no comedy of any author has laboured under so heavy a burden of irrelevant scholarship.

The Frogs is a play about plays and playwrights, tragedy and tragedians. Its action concerns the journey of the God of Tragedy, Dionysus, to the Underworld, with the purpose of resurrecting the poet Euripides, who had died shortly before the play was produced. Thus, argues Dionysus, the tragic stage will be restored to its old glory and his own worship preserved. In the second half of the comedy, Aristophanes allows Dionysus, without explanation, to depart from his declared intention. Once he has arrived in Hades, he does not simply take Euripides back to earth. Rather, he presides over a debate between that poet and his illustrious predecessor Aeschylus, announcing that whoever wins the contest shall be his first choice. Whether or not it was this section of the play that most pleased the ancient audience, it has certainly been the principal delight of modern scholars, and one scene in particular has been turned into an angrily contested tilting ground where many a critical lance has been shattered, not only in the name of Aristophanes but on behalf of Aeschylus and Euripides also.

I refer, of course, to the famous 'oil-flask' scene[1]. After sweeping condemnations have been uttered on both sides, the tragedians turn to attacking each other's work piecemeal. Euripides has just assailed Aeschylus' prologues on the grounds of obscurity, arguing that they are repetitious and confused. Aeschylus now retaliates by forcing Euripides to quote a number of examples from his own prologues. He reduces each in turn to absurdity by interrupting just before the end, and substituting for the proper words the tag 'and lost his oil-flask' (*lekythion apolesen*). For all its critical importance, the scene is a very short one, and I quote it in full here:

Aesch. Now, by Zeus, I won't go pecking at his prologues word by word. With the help of the gods, I'll destroy every one of them with an oil-flask.

Eur. My prologues with an oil-flask?

Aesch. Just one oil-flask. You write them so that everything will fit them — a sheepskin, or an oil-flask, or a knapsack. They all suit your iambics. I'll demonstrate immediately.

Eur. Oh you will, will you?

Aesch.   I will indeed.

Dion.   It's time for you to quote.

Eur.   'Aegyptus, as the tale is widely spread,
         With fifty sons fled in a sea-borne car,
         And reaching Argos ....'

Aesch. Lost his oil-flask.

Dion. What was that oil-flask? It'll be sorry! Quote him another prologue, so that I can have a second look.

Eur. 'Dionysus, who with thyrsus and with skin of deer
His raiment, on Parnassus in the torchlight
Leaps in the dance ...'

Aesch. Lost his oil-flask.

Dion. Oh dear! That's twice we have been struck by this oil-flask.

Eur. It won't be anything. He won't be able to attach his oil-flask to *this* prologue.
'There is no man who's blest in everything.
For either one is nobly born and has no livelihood,
Or else a commoner ...'

Aesch. Lost his oil-flask.

Dion. Euripides.

Eur. What is it?

Dion. It seems to me you ought to take in canvas. This oil-flask is going to raise a great wind.

Eur. No, by Demeter, I wouldn't think of it. It will be knocked out of his hands directly.

Dion. Come then, quote another; and beware of the oil-flask.

Eur. 'Cadmus, once leaving the city of Sidon, Son of Agenor ...'

Aesch. Lost his oil-flask.

Dion. My dear sir, buy the oil-flask from him, before he smashes our prologues.

Eur. What? I buy him off?

Dion. If you take my advice.

Eur. No indeed, for I have many prologues to quote where he won't be able to fit an oil-flask in.
'Pelops, the son of Tantalus, on his way to Pisa
With swift horses ...'

Aesch. Lost his oil-flask.

Dion. You see, he's fitted the oil-flask in once again. My friend, do all you can to buy him off. It's a fine flask, and you can have it for an obol.

Eur. No, by Zeus, not yet. I still have plenty left.
'Once Oineus from the earth ...'

Aesch. Lost his oil-flask.

Eur. Let me quote a whole line before you interrupt!
'Oineus from the earth won a beautiful harvest,
And while he offered up first fruits ...'

Aesch. Lost his oil-flask.

Dion. While he was sacrificing? Who took it?

Eur. Let it pass. Let him find an answer to this:
    'Zeus, as the tale is spread by truth ...'
Dion. He'll finish you off there. He'll say 'Lost his oil-flask'.

I ask forgiveness for the painful literalness of this translation;
but I shall argue later that the interpretation of this whole passage
materially affects the way in which it must be translated, and to
offer more than a literal version at this point would be to beg a
number of important questions.

Editors have found this scene a constant challenge, and have
offered widely differing explanations of its meaning. Why is it
funny? It seems as though Aeschylus is meant to be attacking some
noteworthy feature of Euripides' prologues, just as Euripides had
previously done for Aeschylus, but which? What specific point of
style, if any, is Aristophanes parodying here?

Various solutions have been propounded. For the sake of
brevity, it will be more convenient to consider them in groups
rather than to examine editors individually, for the suggestions
commonly offered to this date are of three principal types. Firstly,
it has been suggested that Aristophanes is presenting a metrical
parody here. The oil-flask tag introduces a tribrach in the fourth
foot of the iambic line, thus:

$$\cup - \mid \cup - \mid \cup \quad \overline{\text{le}} \mid \text{kythion} \mid \text{apo} \mid \text{lesen.}$$

Perhaps Aristophanes is making fun of Euripides' weakness for
breaking down the formal metres into new patterns, and resolving
iambics into collocations of shorter syllables.

It is, of course, true that Euripides liked such changes and
resolutions. A study of his metrics has been one of the most
valuable methods of dating his plays. But so far as this scene is
concerned, such metrical eccentricity seems insufficient justification for a lengthy parody. We can only say, with Professor
Stanford, that 'in general Euripides is fonder of tribrachs than
Aeschylus; but this is hardly a matter for concentrated ridicule'[2]. Even if we make the fullest allowance for the known
sensitivity of the Greeks to metrics and rhythm, it is difficult to
suppose that Aristophanes would have considered so nice a point
sufficient to amuse a mass audience.

Secondly, the scene has been taken as a parody of Euripides'
subject matter, his alleged fondness for low life, and his weakness
for introducing domestic subjects into his plays. The oil-flask was
one of the most common domestic objects, carried by every Greek
and used to anoint and so clean his body. The other objects
mentioned by Aeschylus at the beginning of the scene, the

sheepskin and the knapsack, are similarly humdrum. It was this argument which led Gilbert Murray to suggest 'and found his old umbrella gone' as a suitable translation for *lekythion apolesen*, on the grounds that an Englishman's umbrella was as familiar to him as his oil-flask was to the Greek[3]. Could we say, then, that the point Aristophanes, through Aeschylus, is making is simply this; that Euripides' degrading of tragedy to deal with the sordid and commonplace means that any object, however humble, can find a place in his plays?

The difficulty here, of course, is that Euripides' tragedies do not really reveal the preoccupation with the domestic that such an explanation would require. A critic once said of Shakespeare that, in the last analysis, whatever you say about him is true. By the same token, whatever you say about Euripides is wrong. He is a writer who defies easy classifications, and the popular image of him as a sort of Greek François Villon has little basis in fact. His language is, as far as we can see, closer to the vernacular than that of Sophocles, and far closer than that of Aeschylus, but bears as little resemblance to everyday conversational Greek as that of Christopher Fry does to conversational English. As for his use of a domestic vocabulary, it certainly does not appear to the extent that these commentators would have us believe. Even granted that Aristophanes is exaggerating considerably — and this is usually a safe assumption to make — or that, as he so often does, he is objectifying for the sake of simplicity and making Euripides' alleged vocabulary stand for his whole attitude towards the subject matter of drama, he is erecting his parody on such a slim foundation that we might ask again, as in the case of the metrical argument, whether the audience could reasonably have been expected to understand it. In addition, as Stanford points out, the prologues quoted do not obviously suggest this. On the contrary, they are uniformly noble and elevated in style and subject matter. If this was the joke that Aristophanes was making, one might have expected him to select examples that came closer to his purpose.

Thirdly, it has been suggested that the parody is syntactical, implying that (here again I use Stanford's words) 'Euripides' opening sentences were constructed on a monotonous pattern, beginning with a proper name (all here except 1217) and containing an early participle.' Stanford himself accepts this solution as the likeliest, although as he immediately points out, this criticism strictly applies to only one of Euripides' extant plays, the *Iphigeneia in Tauris*, quoted in this scene, vv 1238-41. So we return to the same bewilderment. Even assuming that the lost plays of

Euripides contain more examples of such a syntactical structure than the ones we have — and this would be a curious circumstance — if this is the intended joke, it is conjured out of thin material.

The difficulty is apparent. Ingenious though these theories are, the text seems to fit none of them particularly well. One cannot help feeling that, if Aristophanes had been primarily concerned with any of these matters, he could have made his point with greater clarity and force. Why be so tortuous, so unnecessarily obscure? As it is, Euripides' penchant for low-life situations, genuine or not, is dealt with adequately elsewhere in the play (vv 948ff., 1301ff) and there would seem to be no reason for reiterating it with such undue subtlety here. It is not the business of a comic poet, particularly one writing for a popular audience, to restate obscurely something that has been stated with perfect clarity already. At the risk of labouring the point, let me insist that the requirements of performance are paramount. The explanations I have cited are those that have, not unreasonably, occurred to scholars working in the privacy of their studies after long and detailed scrutiny of the texts. It is much less credible that they would have occurred to the Athenian audience in the first shock of performance, or that Aristophanes could have expected his spectators to remember, on the instant, that Euripides was sometimes guilty of introducing a tribrach into the fourth foot. It is unlikely that a comic scene, in so important a position, would have been based on a technical detail of prosody, or for that matter, of syntax. Such things are for the scholiast, not for the noisy, critical fifth-century audience.

The reaction of modern audiences, when this is ascertainable, also serves to suggest that the explanation of this scene is not so esoteric as the commentators would have us believe. In the several presentations of this comedy in which I have participated, as director, as performer, or as spectator, the oil-flask scene has regularly proved one of the most amusing sequences of the play. This has been true not only before learned university audiences, where one might expect such a reaction, but before popular groups also, many of whom had never heard of Aristophanes, Aeschylus, or Euripides before the play began, let alone the finer points of Euripidean dramaturgy or the techniques of Greek versification.

The scene supports itself by its own comic logic. May one then say, as Tallulah Bankhead is rumoured to have said of Maeterlinck, that there is less here than meets the eye? Stanford himself, at the conclusion of his summary, seems to agree, suggesting that 'there may be little more than comic foolery here'. He points out that

repetition is a familiar and self-sufficient comic device. This suggestion is tempting, although Stanford does not go on to develop it. It
may well be that we have fallen into the trap, only too common in
Aristophanic studies, of ignoring the obvious and searching for
subtleties where the author intended none. I should like here to consider this argument further, and support it by a more detailed
examination of the Euripidean quotations that Aristophanes selects
for parody.

Stanford's point, that the repetition of a line or tag can be funny
in itself, by sheer cumulative effect, quite apart from the content, is
well taken. He adduces another familiar Aristophanic passage, *The
Birds*, vv. 959ff, where the Soothsayer's repeated 'Take the book' is
eventually taken up and used against him by Pisthetairus, and the
favourite tag of Hegemon of Thasos, 'and the leg of a partridge'.
Examples from plays of later ages are numerous. Taking a few at
random, we might cite from the Elizabethans John Cooke's *The
City Gallant*, whose catch phrase, *tu quoque*, was used so
effectively by the leading player that the author's name was
forgotten and the play known as Greene's *Tu Quoque* thereafter.
Another well-known instance is in Molière's *Les Fourberies de
Scapin*, where Géronte's plaintive repetition of 'Que diable alloit-il
faire dans cette galère?' has become proverbial. Later still, and in a
different key, we find the duel scene in *Cyrano de Bergerac*, Act I,
where Rostand's hero duels to a *ballade*, each stanza concluding
with '*Qu' à la fin de l'envoi je touche*', his sword finding his
opponent at the last. In each of these cases, the catch-phrase is
employed for its own sake, with no deeper motive, and becomes
increasingly funny through repetition. Outside the legitimate
theatre examples multiply. We can point to the catch-phrases used,
·and often overworked, by film, radio, and television comedians;
again, these are phrases usually unfunny in themselves but
acquiring humour by simple repetition. In the face of so many
examples, it is surely legitimate to suggest that this scene in *The
Frogs* belongs to the same class.

These parallels are of course not sufficient in themselves. To say
that the scene can be interpreted on this more rudimentary level is
not to say that it must, or that this explanation disqualifies all
others. It may be objected that although the repetition in itself is
one of the comic elements in the scene, it is not the only one. I shall
argue, however, that there are certain features in the scene's
structure, the function of which is natural and obvious if we accept
the repetition in itself to be the only joke and more difficult to
explain if we look for anything more subtle. Stanford's objection

to the usual explanations — in terms of metre, subject matter or syntax — is a just one; whichever we choose, it is difficult to show that the lines selected by Aristophanes for quotation have any special relevance. Once we accept, however, that the humour lies wholly in the repetition, the quotations acquire a new significance, and a pattern, which can hardly be accidental, begins to appear.

As any playwright knows, there are certain laws which a comic scene must obey, irrespective of its subject matter. It must 'build', that is, maintain the audience's interest by mounting intensity. It must avoid anticlimax and end on a higher level than it began; it must finish with a flourish, and not be permitted to taper off weakly. This is particularly true of scenes involving the repeated line or catch-phrase, one of the easiest jokes to write, but one of the hardest to write well. The author who embarks on such a series of repetitions has two problems. First, how is he to sustain it? For the catch-phrase cannot be used in the same way indefinitely. If the joke is maintained on the same level, without break or variation for more than a limited time, it will grow tedious[4]. The author must ring the changes. As an example of this, we may examine in detail one of the more modern instances referred to above, the 'galley' scene from Molière's *Les Fourberies de Scapin*[5].

In this scene the servant, Scapin, sets out to defraud his miserly master Géronte. As it begins, Géronte has just entered and found Scapin apparently in the depths of despair. When he asks what has happened, Scapin informs him that he and the young master, Géronte's son, had been walking on the quayside, looking at the ships. A fine Turkish vessel had particularly attracted their attention. The ship's captain had invited them aboard and served them a meal. While they were eating, he had ordered the ship to put out to sea, and sent Scapin back with a demand for five hundred crowns ransom. If this is not met, the son will be carried off to Algiers and slavery.

We may now go to Molière's text.

Ger. What the devil! Five hundred crowns!
Scap. Yes sir, and what's more, he's only given me two hours.
Ger. O that monster of a Turk! He's taking my life's blood!
Scap. It's up to you now. Think of something quickly; save your beloved son from slavery.
Ger. What the devil was he doing on that galley?
Scap. He never dreamed that this would happen.
Ger. Off with you, Scapin; off with you at once, and tell this Turk I'll have him arrested.

Scap. Arrested on the high seas? Who do you think you're fooling?

Ger. What the devil was he doing on that galley?

Scap. We all have our unlucky days.

Ger. Scapin, the time has come for you to show yourself a good and faithful servant.

Scap. Meaning?

Ger. Go tell that Turk to send me back my son, and put yourself in his place until I've got the ransom money together.

Scap. Do you know what you're saying? Do you think this Turk is so stupid he'll take a nobody like me in place of your son?

Ger. What the devil was he doing on that galley?

Scap. He had no idea that things would turn out so badly. Don't forget, he's only given me two hours.

Ger. You say he asks —

Scap.　　Five hundred crowns.

Ger. Five hundred crowns! Has he no conscience?

Scap. Of course, the conscience of a Turk.

Ger. Does he know what five hundred crowns are?

Scap. Yes, fifteen hundred pounds.

Ger. Does he think you can sweep up fifteen hundred pounds in the gutter?

Scap. Unreasonable people, Turks.

Ger. But what the devil was he doing in that galley?

Scap. True, but we don't have second sight, do we? For pity's sake, stop wasting time.

Ger. Here, this is the key to my closet.

Scap. Good.

Ger. Open it.

Scap. With pleasure.

Ger. You'll find a large key on the left hand side, the key to the attic.

Scap. Right.

Ger. Take all the old clothes you find in the big hamper, sell them to the junk shop, and go and buy back my son.

Scap. (*giving the key back*) Are you dreaming? I shouldn't get a hundred francs for the lot. Besides, you know how little time I have.

Ger. But what the devil was he doing in that galley?

Scap. Talk, talk, talk! Forget the galley; just remember we're in a hurry, and you're within inches of losing your son. Oh, my poor master, I may never see you again; maybe at this very moment they're taking you as a slave to Algiers. But heaven will be my witness, I've done my best for you; and if you aren't ransomed, you have only your father's callous heart to blame.

Ger. Wait Scapin, I'll go find the money.

Scap. Hurry sir, I'm terrified the clock will strike.

Ger. You said four hundred crowns, didn't you?

Scap. No, five hundred crowns.

Ger. Five hundred crowns!

Scap. Yes.

Ger. What the devil was he doing in that galley?

Scap. What indeed? But hurry!

Ger. Couldn't he find some other place to take a walk?

Scap. True enough, but don't waste time.

Ger. Damn that galley!

Scap. (*aside*) That galley's hit him where it hurts.

Ger. Here, Scapin, I was forgetting, I've just received that sum in gold. I never thought I'd have to part with it so soon. (*drawing his purse from his pocket and holding it out to Scapin*) There. Go and ransom my son.

Scap. (*holding out his hand*) Yes sir.

Ger. (*making as though to give the purse to Scapin, but still holding on to it*) But tell this Turk he's a criminal.

Scap. (*holding out his hand again*) Yes.

Ger. (*same business*) A scoundrel.

Scap. (*still holding out his hand*) Yes.

Ger. (*same business*) A heathen, a robber.

Scap. Leave it to me.

Ger. (*same business*) Say he's extorting five hundred crowns from me against all right or reason.

Scap. Yes.

Ger. (*same business*) That I'd never give him the money willingly, dead or alive.

Scap. Right you are.

Ger. (*same business*) And if I ever catch him, I'll make him pay for it.

Scap. Yes.

Ger. (*putting the purse in his pocket and turning away*) Off you go, off you go, off you go quickly, and get my son back.

Scap. (*running after Géronte*) Hey!

Ger. What is it?

Scap. Where's the money?

Ger. Didn't I give it to you?

Scap. Of course you didn't. You put it back in your pocket.

Ger. I'm so upset I can't think straight.

Scap. That's obvious.

Ger. What the devil was he doing in that galley? That damned
galley! I hope that Turk roasts in Hell! (*exit*)

This scene, superficially so simple, reveals itself under scrutiny as
a masterpiece of deft construction. Molière plays on the repetition
with skill. Géronte begins by using the 'galley' line four times in
rapid succession. At this point, just when there is danger that the
joke might begin to pall, it is abandoned. The conversation takes a
different turn, and concentrates on ways and means to find the
money. Then, suddenly, when the audience has forgotten it,
Géronte introduces the line again. There follows another gap,
longer this time, before it reappears; finally, a longer gap still,
during which we are convinced that it has been abandoned for
good, until Géronte, on his exit, utters the imprecation, almost as
an afterthought, for the last time. Molière has solved the two
principal problems of such a scene: how to introduce sufficient
variation so that the joke will not grow stale, and how to finish
strongly and cleanly so that there will be no sense of anticlimax.
And the latter, perhaps, is the greater problem of the two. Not only
must the humour be cumulative, each repetition being funnier than
the last, but the episode must end neatly and plausibly on the
biggest laugh of all. Molière, of course, has a self-made solution in
this particular scene. The final repetition coincides with the exit of the
character who utters it, and Géronte's furious disappearance ends the
scene on the high note that it requires. Nor, to return to another of our
earlier examples, does Rostand have any difficulty with the
repetitions in his *ballade*. They are self-limiting, restricted by the form
of the *ballade* itself, and the 'punch-line', the final repetition, is given
the needed emphasis by the long-awaited *coup* in the duel.

No such easy solution is available to Aristophanes. He cannot
play with the repetition as Molière does, forgetting it, and allowing
the audience to forget, for a few lines, only to revert to it with
redoubled effect later on. He is limited by the central idea of his
scene; by definition, the repetitions must occur with predictable
regularity. Every time Euripides begins a new quotation, the
audience knows that Aeschylus, sooner or later, must interrupt
with the 'oil-flask' tag. Aristophanes' problem is to vary these
repetitions so that they do not become monotonous. Nor can he use
Molière's easy way of ending the scene. His characters remain on
the stage. He must find some other way to leave his audience
laughing at least as heartily at the end of the scene as they were at
the beginning, to introduce the 'build' that the scene requires, and
to end neatly.

But Aristophanes is a master craftsman too, and constructs his scene impeccably. Euripides is pressed by Dionysus to submit his prologues for consideration. He begins to quote; Aeschylus interrupts; and the first three exchanges (vv. 1206ff., 1211ff., 1217ff.) are structurally identical. In each case Euripides quotes two lines and part of a third, which Aeschylus completes with *lekythion apolesen*. Experience of this scene in production suggests that the audience needs two repetitions to become aware of the nature of the joke. The first takes them by surprise. With the second, most of them have already caught on. When the third comes, nearly everyone is ready to laugh in anticipation. Three identical repetitions are not too many. Interest is still rising, and in any case Aristophanes has been able to exploit two different types of humour, the laugh that comes from the unforeseen joke and that which comes from the one seen in advance and savoured in anticipation. But he is careful not to continue the same pattern for too long. In repetition jokes, three is the magic number. In the fourth repetition (vv. 1225ff.) Aristophanes introduces his first variation, abandoning the three-line pattern and increasing the tempo. Euripides is now permitted to quote only one line entire, and Aeschylus interrupts him halfway through the second. The element of surprise has been reintroduced. Mentally attuned to three lines, the audience finds the repetition coming sooner than expected, and laughs again. This variation can safely be used for the next repetition also, but no longer. Note that Aristophanes is increasing the tempo in two ways. He not only reduces the number of lines, but also the number of times each line-arrangement occurs; three instances of the three-line pattern, two of the two-line pattern. This gain in momentum is paralleled by Euripides' increasing acerbity.

There is now need of a second variation. In the sixth exchange the tempo is increased again by having Aeschylus interrupt in the middle of the *first* line. The element of surprise is restored. Euripides protests, is allowed to continue, and is interrupted again, in the middle of his second line. This variation is used only once; the ratio is now 3:2:1. This trick of double interruption is extremely effective, but in order to use it, Aristophanes has to choose his lines with some care. Not every Euripidean couplet will permit of two substitutions. In practical terms, Aristophanes is limited to couplets whose first lines begin with a proper noun, and the second with a participle in agreement. As Stanford pointed out in a different connection, the combination of proper noun plus early participle occurs only once in the extant prologues, namely in the

line from *Iphigeneia in Tauris* previously discussed, and this would
not suit the present purpose, as both subject and participle occur in
the same line. Aristophanes has to cast about for a suitable couplet.
It is perhaps indicative of his difficulty in locating one, that whereas
the first five quotations are, with one possible exception, from the
opening lines of prologues, the sixth is not[6]. No doubt
Aristophanes preferred to use opening lines whenever possible, for
the simple reason that these tend to be more easily memorable. Most
of us could identify

> Now is the winter of our discontent
> Made glorious summer by this sun of York

as the opening lines of *Richard III*; we would have to think a little
harder if faced with

> And such a want-wit sadness makes of me
> That I have much ado to know myself.

It is, perhaps, not too forceful to imagine Aristophanes, sitting
with his Euripidean texts before him, skimming through the
prologues to find openings to suit his purpose, but in this case
having to go deeper into the play to find a couplet that suits his
special requirements.

We now come to the seventh exchange, on which the scene ends.
Euripides quotes:

> 'Zeus, as the tale is spread by Truth ...'

and for the first time, Aeschylus does not interrupt. Dionysus is left
to supply the tag. At first this seems weak. Why is Aeschylus silent?
The answer is curious. He does not interrupt because he cannot.
Euripides is quoting the beginning of his *Melanippe the Wise*.
Enough of this prologue is extant to show that the *lekythion* tag
could not have been introduced for another eight lines. The
metrical structure is such that the lines cannot be broken at the
correct place for the substitution of the tag. Here is a problem that
so far seems to have escaped comment. No critic, to my knowledge,
has tried to cope with these mysterious lines[7].

I believe that the answer lies in the problem of comic technique,
of 'build' already noted. Aristophanes is faced with the problem of
ending his scene strongly and neatly. He must cap the previous
laughs with one still louder, and at the same time provide an
effective closure, so that he can leave this theme and go on to
something else. It may be that the mere introduction of Zeus
provided this closure. But I doubt that it is strong enough; and
there may be more sense in his using *Melanippe the Wise* than first

appears, for *Melanippe* seems to have been a play, like *Telephus*, capable of arousing a strong response in any Athenian audience.

Plutarch relates an interesting story about the lines in question. According to him, the play originally began,

Zeus, whoever Zeus may be; I only know by rumour....[8]

This aroused such strong protests from the audience that Euripides had to revise the line; it is the amended innocuous version that Aristophanes quotes here. By quoting this revised version he recalls, more effectively because obliquely, the outrageous original. There can be little doubt, given the truth of Plutarch's anecdote, that the repetition of the line would have had this effect even after a lapse of time. The Athenians, citizens of a small community, had retentive memories for things that concerned them deeply. Good jokes and outstanding sayings remained in currency for many years. In this play alone, Aristophanes can mock the famous gaffe of the actor Hegelochus, who misread a line a Euripides' *Orestes*, three years after it was perpetrated (vv. 303ff.). He can still recall the notorious line from *Hippolytus*, 'It was my tongue alone that swore; my mind remained unsworn' (*Hipp.* v.612). This line is unjustly notorious, perhaps; spoken by Hippolytus, it is an apparent defence of perjury, though in fact Hippolytus does not perjure himself and his death comes about precisely because he refuses to do so. In *The Frogs* Aristophanes uses the line twice, first in vv. 101ff., and later, almost at the end of the play, in v. 1471, the latter instance showing, beyond all doubt, that he could rely on his audience's comprehending the allusion. Yet twenty-three years had elapsed between the two plays. This is a tribute not so much to the intellect of the average Athenian spectator, but rather to the simple fact that in a small community, good jokes die hard.

But such persistence of memory was not wholly the property of the Greeks. An equally striking example may be found in Hugo's *Hernani*. At its first performance in Paris in 1830, several flagrantly anti-monarchist lines created a turmoil in the theatre. When *Hernani* was revived at the Paris Exposition thirty-seven years later, Hugo, grown more cautious, had rewritten them. The audience, with one voice, shouted the originals[9]. Aristophanes would have been able to anticipate the reaction. He ends his scene with a familiar device, a joke which, while apparently belonging to the preceding series, in fact provokes a completely different reaction. With this twist he is able to retain the element of surprise, end his series of repetitions, and accomplish the transition into the next scene. Note also that giving the line to Dionysus, instead of Aeschylus, provides an additional, though perhaps in itself insufficient, variation. I would suggest that Dionysus' line was probably lost in the laughter.

In this lengthy analysis of one comparatively short scene, I may appear to have been myself guilty of the fault that I have attributed to earlier critics, that of breaking a butterfly on the wheel. I defend myself on two grounds. Firstly, this scene, one of the most discussed in the whole canon, seems to me to be a test case of Aristophanic scholarship. Earlier critics have attempted to explain its humour in terms of something external to the scene, with the implication that the audience must be familiar with these extraneous factors before the scene can amuse. I have argued, on the contrary, that the scene is largely self-contained, and that in attempting to find some esoteric meaning in the various quotations, commentators have been considering the scene the wrong way round. Euripides' lines do not suggest the joke. Rather it is the joke, the rudimentary device of the repeated tag, that dictates the choice of lines, and their selection is determined not by their content but by the mechanics of scene construction. Once Aristophanes has embarked on the repetition joke, he is forced to introduce some variation lest the idea grow tedious. This variation cannot, in the nature of things, come in the repetition itself. It can come only in the placing of the repetition. This becomes the sole criterion for the choice of lines. They are selected not for their metre, nor for their syntax, nor for their subject matter, but for simpler reasons. As literary criticism this scene is valueless. It tells us nothing about Aeschylus nor Euripides, though it does tell us a good deal about Aristophanes.

And what is true of this scene is true of a whole mass of Aristophanic scholarship. Scenes and groups of scenes have traditionally been explained in terms of reference to some external factor, when a more reasonable explanation may be found in the innate principles of comic writing, the mechanical laws which every draftsman must obey if he wishes his plays to work. Secondly, the oil-flask scene is an excellent example of the course Aristophanes takes in many other places in his work. The device of changing a joke in midstream, of switching to something which, though on the surface the same sort of joke, in practice belongs to a different class, is the kernel of several of his most important scenes, in particular some of his agon sequences.

To end on a practical note: if the above interpretation is accepted, it presents a nice problem for the translator who aims at performance of his work, and who writes for an audience in the theatre rather than for the reader only. Aristophanes, it has been

suggested, relies for his climax on an allusion highly meaningful to
the Athenian audience of 405 BC. To a modern audience, who have
never heard of *Melanippe the Wise*, it must be unintelligible. The
reader here can turn to the footnotes which the editor has so
helpfully provided for him, but the spectator in the theatre has no
such recourse. Without the necessary associations, which Aristophanes could presuppose and take into account, the string of
repetitions will end not strongly but very weakly indeed. This
would seem, then, to be one of the many occasions when the
translator must sacrifice the letter of the joke to the spirit and
supply a different ending that, although unAristophanic, will at
least avoid bathos. In my own stage version[10] I have adopted the
following expedient. Each tag is slightly different; each rhymed;
and each is slightly less predictable than the one before, thus:

Eur. 'Aegyptus, as the legends mostly tell,
        With fifty youths the foaming ocean crossed,
        But reaching Argos ...'
Aesch. Had his oil-can lost!
Eur. 'Dionysus, dancing on Parnassus peak
        With sacred wand, and wrapped in skin of deer,
        By torchlight ...'
Aesch. Saw his oil-can disappear!
Eur. 'There's no man who is blessed in everything.
        One, high-born for a pittance needs must toil,
        The other, low-born
Aesch. Lost his can of oil!
Eur. 'Time was when Cadmus, great Agenor's son,
        Sailing to Sidon ...'
Aesch. Found his oil-can gone!
Eur. 'Pelops to Pisa once his way did wind
        On horseback ...'
Aesch. And left his can of oil behind!
Eur. 'King Oineus from the soil good harvest won,
        And giving thanks ...'
Aesch. He found his oil-can gone!

The scene ends with Dionysus capping the series with the wildest
rhyme of all:

Eur.   'Zeus, as the tale is told by history ...'
Dion. But where his oil-can's gone's a mystery!

This remedy is far from perfect, but something of the sort is
necessary if the ending is not to fall flat.

Notes

1 Aristophanes, *The Frogs*, vv. 1198-1245.
2 Aristophanes, *The Frogs*, ed. W.B. Stanford (London, Macmillan, 1958), v.1208n. Stanford conveniently summarizes the various arguments.
3 Gilbert Murray, *Aristophanes* (New York, Oxford University Press, 1933), 122-5.
4 A good example of the repeated-line joke badly handled occurs in Shaw's *The Doctor's Dilemma*, with unfunny repetition by Walpole of the phrase 'nuciform sacs'.
5 II.7.
6 So the scholia; they come from *Archelaus, Hypsipyle, Sthenoboia, Phrixus, Iphigeneia in Tauris* and *Meleager* respectively. There is some slight doubt about the first. Aristarchus is cited to the effect that vv. 1206ff. were not the first lines of the *Archelaus* but occurred later in the prologue. But this discrepancy is not serious.
7 See J.U. Powell, *New Chapters in the History of Greek Literature*, Third Series (Oxford, Clarendon Press, 1933), 115; and D.L. Page, *Greek Literary Papyri* (London, Heinemann, 1942), Vol.I, 118.
8 Plutarch, *Amator*, xiii, 756c.
9 See André Maurois, *Olympio ou la Vie de Victor Hugo* (Paris, Hachette, 1954), 476.
10 P.D. Arnott, *Three Greek Plays for the Theatre* (Bloomington, Indiana University Press, 1961).

PETER THOMSON

Henry Livings and the Accessible Theatre

At the end of February 1968, I recorded in one of those notebooks that are a destined nightmare for my executors a student performance in the Manchester University Theatre of Henry Livings's *Stop It, Whoever You Are*. The note reads:

> A coach-load of working wives screamed with laughter at it. It was funny — overdone a little perhaps — but funny. 'Not for the serious theatre-goer,' said Pauline Clark on February 28th. What did she mean!?

What, indeed? I can't for the life of me remember who Pauline Clark was, but I remember that coach-load of women. They were the kind of audience you used to hear sometimes on 'Workers' Playtime', prepared to bust a gut if the opportunity arose. And it arose. No stand-up comic in my lifetime has neglected the comic appeal of the lavatory to the English housewife, and there is nothing merely incidental in Livings's setting some of *Stop It, Whoever You Are* in Perkin Warbeck's place of work, the men's lavatory of a northern factory. Working wives laugh more readily and less self-consciously than any other group I know, and the hilarity of this party continued in the foyer when the play was over, and all along Devas Street to the waiting coach. For one brief night, on 27 February 1968, the University Theatre had felt like a genuinely 'popular theatre', and it had been made so — the point is important — by its audience.

Pauline Clark, it will have been noticed, made her observation on 28 February, when the audience was, presumably, a much more typical one. Smaller too, I expect. As Sol Hurok said, 'If people don't want to come, nothing will stop them.'[1] Many 'serious theatre-goers' have an attitude to Livings's plays very similar to Pauline Clark's. The bawdy mockery of respectable middle-class avarice in *Honour and Offer* was lost on Robert Cushman, who admitted that 'the play's action, and its hold upon my attention, became in course of time so tenuous that I ceased to bother,' but he spotted the symbols like a worthy Ibsenite:

Henry [Cash] keeps bees, and two hives are prominently placed on John Bury's stunningly green set. One contains workers and the other drones and their function ... is to serve as a metaphor for the human action. Could well be; it's difficult to see what else they're there for.[2]

They're there, Livings would surely have said, because Henry Cash keeps bees. I didn't see John Neville's production of *Honour and Offer*, and it may, of course, be true, as Cushman suggests, that the actors lacked 'spirit for the enterprise', having already read the first night notices. To stage Livings at the Fortune Theatre in London was probably inviting frost-bite, but Cushman sounds to me an inappropriate audience for Henry Livings anywhere on God's earth. So, let's face it, is Martin Esslin, who does his best to be admiring about another production that I didn't see, that of *The ffinest ffamily in the Land* at the Theatre Royal, Stratford East, on 27 July 1972. Sending Martin Esslin to review *The ffinest ffamily* is a bit like asking for Grotowski's comments on *Oh! Calcutta!* He's more likely to see the dangers than the joke. 'It is all very funny', Esslin concedes, but 'it fails as farce'; and his review proceeds to analyse the play's failure to fit into a genre whose laws Esslin assumes to be about as accommodating as the laws of cricket[3] — but no more so. What is it, in the 'serious theatre-goer', that makes preconception such a blight on enjoyment? 'I might have enjoyed it if it hadn't been Shakespeare' was a common enough reaction even to Peter Brook's magnificent production of *A Midsummer Night's Dream*, and definitions of comedy, tragedy, farce and melodrama are constantly seeking to impose limits on the very playwrights from whom they should receive their impetus. So it is with Esslin when he sets about reviewing one of the most inventive elaborations upon impossibility since *The Government Inspector*[4].

The events of *The ffinest ffamily in the Land* occur because Mr Harris loses the key to his council flat, and because the man who gets the only duplicate, like Gogol's Khlestakov, has never had such a captive audience before. Since this man ends the play by falling out of the window, it is of some importance that the flat is on the sixteenth floor. And that's where the trouble begins for Martin Esslin:

> ... if someone loses his key in a 16 storey block of flats, all he has to do is to go downstairs to the caretaker who has a master key and get himself let in. None of the characters thinks of this device. Why? Only so that the play can go on?

Not only. Mr Harris has a problem with his trousers, Enoch Harris has his transistor radio ear-plug in, and why should Mrs Harris do it? She's always having to do things. Perhaps Esslin's difficulty is not that he doesn't believe in the events of the play, but that he can't trust its characters. He even grows impatient with what looks to him like writer's negligence:

> There isn't even an attempt to indicate that the block has no caretaker, or that the caretaker is out, or uncooperative or whatever. Result: unease, and disbelief.

And then again, why don't the neighbours do something about the crazy Khlestakov with the key? Livings has evidently thought of that one, but not hard enough:

> To show there are no immediate neighbours there is a line in the dialogue that the Harris's flat is the *only* one on the 16th floor. Not only are penthouses rare in council tower blocks, but the flat door is clearly marked 1606, which seems to indicate that there are at least five other flats on the landing. All these factors severely impair the *inevitability* of the events we witness, and inevitability is the mainspring of farce.

Inadequate performance is not an issue this time. 'Henry Livings himself directs: and very well. The acting is uniformly strong ...' The fault, as far as Esslin can tell, is in Livings's misreading of farce:

> Farce in a way is the most naturalistic of genres: the wildest goings on *must* take off from the everyday. Here the set is so real that everything hinges on the reality of the madly absurd. I, personally, simply cannot take a situation in which four people remain for more than two hours on a draughty landing late at night without making one convincing attempt to get an extra key. It makes me too uneasy to enjoy the admittedly delicious fun that is supposed to flow from that unlikely premise.[5]

I would not have spent so long talking about Mr Esslin's disappointing piece of writing if it did not point up so clearly the problems that confront such a writer as Henry Livings in the existing English theatre; for here is the intellectual critic backing the 'serious' audience's pre-emptive bid against a popular theatre. The implication, after all, is once again that Livings is 'not for the serious theatre-goer'; and since the working man, who goes for fun, feels as out of place in the kind of theatre that might stage Livings as a *voyeur* in a Methodist Church, 'not for many people at all'. I mean, here we all are at a Conference on Western 'Popular Theatre', knowing full well that in England we haven't got one any more, that the two words can only be placed together after a process of re-definition has been undertaken, and, what's worse, that we can't do anything about it. If people like us, people with a confirmed interest in drama, stay at home the theatres will be empty. What is more disturbing is that so long as we keep on going they will remain half-full. You open a theatre for the people in England — at the Midlands Arts Centre, at the Round House, above all at Stratford East — and before you can say 'Joan Littlewood' the *Sunday Times* has spotted it and *Theatre Quarterly* does a 'Production Casebook'. That was why Stephen Joseph, a passionate advocate of a popular theatre, went first of all to unfashionable Stoke (which is unfashionable no longer) and then to the holiday audiences of Scarborough with his extravagantly daring repertoire of new plays in-the-round.

Henry Livings has worked with both Stephen Joseph and Joan Littlewood, and the influence of Stratford East in particular, and of the astonishing lady who has been its despairing inspiration, is apparent not only in his plays but also in what he says about them. When he was working on the production of *The ffinest ffamily*, for instance:

> It took Joan Littlewood to point out to us, with excoriating force, that the lift door has to be real and consistent. No cheating, no word cues for the stage management: you press the button, beat, the doors open, beat of three, the doors close like a steel trap. If you interfere with the doors, they stop for a beat, retreat, beat of three, and slam closed again. Similarly with her innate sense of real theatre (in contrast with the decorated trivia she abominates) she made us see that the TV set is the ikon of the last scene as the lift doors are of the rest of the play: it has to be real, plugged in, and stage centre.[6]

An actor as well as a director, he is deeply and naggingly involved in the processes of a play's production, but his emphasis is consistently on two things, the *reality* of what is said and shown and the *audience* that hears and sees it.

It is on the nature of their reality that Livings's plays are most frequently misunderstood. He has written himself:

> It's possible for us as artists to sit, eager and earnest, telling the most detailed and solemn lies; and such is the audience's need for reassurance and discovery that they will convince themselves that

they're enjoying themselves. They will tell themselves they're enjoying themselves, but they won't come again, unless they're masochists. They're the ones who say 'I love the theatre, I do, used to go a lot when the wife was well.'

This is from an open letter to David Scase, who has both worked with Joan Littlewood and directed a number of Livings's plays; and it goes on with the characteristic double emphasis on the reality and its audience:

> To say that what you enact on stage is truer because you add and invent more detail than is seen in everyday life is false. It's a more detailed and inventive enactment, that's what it is; and by the way, you've forgotten the theatrical truth, which is that there's somebody out there watching you. Not you, David; you know: *you*. The best comment I know on this is Magritte's beautifully detailed painting of a revolver, titled 'This is not a revolver.'[7]

There is nothing necessary on the stage of a Livings play but what is *used*, and that can be no fragile cardboard mock-up. If it's a door ('You can't have a farce without doors', I remember hearing him say in a radio interview when the musical door of *Eh?* was mentioned) you need to be able to kick it; if it's a boiler it sounds like one; if it's a lift it's as operative as Pinter's dumb waiter. And there's to be none of this play-acting. Real people (the open letter to Scase is headed 'Let's Make a Theatre for Real People') don't go much for play-acting. They're likely to greet it with some such comment as Mrs Harris's to Enoch: 'Be quiet Enoch, or I'll set fire to you.' 'Speaking for myself,' writes Livings,

> I prefer not to be kidded. I'm happy to see a man standing there in *puribus naturalibus*, doing what he does best. I'll go further: when a feller comes on disguised to the eyeballs, limping about the place and spluttering 'Ah Jim Lad!' I can tell who it is.

When the first Drama Department Summer Company was staging *Big Soft Nellie* in the Manchester University Theatre, Livings came to a rehearsal. I don't know what he really thought, but he didn't *say* anything very complimentary, and he did his best to stop the actors telling lies. I remember in particular his saying of Stanley, who can easily be read (and probably still should be!) as the product of a Dickensian inventiveness, 'I know him. He works in [I think it was] Oldham.'

What Livings does — it is the basis of his comic method — is to ask himself what people would do or say — the kind of people he writes about and is careful to live among — in a particular situation, and then double it. That is not unique, of course. If it were, the people he's writing for wouldn't understand it. It's as familiar as *Dad's Army*. But very few writers have been able to sustain the method without becoming its victim, and even fewer have Livings's linguistic agility and his sense of the performer's timing. Livings does not depend, as have most recent writers of popular comedy, on making his characters endearing. Henry Cash, in *Honour and Offer*, is quite as pompous and verbally self-important as Captain Mainwaring of *Dad's Army*, but much nastier. Our sense of his avarice makes an important contribution to our laughter at his carefully worded rebuke of Alfred Thring, unfaithful husband of the nubile Doris:

> Unhappy years [Henry remembers] watching your lechery [to say nothing of his own!] and deceit of this lady, up whose shoestrings you are not worthy to lace.

And the Harrises live in a dog-eat-dog world of deceit and self-interest, in which, admittedly, Mr Harris is more put upon than putting. If this is the finest f-- [prudent censorship cut out this word from the play's title too!] family in the land, God help the slipping land! But if Henry Cash, middle-class avarice and all, can make us laugh at his language, Mr Harris, working-class meanness and all, can turn on a virtuoso performance — if he's played by anything of an actor — when he first gets out of the lift. This is the stage direction:

> Enoch joins his parents and they set off for the door of their home, Mrs. Harris leading, Mr. Harris groping for his key in his pocket; the lift doors slide closed eventually. Mr. Harris stops, and his family stop with him and watch. Mr. Harris withdraws his hand from his pocket, baffled. Tries the same pocket again more thoroughly, without result. Withdraws his hand furtively; considers the problem, glancing at his wife. Gives her a forgiving little smile, and goes confidently for the other trouser pocket: the key isn't there either, there being a hole, which he examines carefully and with wonder. Tries the first pocket again. Tries the second pocket again.
> Pause for inspiration and hope. None comes. Tries whistling. Tries a sidelong, casual stroll back to the lift, with surreptitious glances at the floor on the way. Still with his eye on his family, he jabs a finger at the lift-call button. Hits it at third go, and the

door seems to take about a fortnight to respond. He leans casually into the lift and looks round it briefly as one who should express a passing interest in the material covering the floor. Nothing. As the lift door closes again he returns nonchalantly to his wife and son, one hand jingling desperately at the change in his pocket.

Eventually the lift will descend slowly to 'G' [from 16!] and return. Mr. Harris glances at his impassive wife; starts to work his way through his jacket pockets, patting each pocket before exploring it: one, two, breast pocket, inside pocket. His movements are beginning to be nervous and jerky as his mind and silent lips race over the places the key might be other than on him, although he attempts a worldly busyness in his search. Remembers the other inside jacket pocket suddenly, pats and tries that. Remembers the change pocket in the waistband of his trousers, pats and tries it. Remembers the ticket pocket within his jacket pocket, pats and tries that. Searching the pocket of his flapping raincoat busily and with diminishing hope, tugs out his hands. Thrusts his hands back in the raincoat pockets and waits for something dreadful to happen.

And after all that, the first words are spoken:

Mr. Harris (to Enoch): I don't want to have to tell her.
Enoch [who has his ear-plug in]: You what our dad?
Mrs. Harris: You can't find the key can you?
Mr. Harris: No love.

It is, of course, a scene for a mime — for Buster Keaton or, in view of the threatening presence of an outsize Mrs Harris, for Stan Laurel. Its derivation is recognizable to any audience, and that is part of its appeal.

I learnt as a boy, at Sheffield pantomimes and variety shows, that you often laugh at comedians because you laugh at comedians; not because they say or do anything funny in itself, but because they know how to tell you to laugh. Livings must have learnt it, too — in Manchester, Liverpool, Oldham, or wherever. As well as giving his actors funny lines to say, he offers them countless silent hints for the extraction of those compulsory laughs that get an audience going to the point where it can no longer help enjoying itself. Reading *The ffinest ffamily*, I was repeatedly reminded of matinées at the Sheffield Empire and its rival the Lyceum in the years immediately after the war. The Harris trio, whose bullying and bustling is only a mask for dependency, reminded me of 'we

three in Happidrome' — Ramsbottom, and Enoch, and me —
whom I saw in *Aladdin*. Livings makes an alert comment on family
relationships in his note to the published text:

> Since nobody goes anywhere much in this play, the actors have to
> observe the geography of the character relationships acutely and
> constantly. There's a certain distance you stand from people,
> according to your relationship with them: that's what I mean by
> 'geography'.

Pantomime comics have always done that, hiding behind a
protective principal boy when threatened by Widow Twankey's
rolling-pin. Mrs Harris trying to get through to Enoch recalled the
forlorn efforts and vigorous insults of Nat Mills as he thrust simple
information into one of his wife Bobbie's ears and almost *heard* it
fall out of the other. But it is, above all, the word-spinning comics
— Albert Modley was the one I knew best — who help me to
apprehend the popular appeal of Livings's plays. He wants actors
who are prepared to stand there in *puribus naturalibus* and say the
lines their character allows them.

There is nothing unexpected in the primacy of language in
popular plays. Linguistic cadenzas have been a feature of every
popular dramatic style from mummers' plays to melodrama. I won
my first girl-friend on an Easter-hike by writing a poem she
couldn't understand, but marvelled at. In pleading for an
'accessible theatre' and writing brilliant verbal extravaganzas,
Livings is not being inconsistent but perceptive. The people he has
in mind love language and its foibles. 'Your dad's about as much
idea as a mop-bucket,' says Mrs Harris to Enoch when he carries
Mr Harris's timid request for furniture in their empty council flat:

> he can do without furniture or he can work! he's got a choice of
> two! If he thinks he can get you to come suckholing round me for
> furniture while we've paid for the washing machine he thinks
> shit! Let him get himself a job if he can't stand his own home!

That coach-load of working wives would have roared at that. It's
written for them.

I've not said enough about what Livings means by 'reality', and I
must move on to discuss his sense of an 'audience'. The two are
related, of course. 'Reality' is whatever an audience of *real* people
recognizes. It may be Valentine Brose's anxiety to grow
mushrooms in a boiler house, or Henry Cash's unrequited
affection for bees, or Enoch Harris's addiction to his transistor ('I
think I'll try and get Radio 3,' he says in a moment of

self-aggrandisement), or your next-door neighbour's unlikely habit of bottling sailing-ships. Something that real people, who are always ridiculous until they're ill, do, or something they might say. Most people care about something, and it is an aspect of Livings's generosity to applaud those eccentricities by which we identify ourselves. It is a generosity he expects from his ideal audience, and he has no other in mind:

> Here we come, grasping our carrier-bags, with never exactly the right amount of sandwiches, but willing enough to provide *some* nourishment for ourselves. We are more than willing to laugh, cry, or be impressed; we plan to take part in the telling of a story, a story we can care about, told by artists with whom we dare entrust our imaginations. In my experience, we like especially reassurance and discovery. 'Oh yes,' we like to say to ourselves, 'that's right. And how clever of us to be here to see it, and to spot it with such joy'.

His concern for the audience is constant:

> Let us now tell them this fine play we have chosen, with clarity and clean fingernails. Can we see these friendly people we have invited? Good grief, you couldn't even play bingo in this gloom, what is it? The flicks? Can they see us? Put more light on the stage. I can't for the life of me see why people stay up all night fiddling with lamps which ought to be pointed at the stage any-way. The activity is quite meaningless without the people in front, so let us accept their benign presence with the calm elegance of a good tumbler, the zest of a clown and the easy grace of tigers ...

The convention of direct address is irresistible to him, as it is to any comedian. 'See you in the next act,' says Ponce Weatherby just before the interval of *The ffinest ffamily*, suddenly addressing us from the sixteenth floor of the council flats. Henry Cash takes us more frequently into his distasteful confidence. When Doris Thring is sent out to seduce him, for instance, he 'stares at her, and then addresses us':

> I'm surrounded by the dissolution of standards; I should build an ark. Doris is remarkably close; by casually raising a hand, as for instance to adjust my tie briefly, I could brush against her thigh, twice. I wonder if she'd notice, or remark on it in any way? [*Doris lays her hand warmly and friendly on his thigh. To us.*]
> How can I tell what she means by that?

The extreme example, and one about which I remain unhappy, is the inset game of bingo in *The Little Mrs. Foster Show*. The relevance of bingo to the points the play is making is clear. But what is Livings expecting of his audience? You'd find more bingo-fiends in Liverpool Cathedral (Anglican brick or stained-glass Roman) than in Liverpool Playhouse, where I saw the play in 1966; and the middle-class audience played a part instead of enacting a truth. But what if the play were performed to a bingo-playing audience? Wouldn't the effect be to expose that audience to the falseness of its position in the intellectual theatre rather than to the worldly heartlessness of playing bingo while Rome burns? The play *wants* to attack the exploiters, who can make a profit out of gangrene, bingo, broken hearts and civil war. The peculiar actor-audience resonances set up during the bingo inset tend rather to affect the exploited, to reduce the reference of the explosive theatricality of the scene to the point where the main objects of satire are those people who do not realize that bingo and the serious theatre are mutually exclusive — those are Livings's 'real' people, surely, and he puts them at risk.

Livings's chief appeal to his audiences, though, is through language. He and John Arden, the two dramatists whose concern for a people's theatre has lasted the longest of the post-war generation, are also the most verbally obsessed. The point is one I would like to illustrate by following a conflict in *The ffinest ffamily in the Land* — the basic conflict, which isn't of man against man, but of word against word. The play describes a struggle for survival, in which a love of language is the only life-saver (and death-dealer!).

From their first entrance the Harrises establish a bludgeoning and unexpectedly precise vocabulary. They like their words to do a lot of heavy work:

Mrs Harris: You have to have the key don't you? Oh yes.

Mr Harris: I'm a masterful and jealous man Dora, you know that.

Mrs Harris: You are on a Thursday when the smell of beer gets up your nose; well you see the results.

Mr Harris: I know them Whisters; lustful hounds they are mostly; when my good lady leaves her castle I want the key in my pocket. Women are weak vessels. Thank God.

Mrs Harris: (slightly mollified): Don't think you can get round me: you're rude. Enoch won't know what to make of us.

Mr Harris: I can't help my longings and imaginings Dora.

Mrs Harris: Out here on the landing an' all.

'Longings and imaginings.' The phrase is striking enough to suggest that the Harrises have dreams that can't always wait for sleep. Much later, Mrs Harris will remember: 'there's no knowing what a man'll do when he's desperate with passion; Mr Harris once spilled a whole cup of cocoa all over the pillow.' For the moment, their attention is on the lost key, and on Enoch's failure to get himself married to their illegal lodger (you can't have lodgers in a council flat!), the dolly-bird Corrie. 'I told her,' Enoch protests, in language chipped off the parental block, 'how I felt locked and trapped in the inevitability of my fate, due to my character and circumstances. I couldn't reach through to her somehow. If you had Whist on a different night it'd help: Thursday's ''Men Only'' at the Club; it's holding me back our mam.'

By the time Corrie gets back with a young man she's picked up at the dance, Mrs Harris has got her hand stuck in her husband's pocket. Their doomed concern for respectability sends them scuttling away, leaving the landing to Corrie and to Ponce Weatherby. In an early chapter of *Sexus*, Henry Miller describes an occasion on which he became suddenly so intoxicated with language, so brilliantly articulate, that the assembled drinkers greeted the end of his speech with a spontaneous round of applause. That is the kind of linguistic force that Ponce brings into the play, not immediately, but as his confidence grows and he discovers the power of words to dominate.

> When I've got the right people round me, forward-thinking, young, strong and straight-limbed, ready to look at life with a steady gaze, then you'll see; all the word-power I've stored up will surge out, I'll straddle my fate, and the fate of many. Just now I'm looking round, but I have the strength of purpose, I shall conquer.

Henry Livings's note on the character of Ponce Weatherby is an important warning to actors:

> ...physically and socially he has heretofore failed [and] the Harrises are the first people ever to listen to him with any attention ... He's cheerful, shifty and egregious, but the dangers and outrages he represents to the family are real because their imaginations are caught, and because they have nothing else; not because he has any natural authority to carry out the fatuous propositions that flit through his disorganized brain. Many followers of Hitler spoke of his penetrating gaze; my contention is that they needed him to have a penetrating gaze; in a more

stable society the neighbours would inquire to know who's that goggly-eyed feller, there's an operation you know.

That, of course, is typical of Henry Livings's seriousness. He's not funny in the teeth of life, but funny because they turn out to be dentures.

Ponce's 'spell' begins when he assures Corrie that:

'You'll find experience with me will bear out what I say: my body expresses my philosophy: life should be continuously orgasmic, not a despairing search for peaks of sensual perception, but enhanced, dilated.'

But he meets early resistance from the Harrises. When he offers Corrie 'unguents', Mr Harris repels the threat to his vocabulary:

She wants none of your unguents, skedaddle. Unguents forsooth; I had hopes that Mrs Harris would go down to her grave without having her ears soiled with such words.

Mrs Harris declares more open war on Ponce's high-fallutin' turns of phrase when she shouts at him, locked by now inside *her* flat, 'Open this dirty stinking rotten flaming blasted festering door!!' And Enoch pipes in with an incitement to physical violence expressed in language that Ponce the powerful would certainly reject: 'Break off his arm and hit him with the soggy end our dad.'

Mr Harris's attempts at violence are a failure — you can't do much when you need your hands to hold up your trousers, and anyway Mrs Harris is the wrestler in the family. They find themselves being caught in Ponce's language. When Enoch assaults Corrie in the lift, his parents describe it like this:

Mr Harris: I glimpsed, Corrie and Enoch, no more than glimpsed; and wild horses wouldn't open my lips.

Mrs Harris: There's a beauty in young passion, naked and unchecked, the soft forms and the lithe unashamed limbs entwined, that would be unseemly in persons of age and responsibility.

Mr Harris: Don't think, you two, that your mam and I have forgotten.

Mrs Harris: The sweetness is still in the blood and the heart; that never goes. I'm still young in heart, aren't I Milton? Ask him.

Mr Harris: Still young in heart, yes....

Mrs. Harris: .... young in heart, yes.

Mr Harris: We live again, through you.

Mrs. Harris: Be as happy as your dad and me, that's all we ask:

> he can still take the strength from my legs.
>
> *Mr. Harris:* Just now, you'll be thinking you're the only two in the world, alone and floating in your cloud of sparkling sensuality, each longing for the others touch, hardly daring to believe your newly aroused senses; your every delicate fibre yearning to know again the rosy fire flooding through you from your loins.
>
> *Mrs. Harris:* .... loins, yes....
>
> *Mr. Harris:* .... loins, yes; trembling in a glow that you can't imagine any other creature has known; but your mother and I understand. We may smell a bit by now, but we have looked on the true face of love.

This is language they know — from inexpensive women's magazines and teen-age comics. It is also, of course, the assumed norm of language and emotion on which the *News of the World* relies for the immediate appeal of its detailed deviations. But the Harrises are insistent that they have sources of language of their own — they picked up 'stertorous' at the St John's Ambulance Brigade, for instance. Ponce's reminiscent vocabulary of romantic release shifts their fantasies. If Corrie agrees to sail with Ponce on the ship on which he's a steward, she will be agreeing to work with him in the mysterious 'abroad' as a call-girl. Mrs Harris encourages her. More than that. She'll go with them, to do the whipping and specialities. One worry lingers from the old linguistic world: 'There'll be a glass in the cabin won't there? For my teeth?'

All this is very well, but what about Mr Harris? He decides to fight — with words this time:

> Ridicule is the best weapon. I shall mock Mr. Weatherby out of here, mock him ...

but the pressure muddles him:

> ... it's hard. But tyranny can only go so far as it's let, and there's always that limit further than which ordinary folk will not let it go over ...

The promised flyting match never comes off; you can't put in an unnecessary preposition without weakening your hold over a man like Ponce Weatherby. Ponce unnerves Milton Harris by kissing him, even trying to force his tongue between the protesting lips (the hands are still needed for the trousers). 'Mr. Harris has a weak heart,' warns his wife. 'Keep still and I'll try and miss it,' says Ponce.

At his moment of triumph, Ponce sneaks into the flat, forces the electric meter, and falls out of the window. All you can see is his desperate finger-tips. Corrie and Mrs Harris pull him up by his blazer; it has to be the women, since one man has a transistor and the other his trousers to take care of; and when Ponce is almost in the room, off he goes again with his words: 'the cold steel gauntlet of fear that nobody takes up, its scales shining like corpses in the dark'. One final heave, and off comes the blazer. There's a ten-second silence, then a distant cry. 'Mrs. Harris peers out and down, listens to the cry, and watches the impact that follows it, and then turns and walks stiff-legged over to the television and switches it on.' 'Nobody's noticed him yet,' says Enoch, having had the decency to drop Ponce's blazer after him.

We don't need Livings's comparison of Ponce to a variety comic to remind us how much of the play depends on music-hall routines — and on an audience that comes ready to laugh. I've talked about it in some detail because it seems to me worth talking about, and because Livings's is a name too little mentioned in the modern theatre. It's almost fifteen years since John Russell Taylor called him 'essentially the sort of dramatist who should come to critical approval by way of popular success rather than the other way round'.[8] But where, in the English theatre, can the popular dramatist find his audience? Ken Campbell has taken his Road Show into pubs and working men's clubs, but he hasn't tried his full-length plays there. You need horses for courses. Meanwhile, revivals of Livings's plays are growing rarer — much rarer than they should be — and there has been no major new work for the stage since *The ffinest ffamily*. Will there be? In his new book, *Arden: A Study of His Plays*, Albert Hunt sounds a gloomy note:

> It isn't, to my mind, surprising, that the Ardens, Joan Littlewood and Henry Livings are all, virtually, exiles from the British theatre. All of them belong to a comic tradition which has no place in the theatre establishment: and they belong to that tradition because the political attitude they instinctively take up has led them to a rejection of the values the legitimate British theatre still expresses.... The problem facing [them] is that they don't belong either to the nineteenth-century hangover which is represented by the official theatre; or to the arty decadence of the avant-garde. They are solidly rooted in a popular tradition: and so they aren't taken seriously, either by the guardians of established culture, or by the non-thinking underground.[9]

That is only too true. Livings writes as a professional, and has to earn his keep. However worthy in themselves, his acclimatization to the English factory-belts of plays by Gogol, Tolstoy, and Hauptmann is a scant use of his originality. Even the *Pongo Plays*, which will always work if you can find the comedians to play them, make a wry, implicit comment on Livings's sense of his place on the contemporary stage, a joking Kyogen among the Noh pack.

Some time before 1965, Livings wrote a 'front cloth solo' called *Watch the Bucket*. He wrote it for and played it himself, and it reads now as a prophetic comment on his isolation. There's this man, and this pile of dung, and this bucket. The dung is invisible; the bucket isn't. Nor, of course, is this man. He gets nervous when he realizes we're looking at him, and the nervousness breaks out sometimes into offensiveness. Watch the bucket! he shouts at us when he's trying to be unobtrusive. There he is, all innocence, walking off the stage, not as quickly as he might have done if his natural shyness were not tempered by natural exhibitionism, and suddenly BANG into an invisible barrier. It's all round him. He's trapped. By an invisible wall? By the *need* to write plays for a theatre of which he doesn't approve, you might say. Eventually — that mixture of shyness and exhibitionism again — he decides to clown for us and to conceal himself:

He seizes the bucket and puts it over his head. Removes it.
There is a feeling of earthy nobility inside this bucket; I wish I could share it with you.
Tries the bucket again. Takes it off again.
There wouldn't be room. And anyway, you might not all appreciate the smell.
Bucket swiftly on. Intones hollowly within.
I should like to speak a message to those in this place that will listen: those who love me as I love them, notice the order.
Whips the bucket off his flushed and cheerful face:
It's infinitely less shaming and disconcerting in here than out here.
On again with the bucket.

It needs to be known that Sweaty Nellie has tender, shapely breasts, and that the set of her shoulders is EXACT, notwithstanding the serious nervous acne that wounds her face. The broken teeth and white stringy bowels of my aged and dear friend John do not make him less firm and generous a friend; and the sad nightly spite and battle with his loving wife which keeps the street waking and hollows his happy laugh at all times, waters my love and respect for this man.

Takes the bucket off his head and peers inside. Screws his head round to read upside down inside.
That's the first time I've ever seen that written inside a bucket. *He goes, carefully circuiting the pile ... Leaves the bucket offstage and returns to bow, planting one foot firmly into the pile. Sees it at the nadir of his bow. Extracts his foot with distaste, and exits, keeping the soiled trouser-leg well away from the other.* [10]

Exit Henry Livings with dung, still carrying a rare and curious interest in the sources of language. A man with a lot of plays in him, and hardly anywhere to put them.

Notes

1   Obituary in *Time*, 18 March 1974.
2   *Plays and Players*, July 1969, 51.
3   The analogy is mine. I know of no reason why Mr Esslin should be at all interested in cricket.
4   The comparison is not accidental. Henry Livings wrote a version of *The Government Inspector*, setting it in a northern English community.
5   *Plays and Players*, October 1972, 47.
6   From the Author's Note to *The ffinest ffamily in the Land*, 1973.
7   The open letter to David Scase is published in *Theatre Quarterly*, II, 6, April-June 1972, pp. 5-7. All subsequent quotations from Livings's non-dramatic work are from this letter, which is entitled 'Let's Make a Theatre for Real People'.
8   *Anger and After,* (Harmondsworth, Penguin, 1963), 259.
9   (London, Methuen, 1974), see 141-2.
10   Published in *Encore*, No. 54, March-April 1965, 24-7.

MARIAN HANNAH WINTER

Popular Theatre and Popular Art

Popular art and popular theatre developed simultaneously. To the present day their inspiriting relationship has illuminated what their public believed in, marvelled or laughed at, wept over, was induced to see and wanted to remember. Mountains of ephemera were created to induce the 'wish to see' and meet the 'desire to remember', in short, the advertising and souvenir industries. Such ephemera — admired, then forgotten or destroyed — mostly vanished as irrevocably as the centuries of performers they advertised or commemorated.

Yet the surest guidelines to understanding what made the popular theatre popular can be found in the surviving fraction of handbills, programmes, posters, song-books and souvenir prints. A footnote to remembrance is furnished by the even scarcer commemorative objects in metal and ceramic ranging from crude pottery to *faience fine* (sometimes called opaque porcelain). We can also see which performers — offhand I think of Grimaldi, Liston, Astley, the Franconis, Ducrow and certain animal stars — and which entertainments, such as the circus and pantomime, appealed to all classes and crossed all social divisions. The 'Elephant of the King of Siam' rescuing her imprisoned master by raising her trunk and carrying him down enfolded therein from a tower window was recorded in plebeian Staffordshire. The same scene in Paris formed part of an elegant little series of jewel-coloured prints to ornament expensive bonbon boxes. I only mention for the record toys and children's books inspired by theatrical performances of all types provided they were popular; the eighteenth-century optical views; and nineteenth-century magic lantern and stereoptican slides. Toy theatres are an inexhaustible mine, with English penny plain and tuppence coloured indisputably the major lode.

From the Middle Ages, when documents become available and explicit, there were three artistic levels concerned with the theatre, which I shall take in its largest sense of entertainment for onlookers including such fringe attractions as menageries, human and scientific phenomena, hypnotists and future-predicting somnambulists. The first two levels comprise pictures and objects which served as advertising, or souvenirs which could be purchased on the fairgrounds, at the showmen's booths, from stands or from ambulant merchants on the boulevards and bridges. It is the style and execution as well as material (quality of paper or clay primarily) that set them into two categories. With one eighteenth-century exception my illustrations have been taken from nineteenth-century work because there is a possibility of assembling sufficient examples for comparison from several countries — England, Scotland, Ireland, France, Germany, Italy, Austria, the USA, Hungary and Denmark — to cover the whole spectrum of popular theatre as seen by popular artists.

These range from popular prints (although I have never felt that this accepted English equivalent term really translates the more nuanced French *imagerie populaire*) to a second level — prints generally, folk art and much else more which does not concern us here — which Pierre-Louis Duchartre, expert on the *commedia dell'arte*, describes as *imagerie demi-fine* or *imagerie bourgeoise*, for which an equivalent in other languages is even more difficult to find. In France this *imagerie demi-fine*, although not confined to the capital, was a speciality of the print publishers on the rue St-Jacques near the Sorbonne. Duchartre and Saulnier's indispensable work on the subject is titled *L'Imagerie Parisienne*[1]. The tendency at present, even in France, is to englobe all types of prints which are not in the domain of fine art as 'popular prints'. In the series on popular prints in various countries (so far France, Germany, Italy and The Netherlands have appeared and England is expected momentarily) this is the procedure which has been followed[2].

Personally I accept this combination as a matter of convenience and because the lines are sometimes blurred. I would, however, question the description given in blurbs of Hyatt Mayor's recent *Popular Prints of the Americas*[3] as 'prints for people who don't care about art'. They cared a good bit about it, and their ideas of art extended the boundaries established by the term 'art print'. What was portrayed was more important than the portrayer's technique in presenting the subject.

Finally, at the summit level — from the often anonymous monastic illuminators through Breughel, Jan Steen, Callot, Carmontelle, Watteau, Vernet, Landseer, Boilly, the over-exposed Impressionists and Picasso, and a number of figurative painters currently active — beaux-artistes have always been attracted by the popular theatre. Their names are by and large well-known and not my concern today. The major number of my illustrations will reflect either style or techniques or viewpoint of basic popular imagery.

However, just to present the three categories as terms of reference to launch the illustrations which follow I shall use a selection from those of one theatrical dynasty in which I am gradually becoming something of a genealogical expert: the Price family.

The child acrobats, *les Frères Price*, are presented in what may have been a small poster which could double as a souvenir print (see Plate 6). The style is crude, naive, forthright and in the spirit of the popular print. It was published by Simon of Marseille. Precisely the same act, engraved a century earlier, showed *les Enfans hollandois*, a celebrated troupe or troupes — for several used that name — in the mid-eighteenth century. Billed also as the Piccoli Olandesi and the Dutch Lilliputians, they appeared in fairs all over the Continent and in London. This latter was a small souvenir print, and although trimmed of all identifying information was *demi-fine*, probably from the rue Saint-Jacques and therefore *imagerie parisienne*. It shows the persistence of this classic act and yet another style of recording it.

In 1855 the children Emilie and Ferdinand Price were appearing at the Porte St-Martin in Paris. A lithograph which shows them in a *pas de deux*, probably *paysanne*, is more souvenir than advertisement and almost certainly destined for a wealthier clientele than the Marseille *frères Price*. The Price family archives held by Madam Tilly Price Rancy have many photographs of later generations of Price children and adults in the same type of performances illustrated by these two prints. Among these photographs was one of the musical clowns *John and William Price*, which has permitted identification of the *Portrait of a Clown* by Renoir in the Kröller-Müller Museum at Otterloo as a *Portrait of the Clown William Price*. This is clearly in the province of beaux-arts and not in that of works under consideration.

Technically the popular prints flourished in woodcuts and lithographs. Save for a limited number of late seventeenth- and early eighteenth-century examples, engravings, etchings and aquatints were primarily techniques for the *imagerie demi-fine* or for art prints. Typical of the rue St-Jacques *imagerie* were the innumerable engravings, hand-coloured, of the various attractions

Plate 6. The child acrobats, Les Freres Price

at the Cirque Franconi, issued by Chéreau, one of the most celebrated dynasties of publisher-printers in Paris. The first Chéreau, Francois Ier (1680-1729), after an apprenticeship and some years with his master Gérard Audran, took over the bulk of his stock and copperplates from Audran's widow and established his own shop, as engraver and print dealer, in 1718. A century later descendants were still active. In all countries the *imagerie demi-fine* and the art print flourished principally in capital cities. Popular prints were certainly produced in the great capitals as well, but the important centres were clearly provincial. Parenthetically, because it is really difficult to fit in anywhere, I must mention a peculiarly Italian speciality, which Binney has noted in his recent catalogue of Italian dance prints[4].

> Its paper is never of the heavy, durable variety; it is almost never colored. It is often accompanied by a dedicatory verse (even to the use of 'D.D.D.' meaning 'the dedicators' or 'Gli Ammiratori' — 'the admirers'), and it frequently appears that little care was spent on its printing. It is a more spontaneous production — and for a simple reason. It is primarily a tribute to the dancer depicted.

I can add from personal observation of documents that actors and equestrian performers were also so honoured. These tributes to the performer were distributed in the theatre during the performance and often tossed upon the stage during curtain calls.

To return to the popular print elsewhere, the style can often deceive in dating if there is no other clue than internal evidence given by the print itself, for there was a time lag in the work of provincial artists. I know of Calais posters for performances dated from 1816 through the 1820s which continued to be issued with borders showing *commedia dell'arte* characters from well-worn woodblocks dating back to the mid-eighteenth century. When a new process such as lithography became the general process, for several decades many provincial artists continued to achieve woodcut effects. Even in the great cities there was always a certain number of artists who had affinities with earlier techniques. A scattering of samples might include: a small poster for the Juan Porté circus in Vienna, circa 1819, lithographed by Trentsensky. It shows a Hell's Mouth which might be copied from a medieval manuscript illumination, and emphasizes the persistence of a theme which is at the very origin of Western theatre. Next there is an actual woodcut of a lady lion trainer in a *tutu, Dompteuse — Marché St Pierre*, which stylistically might date from the late

Plate 7A. Poster of the trainer Bidel with his wild animals
Plate 7B. The equestrienne, Adah Isaacs Menken

eighteenth or early nineteenth century — but the costume is one which would not have been found much before the Second Empire and the performance is in Paris. A considerably later poster of the trainer Bidel with his mixed wild animal group is of remarkable technical sophistication, from a Paris atelier (see Plate 7A). It is dated in manuscript '1874', which would be right for Bidel in Paris. At first glance it appears to be a woodcut. The 'A. Mary Sc' signature instead of 'Del' implies the same thing. Yet in principle a poster of this size cannot be a woodblock, certainly not in one piece. And the obvious joinings in the border do not seem to indicate four woodblocks. A number of experts such as Duchartre, the Proutés and Michèle Richet have puzzled over this poster — and the only firm conclusion was that a number of processes, including hand-colouring with pochoir, were involved. The cross-hatching and stippling (probably with tulle) are remarkable. There is the publisher's address: *'Typographie Morris Père et Fils, rue Amelot, Spécialité pour Affiches Imprimées en plusieurs couleurs'*. The rue Amelot is right off the rue Filles du Calvaire, site of the Cirque d'Hiver. The clientele was to hand. When an artist such as the rope walker Kremo arrived in Paris with his own posters, executed by the M. Deutsch printing company of Budapest from a drawing by one 'Fredy', Morris Père & Fils inserted the little printed text indicating the place and time of performance.

The posters I have discussed so far are quite straightforward and literal. Apart from a certain exaggeration — 'One Hundred Wild Beasts' for example — the performer is presented in a plausible setting. There are a number of posters, however, which are strange and to be marvelled at, and sometimes even disquieting. Many fall into a category that I identify to myself as 'pre-surrealist'. They occur in all the countries for which these prints exist and they are almost all stock posters — that is, a subject already made up in which the performer's name and place of performance will be inserted. They were often sold to travelling fairground artistes who had run out of their stock of posters and handbills whilst on the road, and who knew in which provincial city they could replenish their publicity handouts. Obviously magicians and prestidigitators merited a presentation which stressed the marvellous. A decapitation number appears in a lithograph which could serve either as a souvenir print or small poster, published by the printer Robin, artist anonymous, in one of France's greatest centres of popular print-making — Lyons. Another number which was popular in fairground booths, theatres and even middle-class salons — the hypnotist and his subject, who usually predicted the future while in trance — was recorded in a print by Charpentier of Nantes. The mystic quality of the performance was emphasized by costuming the subject in the Druidess robes of Bellini's *Norma*.

In essence human beings impersonating animals can be disturbing; there are deep magico-religious, centuries-old legends involved. The most cheerful of these impersonations was the rôle of Jocko, hero of the long-lived Mazuriad, *Jocko ou le Singe du Brésil*. He is depicted in a small poster and/or souvenir print by the firm of Maquin in Montpellier. Contortionists such as the Carsley Howells, who impersonated snakes, are set admirably in contrast by their portraits in off-stage suits, respectably like everyone else *not* theatrical, from the German firm Hoenig, probably a Hamburg printer. The most celebrated German firm which specialized in theatrical subjects, Adolf Friedlander, was located in Hamburg. So too was a cluster of other printers, including D.H. Michael, who issued some splendid trained dog and monkey posters, and Wilhelm Rohde, who specialized in variety artists. Hamburg developed an international theatrical clientele which carried over well into the twentieth century.

The most curious of the contortionist posters is one of the Berg Brothers — a Spanish 'Hermanos Berg' on a lithographed poster by Widman of Copenhagen (see Fig. 12.1). The mixture of an almost calligraphic technique and surrealist exaggeration of the poses is notable. Somewhere among the oddities should go a fairground number which fell into disrepute only toward the end of the nineteenth century, and was described by Gaston Escudier at the period of its decline[5]. This was known as 'challenge wrestling', and occurs at the English fairgrounds as well. The wrestlers appeared first in the parade before the booth, flexing muscles, and perhaps staged some exhibition matches, then challenged the local champion or any other volunteer. The matches were rough, particularly when that peculiar type of French wrestling, *la savate*, in which kicking one's opponent is a desirable and fair move, was chosen. There was a scene in Carné's *Les Enfants du Paradis* in which Lacénaire's minion Avril swaggers up to toss Baptiste out of an underworld dive and in a split second Baptiste has launched a lethal *savate riposte* — a kick in the *bas ventre*. A crude but vigorous print by Fernique of Paris, who made a speciality of these, shows a preliminary series of exhibition holds. The firm of Gubian in Lyons also issued a series of wrestlers, as well as other fairground and circus attractions, in oblong plates which seem intended for souvenir albums. Another entry in the 'marvellous' category, and most certainly for a fairground theatre, shows two albino giantesses, called twins — and very likely they

Figure 12.1. Poster of the Berg Brothers, acrobats

were — with a dwarf dressed as Napoleon III, which places it before 1870, to emphasize their height. Anyone who has read Lord George Sanger's *Seventy Years a Showman* or Escudier's *Les Saltimbanques* will know the various techniques used to make 'giants' appear more gigantic. And just to show that my generalizations about provincial and capital city print characteristics can be occasionally disproved, a poster-souvenir print illustrating this number was issued by Prodhomme of Paris.

Circuses were especially favoured by the printers because their consumption of posters was enormous. The riders alone furnished material for an infinite variety of prints. Among them there is an exotic number of Gustave Price, astride a tandem of doe and deer, costumed as an American Indian, issued by Kiersdorf of Ghent. There was the equestrian pantomime performer who specialized in the Napoleonic circus epics which were a major attraction of the Cirque Franconi. And there was the great pantomime draw — *Mazeppa* — in which countless lady riders after 1861 attempted to duplicate the success of Adah Isaacs Menken (see Plate 7B). This poster is not only exceptionally handsome but also one of the earliest produced by a firm which was to become internationally famous: D & J Allen of Belfast. They were established in Belfast in 1858 and thirty years later opened the first of their several branches in London. The equestrienne seems to be a very definite likeness of Menken, who was touring all over the British Isles after 1864, when she had made her London début in *Mazeppa*.

Posters of animal trainers range from crude and rather unpleasant ones, such as a bear trainer by Delor of Toulouse, to brilliantly fantastic and witty examples, such as a thief surprised to find that the victim he is robbing is a horse and that two policemen (also horses) are leaping through the window to arrest him. Titled *Emilio and his Poney Pantomimists*, this act was immortalized by the prolific Louis Gallice, who was artist as well as publisher in Paris. There are crazily logical touches such as an ancestor portrait (equine) on the wall and bearskin rug on the floor. From the Museo Correr in Venice comes a print of an Italian pantomime company which featured a trained dog, who is shown barking at a fop and trying to nip his coat-tails. This Compagnia Vergnano is recorded in Gandini's Modena chronology for 5 November 1844: 'The company directed by Vergnano has combined with the equestrian company Ghelia-Tourniaire' to jointly produce the pantomime *Mazeppa*[6].

French collectors of the last century were particularly astute in appreciating the qualities of the English theatrical posters. Like their fellow-collectors in England — in fact like collectors all over the world — they acquired what were termed *maîtres de l'affiche*: the undisputed poster 'greats' such as Lautrec and Forain, followed by Steinlen, Chéret, Capiello, Dudley Hardy, Will Bradley, John Hassall, Aubrey Beardsley and all the internationally famous names whose work was regularly reported on in *The Poster* and *Maîtres de l'Affiche*. But the French quietly kept adding works by anonymous artists, and most particularly those issued by English firms. I doubt that any single collection in England can match the English poster holdings in the Paris *Musée des Arts Décoratifs*.

Recently this museum has found in its reserve cabinets a hitherto untouched collection of another 400 English posters, almost all by anonymous artists and many issued by Stafford of Nottingham. They are presently being catalogued and will eventually be available to scholars. One of the most interesting items in the *Musée des Arts Décoratifs* 1972 exhibition of English posters in the 1890s was a tremendous photomural blowup and montage of old photographs of London streets with their hoardings a veritable mosaic of posters. Typical of the Stafford productions is a remarkable study

Plate 8A.
A Stafford & Co.
poster of acrobats

Plate 8B. A Louis
Gallice poster of
the 'American'
artiste, Bares

of acrobats (see Plate 8A). In all Stafford work the colours are remarkably beautiful. They manufactured their own coloured inks. A later Stafford print, from its small format, was probably issued as a souvenir for a lion tamer's act. Stafford also produced posters, souvenir programmes and an illustrated journal for Buffalo Bill during his European tours.

Posters generally started moving out of the crudely popular category into that second level of *demi-fine* popular art. As the nineteenth century ended examples of both types could be found in the productions of Latscha, a Parisian printer who occasionally designed as well as edited his posters. Sometimes they were for well-known performers such as *The Borbonel*, a fixed trapeze act mentioned in Thétard's *Merveilleuse Histoire du Cirque*. Just as often they were commissions for a now-forgotten act of four dancer acrobats, *The Four Vincents*. No matter how badly drawn and poorly designed, Latscha's posters are endlessly fascinating in unexpected details. The tremendous brooding eagle which hovers over the trapeze for no conceivable reason on the Borbonel poster is matched by a presentation of one of the female members of the Vincents, costumed in a frilly rose-coloured gown and wearing long black gloves and stockings. She is pictured in a hand-stand in which the functions of arms and legs are reversed, and her face smiles out at the public with the unconcern of a disembodied Cheshire Cat. Another prolific Parisian poster firm, whose director sometimes signed as artist, was Louis Gallice. His poster of the 'American' artiste Barès is probably best described by the current phrase 'high camp' (see Plate 8B). I have been trying for some time to identify this Barès, improbably draped in an American flag with six-pointed stars. The only other poster of Barès that I know is a quite banal equilibrist advertisement in an unexceptional clown costume and make-up. In fact absolutely no resemblance to this poster.

As a record of a number which is no longer often seen there are several posters of 'living statues'. *The Conradi* appeared in 1882 at the elegant Hippodrome au Pont de l'Alma in *Poses Plastiques* and on a Chéret poster for that programme. A poster for their appearance at the Ambassadeurs-Champs Elysées in 1884 was made by one of the most prolific of all French firms — Charles Lévy's *Affiches Américaines*. Others of this firm are issued at the same period and same address by *Émile Lévy*. This was a period when 'Américain' had a certain exotic chic. The Lévy posters range from those which are poorly drawn, unattractive and with nothing other than documentary value to recommend them, to some very effective examples such as the 1883 *Le Ballet Noir* for the Folies

Bergère and the sought-after bicycle advertisements.

Another living statues — *Gems of the Great Masters — Raffael and Rigaretto's Troupe of Male and Female Living Statuary* — was 'del' and 'lith' by Signor Rigaretto himself. The vogue for living statues extended to Sweet Caporal cigarette cards, which showed members of the Espinosa family in plastic poses, probably from one of their ballet pantomimes. The Espinosas were a famous dancing dynasty who toured the United States and settled in England. There is to this day an Espinosa School of Ballet in London.

There is only a token representation in this group for the American companies, which were brilliant, prolific and flourished in the latter half of the nineteenth century from coast to coast. In themselves they warrant a volume. In 1956 the Library of Congress began to undo bundles of paper which had been stored in the bowels of the Library, mostly tied with string and otherwise unprotected. These included thousands of documents which had been submitted for copyright purposes, amongst them uncounted theatrical posters. Many were stock posters which could be adapted for any performers specializing in the type of act depicted. The paper was often so stiff and brittle that it could not be unfolded until treated in the Library's bookbindery. In June 1963 the Library first displayed some of the gems from this collection. John Canaday in his *New York Times Review* mentioned the firms of Morse M'Kenny & Co. of New York and Russell Morgan of Cincinnati and New York. The latter firm's productions are interesting for the period around 1870 when they produced colour woodcuts by an artist named Joseph W. Hart at a time when lithography had already taken over with so many companies — and was shortly to do the same with them.

A print of the famous Majilton Family (Frank, Marie and Charles), eccentric dancers in the pantomime *Spectresheim*, was produced by W.J. Morgan of Cincinnati (probably a branch of the Russell Morgan family), in a small format which could certainly be used as a souvenir print. It makes an amusing contrast with a French souvenir of an extravaganza based on the American play *Rip Van Winkle*. Another American print which is posterlike in text but souvenir print in size 16¼'' w x 23'' h) is an elegantly finished lithograph by the New York firm of Robertson, Seibert & Shearman. It has a French text, *Les Artistes Américains de Bonfanti*, and shows the negro dancer Jean Ritter in *travesti*, performing Fanny Elssler's Cachucha and other of her dances, in vignettes which surround his full-length portrait. Both of these small-format souvenir-print type of posters are from the Dessolliers poster collection and were presumably so used. There were, however, analogous French posters, particularly for cabarets and music halls, in which the small format was nevertheless more exclusively 'poster' in feeling.

Two drawings which I believe may have been studies for prints, circa 1820, have sufficient technical quality to have been destined for the more expensive 'art print'. The last poster I shall consider is of such technical virtuosity that it transcends the usual commercial work for music hall turns, and is certainly one of Louis Gallice's masterworks. It shows a pair of dancers in costumes completely wired for electricity — in costumes decorated with thousands of small lamps: *Les Loëbert*[7].

The majority of exhibits have been posters or small format prints which could serve both as shop-door poster and as souvenir. This is not because of a lack of other types of prints in all the countries concerned. The sheer number of posters produced, and the fact that during the later nineteenth century many Continental collectors were actively acquiring popular and often anonymous works, ensured survival of enough examples to make comparisons between countries and between styles. The fact that in France and the United States it was mandatory for two copies of all posters to be deposited in the *Dépôt Légal* and Library of Congress, respectively, also helped — although for generations thousands of prints perished through neglect in the Library of Congress cellars and *Dépôt Légal* copies were often discarded or abstracted and quietly sold. Even today, *Dépôt Légal* copies of prints with the printer's signature and dated note guaranteeing that the edition would be *'conforme à l'exemplaire'* turn up in dealers' rooms.

I would like to finish not with a poster but with another type of popular print, an ancestor of the comic strip. This was the sheet which told a complete story in four or five rows of four rectangular boxes each, a speciality of firms such as Pellerin in Epinal or Gangel, later Gangel and Dembour, in Metz. Known generically as *imageries d'Epinal*, they were devoted to fairy tales, popular novels in summaries, moral fables, theatrical productions and almost every phase of activity which might interest a child or tempt his parents to purchase.

It was inevitable that this form of print should be adapted for publicity purposes. The ultimate in persuasion, containing several new elements of advertising logic, is found in a crude Parisian lithographed handout imitating this type of *imagerie d'Epinal*. There are four rows of boxed vignettes, each $2\frac{3}{8}$ x $2\frac{3}{4}$ ins, with descriptive texts underneath. The sheet is titled *L'Enfant Studieux ou à Quoi Tient la Destinée*. It was distributed by the *Cirque Métropole* in Paris during June 1907. I think that few of the popular prints I know which have been the subject of structuralist studies offer more points of interest than this one, which I do not believe has received attention to date.

The milieu, immediately obvious from father's baggy trousers, red cummerbund and heavy shoes, and Maman in an apron washing up, is that of a blue-collar working-class family. Little Henri, home from his *lycée*, has started work on one of the *Cirque Métropole's* publicity handouts: a model circus to cut out, colour, mount and present at the circus box office in exchange for a matinée ticket (probably Thursday, midweek school break in France until replaced recently by Wednesday). It was a not unlikely gamble that if the lad actually did complete the model Maman and any other children in the family would accompany the winner.

A version of this type of cut-out may still be seen on cereal boxes, further refined because the cut-out is actually printed on the container and does not necessitate extra expense in paper for the manufacturer. The subject is accompanied by an offer to send an explanatory booklet for anything from 10 to 25c — or five similar box tops. The latter method means working through five boxes of the same breakfast food in reasonably short order to meet the offer's time limit. Unless faced with the indifference of a particularly canny or blasé child, the manufacturer can't lose on this gimmick.

Little Henri, then, longing to see the circus, completes the model and Maman does indeed take him with his admiring small sister to the *Cirque Métropole*, where a free ticket is given Henri and two admissions are paid. The performance is traditional. The school rider, like all celebrated *haute école ecuyères* of the period, rides side-saddle, *en amazone*, and has been given a title. Indeed, there were celebrated centauresses who married into the aristocracy and the Baronne de Rhaden actually belonged to it. Another scene names the performer and the drawing, though maladroit, is recognizably the clown Footit, familiar even today through the Lautrec prints and drawings.

At home that evening little Henri tells his father about the wonders of the *Cirque Métropole* and resolves, even if he has to pay for a ticket, that he wants above all to go again. Working to gain something he enjoys proves an incentive for Henri to rise above the family background. It is still not the moment when he would be pictured as a bank director or a president of the

République. Jargonwise, such upward mobility for a working-man's son in France at that time would have been unimaginable. But — with talent, hard work and a seat at the circus as incentive — he has presumably been able to win one of the competitions for training as an architect — that held annually for a scholarship in Rome, perhaps. The final vignette shows him as architect of the next World Exposition in Paris, Mama and Papa looking prosperously middle-class, and Henri now a distinguished person escorting other distinguished persons — perhaps President Fallières and his guests — around the Exposition. This little history is a basic challenge to the unwritten law that anything you enjoy is probably bad for you, if not downright immoral, and will lead to a sorry end — particularly if you belong to the lower classes. The time had arrived when the purchasing power even of the lower classes had become a high power objective.

It is a logical advertising presentation of the old theme, so popular in the Anglo-Saxon world, of the poor lad who makes good through industry and perseverance. In England Dick Whittington and Hogarth's Industrious Apprentice, who both end up Lord Mayors of London, are classic examples. But in France the Marquis of Carrabas depended on good looks, charm and his intelligent cat to arrive. Going up in the world through industry and above-average intellect had long been suspect in France — there was always the example of Jacques Coeur in warning ... until the Second Empire. This period of the buccaneering entrepreneur, the self-made man and the *arriviste* coincided with a tremendous advertising boom. It had been forecast by Balzac in the lyrical advertisements of César Birotteau or in the prototype young man-on-the-make, Lucien de Rubempré. A whole new world was opened to popular art, and for yet some decades its particular artistic elements triumphed over mass production. That part of it devoted to the theatre remains a key to the taste and ways of thought for successive periods, and rivals the written word as the scholar's documentary evidence[8].

Notes

1   Pierre-Louis Duchartre and René Saulnier, *L'Imagerie Parisienne* (Paris, Grund, 1944).
2   Series on *Imagerie Populaire*, printed in Italy by Electa

Press, Milan, 1956-72. The procedure has been accompanied by anguished cries of protest from the purists, particularly when confronted with chromo-lithographed postcards included in the Italian volume.

3 Published by Crown Publishers, New York, 1973.

4 Edwin Binney 3rd, *Sixty Years of Italian Dance Prints 1815-1875*, Dance Perspectives 53 (New York, 1973).

5 Gaston Escudier, *Les Saltimbanques* (Paris, 1874).

6 A. Gandini, *Cronistoria dei Teatri di Modena del 1539 al 1871* (Modena, 1871), Vol.II, 322. The Tourniaire Circus was the first French circus to tour extensively in Italy. The 'Ghelia' was a Mlle Tourniaire who married into the family. The Tourniaire Circus at that time was exclusively equestrian and could not have presented a pantomime such as *Mazeppa* without collaborators.

7 Reproduced in the *Bulletin — Société 'Les Vieux Papiers'* (Paris), no.197.

8 In addition to the French collections I have noted, there is the John Johnson Collection of Printed Ephemera at Oxford, the Jefferson R. Burdick Collection of Paper Americana in the Metropolitan Museum Print Room, New York, and the Special Collections in the Library of Congress — all awaiting further exploration. I have not seen the collections in the new Poster Museum of Essen, but I know that in addition to posters it has acquired handbills, throwaways and some souvenir prints, all relating to Vienna's Prater. Considerable work has been accomplished during the past three decades in the use of ephemera, but there remains much untouched and unexploited material awaiting the scholar in search of new sources for documentation and illustration.

IRMELI NIEMI

Finnish Popular Theatre

The Finnish theatre has always been a popular theatre.
The Finnish theatre has always been a serious matter of art.

These two seemingly opposite statements can be helpful when starting to consider the popularity of the theatre in Finland. Its popularity means that it has always been intended for the common people. The theatre has never been mastered by a single class or group; there is, for example, no court-theatre tradition. The earliest manifestations of histrionic art can be found in pagan rites and in Catholic Church plays when the audience was asked to participate in the processions and part-songs. But as an independent professional art the theatre only developed in the middle of the nineteenth century.

There had been a period of touring vaudeville companies in the late eighteenth and early nineteenth centuries, but they were all foreign groups performing in Swedish or German. Only a minor part of the population was able to understand their spoken performances, so they often had in their company circus artists, acrobats, and fire-eaters. Essentially non-verbal, these especially appealed to audiences in the cities on the southern coast, Turku, Helsinki and Viborg (now Soviet territory). Even late in the nineteenth century the circus was the kind of entertainment that could connect different language groups. People seem to have money for circus, but for theatre it was different. The Swedish people went to their theatre and the Finnish people went to their own. But it was a long time before the Finns could have any theatre in their own language.

At the beginning of the nineteenth century the long political unity of Finland with Sweden was broken, and Finland became an autonomous Grand Duchy of Russia. Swedish remained the language of the upper class, but among its members a national enthusiasm was awakened which had direct influence upon the future of the literature and the theatre. Could it be possible to raise the Finnish language, well-known for its rich folklore tradition but entirely unpolished, to the position of the principal instrument of cultural life?

Emotional optimism grew alongside political and economic liberalism. At first, the outlook was not very favourable. For a period publication in Finnish was restricted to books on religion or economy. But a national ambition had been fanned into flame and nothing could stop it.

Concurrently, the Swedish theatre developed among the upper-class families, partly professional, partly amateur in character. It became customary to present small plays and tableaux in family celebrations and charity soirées. Sometimes songs in Finnish could be sandwiched in a Swedish play, as happened as early as the 1830s in a melodrama called *The Finnish Girl*, or *The Foundling in the Graveyard*. University students, engaged both in politics and in the arts, were responsible for the first theatre performances in Finnish. However, co-operation between the Finnish and Swedish theatre groups could not be realized in a fruitful way. The first all-Finnish theatre company, the Finnish Theatre, later the National Theatre, was founded in 1872. This theatre had to prove that the language of the common people was able to transmit both the tragic depths and comic outbursts of verbal dramatic expression. Since then, language has been one of the dominating features of the Finnish theatre. The actors did not consider themselves artists or entertainers, but national pioneers devoted to the cause of the Finnish people and language. Its first director, Kaarlo Bergbom (1843-1906), was well acquainted with the European theatrical traditions and brought to the theatre both modern and classical plays. The first great actress on the Finnish stage was Ida Aalberg (1857-1915), a country girl who made an international career as a tragedienne in the style of Bernhardt and Duse. In her own country she became the idol of all theatre-lovers, despite the fact that Naturalism was outside her range.

Although the presentations of the Finnish theatre were well received, the theatre was not appreciated by as wide a public as had been intended, and its popularity was not followed by economic success. The greater number of potential theatre-goers were to be found in Helsinki, the capital, with a population of about 7,000 in 1870 and about 14,000 in 1880. The salaries and expenses of the theatre were kept at a minimum, but the company had to undertake extensive tours to bring in the necessary funds. They criss-crossed the country, stopping for a few weeks to a couple of months in the towns they visited; they received an enthusiastic reception wherever they appeared. These tours gave the public an opportunity of seeing various examples of the theatrical art in their own language. An illustrative anecdote tells of a farmer who, having seen his first theatre performance in Finnish, said: 'Well, maybe one has seen theatre before, but what has it meant when one has not been able to understand it.' The importance of understanding made the theatre something of an educational process.

The Finnish Theatre was soon followed by other repertory companies, each receiving some financial support from a board of trustees and from the government. They formed a basic theatrical structure which still prevails in Finland. In 1887 the People's Theatre was started in Tampere and in 1897 the Country Theatre in Viborg. Although the political climate and general conditions were worsening, popular interest in the theatre was greater than ever. The effect of the professional theatres was reflected in the interest of the common people, especially among rural farm people and urban workers. With the establishment of workers' unions the theatre became a popular activity which suited the young people very well; it gave them opportunities for developing their capacities for expression and for educating their audiences. In many cities workers' acting groups became regular theatre companies. At first all the actors were amateurs and performed without salary, but gradually the manager and the principal actors became full-time professionals. The most important workers' theatre was founded in Tampere, and it is still one of the leading theatres of the country. Its example was followed in many cities, and playing became almost as popular as watching plays.

It was not difficult to make people visit the theatre once — but how to keep their interest alive? During the first years of the twentieth century, especially, the theatre came up against many problems. Theatre-goers found a new sort of entertainment in the cinema and critical opinion was divided as to the artistic and cultural utility of the theatres. At the end of the nineteenth century the director of the Finnish Theatre could still say, 'We are the theatre'; now the public began to cry, 'The theatre is for us'.

The director of the Country Theatre at the turn of the century kept a diary which throws some interesting light on the difficulties of the theatre at that time. Sometimes he himself slipped into the auditorium at the beginning of an important scene and sobbed at the right moment to encourage the audience in their own response. The theatre was the home of actors who were used to long tours and had very little private life. Alcohol was one of the major problems, and the actors were severely punished if found drunk. The director records: 'Every morning I went to the theatre and was prepared to see one-half of the actors drunk and the other half quarrelling. When I found I was wrong, I became happy for the whole day.' Quite often the actors had to take alcohol simply as a means of warming up in the cold and unhealthy houses where the theatre performances were given.

The theatre people were directed by a strong feeling that their work was important to everyone and that everyone ought to understand their message. From the very beginning the need for native plays became evident. Fortunately, at the same time there was a great interest among Finnish authors to attempt drama in their own language, and a few plays had been written in Finnish before the Finnish theatre had ever started. But to win the general public a special genre of popular drama, rural folk comedy, seemed to be most successful.

To trace the origins of the folk comedy one has to go back to old dances and games which formed a part of the yearly celebrations of festival days — Christmas, Midsummer and Harvest time. They met the expectations of the general public, combining a simple fable with a great deal of action and typical characters of a country village. Their language was simple and concrete, and their lyrical moments recall the bold idioms and clichés of folk poetry rather than the complex nuances of literary drama. The familiar settings and characters were also used to point a moral, the chief themes being to criticize superstition, social prejudices and such bad habits as drinking and greediness. The influence of Gogol and Holberg can be clearly seen in the first attempts of the Finnish comedy writers. They include *Silmänkääntäjä* (*The Miracle Man*) by Pietari Hannikainen in the 1850s and *Nummisuutarit* (*The Village Cobblers*) by Aleksis Kivi in the 1860s. Kivi is the greatest representative of nineteenth-century Finnish literature, the founder of both epic prose and drama. *The Village Cobblers* has not lost its popularity during the century it has been played. It is a masterpiece of rural comedy and has also a high literary and aesthetic value. One of the reasons for its continuing success is Aleksis Kivi's inborn sense for the dramatic, the other his extraordinary ability to use the language to express the way of life and the feelings of his countrymen. *The Village Cobblers* was given its first performance by the Finnish Theatre in 1875 and has since belonged to the repertory of most theatres. In the last ten years special festival performances attended by thousands of visitors have been given in the open air in Kivi's home village, Nurmijärvi.

The Village Cobblers can be taken as the paradigm of a folk play. Its characteristics have reappeared again and again in the pattern of the plays that follow: the weak husband who prefers drink to work; the strong and dominating mother, and children who, for the most part, are rather good-natured than clever. There is a disputed will; intrigue develops between the persons trying to benefit from it and those fulfilling the conditions set by it. There are various conflicting love affairs and both true and false marriage promises. Brandy is a powerful catalyst and leads to fantasy, violence and remorse. The end is harmonious, giving a satisfactory solution to the marriage problems and a moral lesson to all participants. Family relationships are restored on the basis that goodness and human kindness will win over selfishness and bad temper.

As a background feature of this comedy one can see the increasing tension between country life and urban life, and this pattern becomes more and more important as new playwrights turn up. It is a subject for both tragedy and comedy. Typically the setting of a tragedy is a city and the setting of a comedy a country village. The social ties in a village are clear and natural, love and money are the traditional stimuli of the action. The atmosphere is familiar and strongly pervaded by natural urges: everyone is looking for someone with whom to mate, old widows and bachelors as well as spinsters and poor servants. The plays very often contain excellent realistic situations and typical characters whose sayings have since become proverbs. The dialogue has the necessary comic overtones, and typical dramatic effects are, for instance, a girl appearing in boy's dress or messages of love being sent to the wrong person. The established social order can be changed only by innocent love which rises above individual ambition.

The most well-known of the rural comedies were written by Maria Jotuni (1880-1943) and Maiju Lassila (1868-1918), but they were followed by a great number of minor playwrights who did not aim at artistic value and literary quality but simply at funny and entertaining productions. They were rejected by the established theatres but were often performed by amateur actors and were thus called 'club plays'. They were written by the dozen and often published by private enterprise or by youth clubs. Many of them were simplified versions of literary comedies using the same motifs and settings but making less demands on the characterization and artistic ability of the performers.

Finland became an independent state in 1917. This gave new emphasis to national feeling, but it also resulted in a split between the classes, and left-wing activities, including workers' theatres, had difficulty surviving on their own. At the same time the institutionalization of the theatres rapidly proceeded. Theatre companies were given financial aid by the government and by municipal authorities. In many cases limited funds led to a fusion of the workers' theatre and the bourgeois theatre and a resultant concentration of their manpower and material resources. The intent in such cases was to offer theatre to all people, but the workers did not follow their actors to the new theatres.

There are at present thirty-two Finnish and four Swedish theatres, all with vast ensembles and large repertoires working in their own houses and serving a total public of about two million yearly. But a widely dispersed population and differences in economic development do not give equal opportunities to all people to visit the theatre. Each theatre has its own public who attend almost all local performances, but a large majority now seems to be alienated from the theatre. In some parts of the country this majority is largely due to a strong religiosity which still considers theatre sinful. The general population now receives its theatre experiences mostly from television serials, the majority of which are imported and have no connections with their life. In the theatre repertoires the native plays have always formed a majority, varying approximately from 30 to 40 per cent of all plays produced.

As a result of the strong influence of television entertainment, the needs for theatrical enjoyment, and increased official support to the theatres, the idea of reorganizing the theatres gained in importance at the end of the 1960s. It was considered unfair that only a small percentage of the tax payers had much chance to see theatre. The aim now was to give as many as possible a choice of participating in theatre performances in spite of local or social aspects. To this end a number of professional touring theatre groups were formed. These groups did not only want to go to different parts of the country with their 'portable theatres', they also wanted to offer audiences an alternative to the traditional repertoires of the institutional theatres. Many young directors and actors, who wanted to experiment in collective methods of production, were highly critical of the hierarchical system of the institutionalized theatres.

There are at present seven free groups, six Finnish and one Swedish. Three of them cater mainly for children and young people. They are all independent and democratic in the sense that the members equally take part in all decisions. The plays are usually written by a playwright belonging to the group or by a team of its members, though a group may also commission a play on a special topic from a writer outside the theatre. The place of performance may be a playground, a classroom or a library, a hospital or a prison hall. The productions and the props are planned so that no special requirements are necessary.

About one-third of all productions have been prepared specially for children. The Ahaa Theatre has visited schools all over Finland. Its plays often combine educational and entertaining elements; it has dealt, for instance, with the problems of cigarette smoking and drug addiction. Examples of foreign cultures and international solidarity are introduced into the performances in the form of songs and scenes. In 1971 it was given a State Award for its dramatization of *Robin Hood*. Another group, the Penny Theatre, has prepared a popular play about children's problems in traffic and described the process of decisionmaking in a way which is easily understood by children. The groups have also produced some revivals of the classics, including rural comedies, which give the urban public an opportunity to confront its own roots in the past. Another typical example is the KOM theatre, with its special politico-social line. Its productions have described critically Finnish history during the last centuries. Its point of view is that of the working class and the players have also selected specific topics such as the immigration of Finnish workers to Sweden and the economical and emotional problems in developing areas. Many of the groups have visited Sweden and other countries and in Sweden have played especially for the Finnish groups of workers living in a poor cultural environment.

The popularity of the new theatre groups is connected with their political awareness. The performances are often followed by discussions, and the groups feel that contact with the audiences is necessary for their work. They have found their way both to working-class people in the cities and to far-away villages where there are no proper theatre buildings and there is little idea of what theatre can be. The groups receive an annual subsidy from the community which covers about 30 per cent of their expenses (compared to approximately 70 per cent to the institutional theatres). Different kinds of co-operation between the authorities and the groups have been worked out. Recently the fourth city in Finland, Espoo, announced that it would finance thirty children's performances of a specially devised play from one of the groups. Similar agreements on a minor scale have been made elsewhere. The groups have given the Finnish theatre a new profile and a new kind of popularity.

During its one hundred years of existence the Finnish theatre has wandered on an ambitious but narrow road. There has been no music hall tradition, nor any pantomime or burlesque, and hardly any puppet theatre. The variety artists have been confined to the big restaurants. But if it lacks variety, the Finnish theatre yet has a depth and sincerity which gives it an opportunity to reach the masses. Its native tone has always been its greatest source of popularity.

Bibliography

Aspelin-Haapkylä, Eliel, *Suomalaisen teatterin historia* (*The History of the Finnish Theatre*), Helsinki, 1906-10.

Koskimies, Rafael, *Suomen Kansallisteatteri 1902-1917* (*The Finnish National Theatre — 1902-1917*), Helsinki, 1953.

Report of the Theatre Centre, Helsinki, 1973 (manuscript).

Tiusanen, Timo, *Teatterimme hahmottuu* (*The Outlines of our Theatre*), Helsinki, 1969.

Veistäjä, Verneri, *Viipurin ja muun Suomen teatteri* (*The Theatre of Viborg and other Parts of Finland*), Helsinki, 1957.

VIVEKA HAGNELL

Is the Established Theatre Popular?

Audience Research among Newcomers and Connoisseurs

When approaching the subject 'Western Popular Theatre' we have to ask ourselves: Does it exist? Is there any popular theatre in the Western world today? The answer depends upon what we mean by popular theatre. If the final criteria for popular theatre is that it is a theatre widely spread, a theatre which a large number of people make use of today, the answer is the television-theatre. Television-theatre is our modern folk theatre according to the criterion that it is watched by a wide range of people. Drama is one of the items on the television programme with a very high percentage of viewers and not only viewers from a high-brow cultural stratum.

The radio/TV theatres and the stage theatre, however, belong both technically and aesthetically to different media. Radio and television constitute a complement but not a substitute for the stage theatre with its direct confrontation between the performers and their audience who are physically present in the same room. And this is not an academic question! According to a new Swedish Government Bill on Culture, stage performances transmitted through TV are to be a relatively inexpensive means of giving quality theatre to all the people in this fairly large country, wherever they may live. During the cultural-political discussions on the subject of state subsidies to certain kinds of theatres, which accompanied the preparation of the bill, it has become clear that it is necessary to consider the effects of dramatic performance on the audience, not only to avoid possibly harmful effects of watching violence enacted, but also to find out how, for instance, stage theatre transmitted through TV affects people (e.g. in terms of activity-passivity, as escapism, or as a stimulus to make conclusions pertaining to their own lives), both in comparison to stage-theatre and to TV-theatre made exclusively for the medium.

What are the prospects for a philanthropic cultural policy? Has the theatre any value in itself? Is the fact that theatre has existed for some thousand years a sign of its inherent value? We do not think so.

We know how institutions and values that have been looked upon as something eternal are now regarded as something obsolete and we are happy that this is the case. It is worth keeping in mind that theatre may now belong to a conquered stage and that the time has come for new media. But in the present situation, when we no longer — as with the mystery plays of the fifteenth century or the theatre of the fairs of the sixteenth and seventeenth centuries — have a vigorous collection of all groups, categories and classes united in and around the theatre as something of vital importance, we must question the conditions of existence and indispensability of the theatre. There have been many well-meaning attempts to give the theatre increased distribution. There are reasons for asking if theatre has a value in itself. Why do people feel no need for theatre in the way they did in earlier centuries? Could it be that the fault lies not so much with the audience as with theatre itself; that it cannot satisfy our demand that it offer justification of our lives.

These were the sort of questions that Romain Rolland posed in 'Le Théâtre du Peuple' when he wanted to devise a theatre which was to serve not only as leisure-time enjoyment for a new group of consumers but which, as he intended to reshape the theatre itself, was to become an arsenal for new thoughts and visions available to the large groups of people who had access to neither objects of art nor political power. The examples are, however, manifold. One could mention Arnold Wesker's Centre 42, Roger Planchon's theatre work at Villeurbanne and many others. Romain Rolland's programme does not allow for the likelihood that his theatre, made by certain groups of people in a given historical situation, will be handed over to new groups of people in a new historical situation. A cultural policy with a limited vision is always liable to fail.

Much of the work that has been done at a young research institute, 'The Institute for Theatre and Film Research' in Lund, Sweden, has been based on these theoretical and historical assumptions. Some of the results are published in our duplicated series, 'Drama-theatre-film'. We have involved ourselves with answering these questions mainly because of the importance we have attached to them.

Much criticism can be directed against conventional ways of conducting audience research, particularly against the weaknesses of interview technique. To many theatre historians, amazingly enough, the computer is not an instrument for rapid and precise tabulation but a sign that the user is not really a sensitive humanist. However, as audience research is a necessary field in modern theatre research on the living theatre, the methods have to be developed and made more ingenious. A combination of focused interviews, physical registration of audience response, scaling techniques and different sorts of indirect questions is, if diligently applied, a way to trace the truth about these matters.

An example of a field study in theatre audience research will be briefly discussed below. The example is chosen mainly because of its cultural-political interest. It has been carried out at The Institute for Theatre and Film Research in Lund by Professor Ingvar Holm, mag. art., Jane Rasch and myself. The aim of the investigation was to study the relationship between *form* (the qualities of the finished performance which can be observed and measured in the interaction with an audience), *experience* (the perception and inter-pretation of and immediate emotional response towards the work of art) and *effect* (the increase in cognitive and emotional experience which the work of art may cause and on the other hand the change in opinions and attitudes which may result from this new experience) with members of an audience on their first visit to the theatre.

What will happen if we invite to the theatre people who have never been there before? How do they interpret what they see in comparison to people who are habitués, well accustomed to the phenomenon? What do they choose to note, what themes do they follow, what do they do after the visit to the theatre, how has the performance affected their lives? It is most important to be familiar with this aspect before one tries to spread theatre, make the distribution system efficient, the tickets easily accessible, arrange baby-sitters for the audience etc.

As there are no theatre productions especially made for newcomers among the adult audiences, the usual first meeting with theatre is a performance from the ordinary repertoire. But is the established theatre in, for example, the Scandinavian countries so 'popular' that it appeals to newcomers? What is the special kind of knowledge one has to have to get something out of a performance today? Does a connoisseur who goes to the theatre regularly get more out of it on account of what he has learnt at the theatre or from other kinds of education? Or does the newcomer get a fresher and more important experience just because he does not see a production with a uniformed eye?

The study mentioned was based on Holstebro, a small commercial town on the west coast of Denmark, quite some distance from the capital. The place was chosen mainly for two reasons: 1. It was a normal state of affairs for people not to go to the theatre, and 2. Holstebro is a culturally expanding town, which is why the opportunity for choosing theatre-going as an alternative in one's leisure time was there. The Danish Theatre with its richly varied touring repertoire regularly visits Holstebro, and the town has one permanent theatre, Eugenio Barba's exclusive Odin Theatre.

The investigation worked with stratified samples of first-time theatre-goers, where certain factors (approach to life, education, place of work, etc.) were controlled. Their reactions were compared to those of theatre-goers who, all their lives, had been to the theatre extensively and who saw almost every production given in the town. In both cases, however, the project involved subjects who had been invited to come to the theatre, not people who had desired to come on their own initiative (800 in all).

Three productions were chosen representing an Artaud-Grotowski line, a realistic-social line (Wesker is a predecessor) and a Brechtian line — approaches to drama equally prevalent in the Scandinavian theatre today. The first production chosen was the Dane Peter Seeberg's *Ferai* at The Odin Theatre, directed by the original Grotowski disciple, Eugenio Barba. It was a strongly physical, psychoanalytical production with fundamental human situations — funerals, weddings, proclaimings of state philosophy, scourgings of faithful subjects, wild cult-worship, rituals, orgies and fights. The second sub-study was concerned with a social documentary play, the Danish Theatre's production of the Swedish author Bengt Bratt's *The Warehouse Manager*. It showed everyday problems at a place of work. The third and last production was Bertolt Brecht's *The Threepenny Opera*, which was another touring production of the Danish Theatre. The purpose behind this choice was to test whether a new audience might be created in a situation where the theatre was represented by three of the most important lines in the stage art of the twentieth century.

The plot of *Ferai* can be told in a few words. An old man, King Frode, is dead. A younger man takes his place and wants to effect certain changes in the state. The people react and the conflict ends with the suicide of a woman, King Frode's daughter. This material, these human situations in the strong, cruel play, mark the starting-point for a process of deciphering which every member of the audience has to conduct himself. What is beneath the surface in the play is irrational and contradictory. The director Eugenio Barba describes his theatre as a theatre for the alpinist:

> I think that the kind of theatre that we are working with, applies to people with very special needs. One can ask why there are alpinists, why some people risk their lives to climb mountains 15,000 feet high, when they comfortably could walk in a park

without risking anything at all. Which of these ways is the better, I do not know. But they feel a need to challenge themselves and to break down limitations imposed upon them.[1] We need no field investigation to tell us that the meeting between Barba and Holstebro is something of a paradox. What strikes us immediately about the expansive cultural town, with its certainty of belief and its pedagogics, and the ultra-theatre which is described in Barba's words about performance is not their similarities. Holstebro numbers its souls in thousands, while Barba speaks of the few, the alpinists.

Barba admits no more than seventy people at the same time to see *Ferai*, as he does not want the individuals to feel themselves being drowned in a mass audience but to be able to react individually. When he was asked about interpretations of the play, his answer was:

When the author wrote a text he built a sphinx. The riddle of the sphinx he does not know. It is the task for the director and the actors to find it. However, in the very moment they do so, they make a new sphinx, the riddle of which they cannot explain themselves; only other people can, the spectators.

The results from the sub-study of the audience showed, among other things, that the group of people who could be designated 'connoisseurs' was quite happy about their experience. They had interpreted the play in terms of beautiful and melancholic young love. They said that they would feel satisfied with their new king (had they been inhabitants of the town of Ferai) and they followed, all the way through the play, the story of him and his wife, the old king's daughter. They had thus reduced the drama to a charming and pleasant theme and declared that they would willingly see much more like it. They had concentrated their attention on two spectacular scenes, one characterized by forceful movement (a fight between two pretenders to the throne), the other by visual beauty and miracle (the suicide and self-sacrifice of the king's daughter). The group of spectators who had never before been to the theatre had, on the other hand, experienced the dangerous and 'difficult', the struggle for regal power and the disastrous conflicts in the play. They had difficulties in taking sides with the rivals. A large group turned back to the dead king and more than 30 per cent of the group were not able to choose between the alternatives. Two scenes where the dead king posthumously played the leading part were especially noticed by this group (irrational scenes difficult to decipher where a white egg — the king's head? — was worshipped as a relic in a ritual procession). The newcomers declined any further invitations to similar kinds of theatre.

The fact that the spectators who had a fairly superficial experience of the performance judged it benevolently is rather more disturbing than that the spectators who had seen something of the dark depths of the play (or of themselves) answered: No more, please! The experienced group did not listen to the appeal to solve the riddle of the performance — they were skilled enough to avoid becoming affected by such summons, while the newcomers were not protected against the Rorschach Test of this kind of theatre. When Barba was interviewed for the investigation he spoke of a theatrical tradition which had only attached importance to the logic of words, which he considered a faulty approach:

> In the theatre the words are not allowed to be revealed through bodily reactions, and thus they cannot express the tension between emotion and intellect, intention and action. When a spectator is confronted with a theatre which is faithful to the contradictory nature of life he becomes confused. This is part and parcel of a conditioned attitude to theatre, in which only a mechanical, one-sided picture of Man is presented.

The following analysis is quoted from our Swedish manuscript:

> From the first scene *Ferai* is an example of the dialectic which Barba speaks of here. The scourging of faithful subjects, the message of brotherhood flowing out over literally grovelling citizens, wild cult-worship of Frode, whose cruelty the whole story expresses: all this provides a stimulus for continued work and problem-solving. It is this sub-aspect that the connoisseurs observe, the problematic, difficult and enigmatic in so much human behaviour. No one in the audience could fall back upon earlier theatre experience to solve the human riddle which was at the base of this production.
>
> If we ignore this contradictory, irrational side of the play, *Ferai* could be a *Romeo and Juliet* (or almost any play!) — but not, take note, the *whole* of *Romeo and Juliet*, only the struggle for power, the possession and the disastrous factiousness have been reduced even in this drama.

It is to be noted that it was this very aspect of *Ferai* that the connoisseurs observed in the experimental situation which the field study had brought about. The habitual theatre-goers considered *Ferai* to be 'a lovely play' and they would like to see many more productions of the same kind. That an audience which has not been spoiled by theatre can actually notice what is 'difficult' about theatre when reacting to scenes, characters and conflicts is the most important result of this sub-investigation so far. At the same time it is understandable that the same audience declines any further invitations; this is something that a living theatre must take as a challenge. When the Odin Theatre received its mandate at Holstebro, it meant the chance to try out exclusive theatre in the conditions of the popular stage. This is what makes it unique — a paradox transformed into cultural policy. This is only one of the possible alternatives for the first meeting of the unknown, previously quite anonymous audience with theatre. But there are also other alternatives.

The second production subjected to investigation was Bengt Bratt's *The Warehouse Manager*. The play dealt with a number of workers in a warehouse. Among everyday incidents, the older manager was sacked in favour of a younger and less experienced man. The play illustrated the routine of the work, but the realism was heightened so as to make the newspaper critics remember Chekhov, Kafka and Ionesco. The setting was, however, contemporary and none of the characters too sophisticated.

Was this a kind of theatre that appealed to the newcomers? Or was it so grey and monotonous that one had to be a habitué to like it? The director professed that he had made the production with the habitual theatre-goers in mind. Had the production, all the same, anything to communicate to a newcomer? Would, for instance, a worker who had experience from a similar kind of milieu as was shown in the performance react differently to other members of the audience?

According to the results of the investigation about 50 per cent of the connoisseurs rated the performance they had seen positively. The figures were the same for the newcomers. Equally large numbers in both groups wanted to recommend the production to their friends and as many as 77 per cent in both groups confessed that they judged the production to be important. The two groups had seen the same performance of the production but they had noticed different things in what they had seen.

For example, in their choice of themes in the performance the newcomers were more fettered by the actions that took place in the room, before their eyes, by the warehouse functioning as a place of work. They were apt to criticize the workers' lack of responsibility in their work. The connoisseurs had recognized alternative themes which they stated as a longing to be away from the given situation, a wish for greater freedom, a fear of authorities, etc. Whilst most of the newcomers interpreted the performance of the play realistically, the connoisseurs often saw openings into an absurd and escapist direction as well. In short, the connoisseurs saw more ways of interpreting the performance and followed the behaviour of many parts of the play (and the characters' dreams back to the past), while the newcomers concentrated upon the two persons who carried the plot, the two managers. They had, quite consistently, considered the scene of change of power as the most important — a decisive turning-point in the chain of events that eventually led to the sacking of the old manager.

It is also noteworthy that a larger percentage of the newcomers had recognized the working conditions in the warehouse from reality, while the connoisseurs found the relations between the workers in the warehouse and the office credible — and were thus a step higher in the hierarchy of the place of work. This difference between the groups reflects the different positions of the spectators in society. Those people who had made theatre one of their leisure-time occupations could also, more easily than the others, express what they thought was the opinion of the playwright, a result that probably depends on the higher general education of this group rather than mere familiarity with theatre.

Bratt's *The Warehouse Manager* was distinguished from *Ferai* at the Odin Theatre chiefly through being a production directly related to working life. However, the group that was not attracted by the theatre in its traditional forms or that at least did not attend the performances offered, had more experience of the type of the work-environment which the play depicts and enacts. As might be expected, the extent of their previous knowledge of the work environment largely determined the degree of the newcomers' empathic response to the play, though this was not invariably the case. One notices, instead, a strange echo of similar results analysed in the study of *Ferai*. One would have expected their interest to have been directed towards techniques of work and problems which reflected political valuations of their work. Instead, it is the strong confrontation between two generations in the warehouse, which was also difficult to analyse, that made the newcomers react. As in *Ferai* there is little of the clear, logical justification of why one should support one or the other of the two men in the conflict or for that matter why the conflict resulted in the crisis it did. The author of the play solved the problem through stating that it is *not* a picture of the labour market but a picture of the absurdities of the struggle for power.

A theatre that, when it works with urgent questions of human relationships, has no answer to give but that, instead, stimulates questions, is in line with the essence of the art form. One can maintain that the struggle of the two men, one of whom takes over the rôle as the warehouse manager, depicts the moments of unpleasant confrontation, difficult points offering material for reflection which are in line with the essence of theatre. A few of these moments were observed by the newcomers in the audience when *The Warehouse Manager* was in repertoire, in a similar way as when *Ferai* was subjected to study.

The third production chosen at Holstebro was Bertolt Brecht's play *The Threepenny Opera*. The director had staged the play as a Danish folk-comedy interlarded with vulgar and coarse elements. The part of Mrs Peachum was an extreme example of this, while the part of Mr Peachum was reduced (38 per cent of his words were cut). It was, however, a choreographic production with a beggars' parade, pop-music and with the romantic poetry emphasized.

Those who had been to the theatre many times before applied an aesthetic model of experience, while the newcomers used a more concrete model of experience. This difference determined the result that the habitués liked the performance better, thought that it had an important message of immediate interest and expressed a wish to see more plays by the same author. They stressed the theatrical devices and subtleties when they criticized the production while the newcomers drew in irrelevant material, such as that the coarse language was offensive. Mrs Peachum completely dominated the experience of the habitués; they liked her because of the acting, not because of her character. They had also enjoyed the smartness of Macheath and the smoothness of the plot more than the newcomers. The newcomers did not pick out certain members of the cast but rather certain scenes. They enjoyed especially the jealousy scene, a scene full of physical activity, and they remembered the scenes between Polly and Mac and the conflict between Polly and the older generation, i.e. they noticed the scenes with an emotional content more than the ideological scenes which the habitués appreciated.

There is a lot more to be said about the reactions of the audience to each of these productions but as it can hardly be done without giving a thorough analysis of each production, it had better be left out.

When theatre historians speak about the audience, they usually mean the people actually in the theatre, watching certain productions. Often the potential audience not yet in the theatre is not included in the definition. The point in this article is *not* that people who are quite inexperienced as far as theatre is concerned should in any way be a better audience than the regulars, but that the new-comers seem often to experience *other* things in a performance than do the connoisseurs — they are often less prejudiced and more open to the interpretation or the message of the director.

This statement is also supported by other investigations made at The Institute for Theatre and Film Research. When *Romeo and Juliet* was staged in Malmö in 1967, three hundred people, drawn from the census register, who would not have gone to see the production otherwise, were invited to the theatre. The theatre critics, habitués indeed, seemed programmed to stress certain scenes (for instance the balcony scene) which the critics, according to an analysis of fifty reviews from earlier Swedish productions of the same play, paid attention to in every production of the play. This tendency may be based upon an assumption among the critics of what their readers want to know. They execute an order for information even in productions where those facts are of minor importance. What the specially invited novices, unfamiliar with the theatre, observed was the specific dimension of the production in question, the reason for the director to produce the play, her alibi for working with this sixteenth-century play. The newcomers were less restricted by tradition and knowledge of expected demands.

Popularization is not a question of the theatre staging old types of plays with simplified typologies, but of touching upon essential subject matter (the situation of man, relations between people, simple things like survival ...), of putting questions like: What is Macbeth basically about, what is Werther about? If the question is thrown to one thousand habitual theatre-goers, they will regard the play as something difficult, incomprehensible, unrelated to the daily problems of survival. But people unaccustomed to theatre may have keys which do not belong to the tradition.

This is not the right place to state which kind of theatre a newcomer should visit to gain a positive experience or how he should prepare himself before going there. The aim of this article has only been to point out how we must take into account the complexities of a theatre audience when we discuss 'popular theatre.'

Notes

1   Holm, Hagnell and Rasch, *Kultur Modell Holstebro* (Cavefors, Lund, 1976).

SINCLAIR GOODLAD

Approaches to Popular Drama through the Social Sciences

At 9.25 p.m. on Thursday, 18 January 1973, 37 per cent of the United Kingdom population over the age of five watched an episode of 'Colditz' on BBC 1 television. Why? I doubt whether even the warmest admirers of this drama series about the efforts of a handful of British officers to escape from a German prisoner-of-war camp would claim that the drama is distinguished by depth of characterization, subtlety of theme, ingenuity of plot, charm of *mise-en-scène* or elegance of style. As an item of modern theatre, 'Colditz' is technically neither better nor worse than many other similar productions. Scholars concerned with the artistic originality of an art form will likely give it but passing interest. However, to the social scientist, any cultural phenomenon which commands the simultaneous interest of over 18 million citizens of these islands cannot but be of the most intense interest[1].

In this paper, I will sketch some of the issues of theory and of methodology which exercise social scientists in approaching such forms of popular drama, and hope thereby to suggest questions which may be of interest to theatre critics and theatre historians.

In form, theatre is of interest to the social scientist as an institutionalized form of social behaviour. In content, it is of interest because it deals in norms and values of society, portraying alternative forms of social behaviour. The major question to which one would like an answer is: does theatre *reflect* or *control* our understanding of the social world? Clearly, such a general question cannot be answered directly: it must be broken down into smaller questions amenable to systematic examination. Any method of breaking a large question into smaller ones implies some form of social theory. It is the symbiosis of theory and method which, in my view, characterizes the social sciences, and which I intend to illustrate in this paper.

The primary activity in any scientific endeavour is that of *classification*. In the physical sciences, experimentation is largely a strategy by which to test (by systematically seeking to disprove) a scheme of classification. An 'explanation' has been achieved when a scheme of classification of suitable comprehensiveness has been arrived at. Many statements in social science *imply* a programme of experimentation, even though, in fields such as sociology and social anthropology, no procedure of experimentation may be specifically mentioned. For example, Georges Gurvitch, in a seminal essay on 'The sociology of the theatre' (1956), writes as follows:

> The theatre is a *sublimation* of certain social situations, whether it *idealises* them, *parodies* them, or *calls for them to be trans-cended*. The theatre is simultaneously a sort of escape-hatch from social conflicts and the embodiment of these conflicts. From this point of view it contains a paradoxical element, or rather a theatrical dialectic which is supremely a dialectic of ambiguity. The theatre is society or the group looking at itself in various mirrors, the images reflected therein making the people concerned, the spectators, weep, laugh or come to some decision with increased resolution. The theatre offers transcendence and relaxation such that the theatre itself remains a completely integrated part of society, an expression of it, and occasionally, capable of guiding it.[2]

Gurvitch's statement suggests that theatre functions in society both to *express* social values and to *determine* them. Typically, the approaches to culture of the social sciences emphasize either the expressive *or* the instrumental aspects. For example, the methods of structuralism are based upon certain assumptions which have been conveniently summarized by Michael Lane as follows:

1. All patterns of human social behaviour are codes, with the characteristics of languages.
2. Man has an innate structuring capacity which determines the limits within which the structure of all types of social pheno-mena can be formed.
3. Relations can be reduced to binary oppositions.   [3]

The endeavour of structuralist methodology is to uncover the deep structure, configuration, or 'gestalt' underlying our percep-tion of and description of reality. Inevitably, the methodological postulate of an innate structuring capacity achieves the status of a theory. But, of course, the assumption of the *capacity* does not presuppose a theory of what the particular *structure* will be. Claude Lévi-Strauss, for example, in *The Savage Mind*, insists that 'the principle underlying a classification can never be postulated in advance. It can only be discovered a posteriori by ethnographic investigation, that is, by experience'[4]. And he shows in this book, as in others, by empirical observation the immense complexity of primitive thought patterns. The structuralist approach to popular drama would be to show the ordered way in which our perception of the world is structured — for example, through concepts of raw and cooked, male and female, sacred and profane, good and bad, even, foreign and native. Emphasis would most likely be not on an hypothesis that popular drama *caused* us to see the world in this way, but that it simply *reflected* the fact that we do so.

By contrast, Peter L. Berger and Thomas Luckmann in their treatise in the sociology of knowledge, *The Social Construction of Reality*, stress that social order exists *only* as a product of human activity (p. 70). For them, symbolic universes are of interest not because they express any deep structure or innate structuring capacity, but because they are the product of institutional order and social interaction. Explanatory schemes, they stress, are highly pragmatic. Proverbs, moral maxims, wise sayings, legends, folk tales, etc. (*cf.* pp. 112-14) are ways through which the individual is systematically taught what is required of him by his society. Symbolic universes, they argue (p. 116), have a nomic function for the individual by putting everything in its right place[5]. Emphasis in the sociology of knowledge is on the maintenance of a world view by repeated reinforcements. And popular drama may be seen as one of many forms of reinforcement. Indeed, in a recent book *Theatricality: A Study of Convention in the Theatre and in Social Life*, Elizabeth Burns has presented just this view of the social function of drama:

> The *social* function of drama, as of children's play (and films, fiction, and, formerly, poetry) is to supply the means whereby social inconsistencies and unbridgeable gaps with which the world constantly confronts us can be tied into the pre-existing thematically relevant world of social reality which has been constructed for us and by us as a total set of typifications. From Greek drama on, the dramatist and the theatre have provided audiences, i.e. representatives or sections of contemporary society, with the means whereby the anomic can be rendered nomic: comprehensible within the structure of relevance within which we can work out our lives. By presenting the possibility of some form of abductive reasoning explanation at some level of adequacy can be found.[6]

Elizabeth Burns's concern is with the authenticating conventions by which the provinces of real life and of theatre are defined.

In trying to sort out what distinguishes a drama series like 'Colditz' from any other drama commonly available, what to study and why? Structuralist analysis is not concerned with causality; and much general theorizing in the sociology of knowledge is little concerned with empirical verification. To avoid the number-crunching idiocies of brute empiricism, it is necessary to propose some hypothesis concerned with uses and gratifications — with the *function* of the form of popular drama for a defined audience. My own study, *A Sociology of Popular Drama*[7], was a modest attempt to use the functionalist model for heuristic purposes. Nowadays, functionalism is very unfashionable — although it is widely practised by consenting adults in private. Functionalist analysis may not offer the last word in understanding the social significance of popular drama; but, at least, it offers a systematic programme for observation and seeks to generate propositions capable of being disproved.

R.K. Merton's paradigm for functional analysis given in the first chapter of *Social Theory and Social Structure*[8] is still the most systematic scheme of analysis available; I will, therefore, sketch its heuristic value. Each of Merton's categories could itself provide the focal point of an investigation. However, the value of the paradigm as a whole is that it subdivides leading concepts so that crucial relationships may be the more readily exposed.

Category 1: the items to which functions are imputed
Although a definition is normally the end point of an investigation, it is important to begin one's investigation with a definition — however temporary. To take an apparently trivial example: milk is ... well, what? To define it, we place it in the broadest possible category and then differentiate it from all other items in that category by its distinguishing characteristics. 'Milk is a liquid.' Too broad. 'Milk is a *white* liquid.' Yes, but so is whitewash. 'Milk is a white liquid secreted by mammals.' A considerable improvement; but mammals are known to secrete other white liquids. 'Milk is a white liquid secreted by mammals for the nourishment of their young.' This final definition incorporates a theory about the use or function of the substance.

It is, perhaps, illuminating to see the sort of difficulties one can encounter if one starts with too imprecise a definition. Is drama, for example, a form of play? According to the thesis put forward by Johan Huizinga in *Homo Ludens* it certainly is[9]. The sweep and comprehensiveness of Huizinga's analysis is hypnotizing. Here, at last, seems to be an analysis which relates drama to other forms of social life.

Huizinga describes the principal characteristics of play as follows (pp. 26-9). First, play is a voluntary activity. Secondly, for the adult and responsible human being, play is superfluous: the need for it is only urgent to the extent that the enjoyment of it makes it a need. Play, Huizinga argues, can be deferred or suspended at any time; it is never imposed by physical necessity or moral duty; it is never a task. It is done at leisure, during 'free time'. Huizinga stresses its *disinterestedness*: not being 'ordinary' life, it stands outside the immediate satisfaction of wants and appetites, indeed it interrupts the appetitive process. When it is a sacred activity, and Huizinga includes ritual in his concept of play, it contributes to the well-being of the group, but in quite another way and by other means than the acquisition of the necessities of life.

Thirdly, play is distinct from 'ordinary' life both as to locality and duration. It is secluded, limited, 'played out' within certain limits of time and place. Huizinga is particularly impressive at this point:

> Play begins, and then at a certain moment it is 'over'. It plays itself to an end. While it is in progress all is movement, change, alternation, succession, association, separation....
>
> More striking even than the limitation as to time is the limitation as to space. All play moves and has its being within a playground marked off beforehand either materially or ideally, deliberately or as a matter of course. Just as there is no formal difference between play and ritual, so the 'consecrated spot' cannot be formally distinguished from the play-ground. The arena, the card-table, the magic circle, the temple, the stage, the screen, the tennis court, the court of justice, etc., are all in form and function play-grounds, i.e. forbidden spots, isolated, hedged round, hallowed, within which special rules obtain. All are temporary worlds within the ordinary world, dedicated to the performance of an act apart.
>
> Inside the play-ground an absolute and peculiar order reigns. Here we come across another, very positive feature of play: it creates order, *is* order. Into an imperfect world and into the confusion of life it brings a temporary, a limited perfection. Play demands order absolute and supreme.

As is well known, Huizinga then proceeds to show the way in which his play-concept is expressed in language; is a civilizing function; is found in law, war, knowing, poetry; is the basis of mythopoeisis; is found in forms of philosophy; in art; and is, indeed, the very central element of civilization.

But, one wonders, are drama and *sport* the same thing? A more rigorous examination of different types of play suggests the need for a firmer classification. This has been provided by, for example, Roger Caillois in *Man, Play, and Games* (ch.3)[10]. Caillois proposes four categories as follows: *agon, alea, mimicry* and *ilinx*. All four, he suggests, belong to the domain of play. One *plays* football, billiards or chess (*agon*); roulette or lottery (*alea*); pirate, Nero, or Hamlet (*mimicry*); or one produces in oneself, by a rapid whirling or falling movement, a state of dizziness and disorder (*ilinx*). Even these designations, he argues, do not completely describe play and he distinguishes between a kind of uncontrolled fantasy which he calls *paidia* and, in contrast to frolicsome and impulsive exuberance, a tendency to bind play with arbitrary, imperative and purposely tedious conventions, to put a premium on effort, patience, skill, and ingenuity: he calls this second component *ludus*. Caillois' disciplined analysis helps one to distinguish between different sorts of games and play.

Under *agon*, he groups games which are competitive, where equality of chance is artificially created so that competitors confront each other under ideal conditions, susceptible of giving precise and incontestible value to the winner's triumph. *Alea*, the Latin name for the game of dice, Caillois uses to designate, in contrast to *agon*, all games that are based on a decision independent of the player, where he has no control over the outcome, and in which winning is the result of fate rather than triumph over an adversary. Not only does one refrain from seeking to remove the injustice of chance; rather, it is the capriciousness of chance that makes all men equal and gives the game its unique appeal. *Alea*, Caillois argues, signifies and reveals the favour of destiny. The player is entirely passive; he does not deploy his resources, skill, muscles or intelligence.

Play, whether *agon* or *alea*, is, Caillois suggests, an attempt to substitute perfect situations for the normal confusion of contemporary life. But one can also do this through *mimicry*. The pleasure of mimicry lies in being or passing for someone else — in illusion, which, Caillois points out, means nothing less than beginning a game: *in-lusio*. With one exception, Caillois points out, *mimicry* exhibits all the characteristics of play: liberty, convention, suspension of reality, and delimitation of space and time. However, there is one crucial difference: the continuous submission to imperative and precise rules cannot be observed — rules for the dissimulation of reality and the substitution of a second reality. Mimicry requires incessant invention.

Finally, Caillois reserves the concept of *ilinx* for games which are based upon the pursuit of vertigo, which consist of the attempt to momentarily destroy the stability of perception and inflict a kind of panic upon an otherwise lucid mind: the activities of whirling dervishes, acrobats, and even children rolling down slopes.

Caillois' analysis tidies up considerably the concept of play. But, clearly, *agon* and *mimicry* can still be found in various combinations inside and outside theatre. Indeed, it is still tempting to see sport and popular drama as offering similar satisfactions. The attempt to achieve suitable definitions in each sphere serves to point out not only the differences but also the similarities. For example, J.W. Loy in 'The nature of sport: a definitional effort' [11] has gone some way towards this. First he describes sport as a game occurrence with the following characteristics: (a) it is playful — being free, separate, uncertain, unproductive, governed by rules, make-believe; (b) it involves competition; (c) it relies on physical skill, strategy and chance; (d) it involves physical prowess. Loy then goes on to deal with sport as an institutionalised game. By doing this, he sees it as a distinctive enduring pattern of culture and social structure. It includes values, norms, sanctions, knowledge and social positions (i.e. rôles and statuses). By pointing to its degree of institutionalisation, and analysing empirically its degree of organization, Loy is able to suggest avenues of enquiry which will help to differentiate sport from drama and, where necessary, to isolate its critical and interesting similarities.

The process of definition is, then, itself very illuminating. Simply to distinguish, as Caillois does, different types of play helps one to locate drama as a sub-category. To define even further particularities within a sub-category advances the process of understanding considerably. For example, Elizabeth Burns gives a definition of 'a play' which emphasizes the element of mimicry:

> ... a play is a ritual form of release from the need to act as undivided selves, a reaffirmation of the multiple existential potentialities we incorporate but cannot realize. This reaffirmation by a single person — the playwright — is lived out by players on a stage before hundreds of our fellows in the audience on a totally acceptable, traditionally sanctioned, and unexceptionable occasion, in buildings constructed for this very purpose, and in an institutional context which is connected with everyday existence in all kinds of manifest ways. The theatre thus reveals itself as a ritual device for the constant renewal of belief in human autonomy for individuals required constantly to submit to the vexacious necessities of consistent, recognisable role behaviour in the world of ordered social life. The actor is the

visible, literally corporeal, vehicle of this ritual reaffirmation, conceived by culturally selected individuals but enacted on the stage *on our behalf*.[12]

Her analysis of convention in theatre and in social life, by defining the *differences* involved, thus helps us to understand the function of theatricality in daily living — and also the hypnotic power of theatre.

Category 2: concepts of subjective dispositions (*motives, purposes*)
Merton next observes that at some point, functional analysis invariably assumes or explicitly operates with a conception of the motives of individuals involved in a social system. It is necessary to state what one believes these motives or purposes to be so that one may decide whether one may take such motivations as *data*, or whether, rather, one should treat them as problematical. For example, to say that people watch drama because they 'enjoy it' is not very illuminating. After all, one 'enjoys' a walk in the park, a plate of egg and chips, etc. Do people enjoy drama for 'escape'? The concept becomes fraught with difficulty when, as in March 1974, the real world and the fictional world coalesce — I refer to the participation of show-jumper Ann Moore in the radio serial 'The Archers' — playing *herself!* Are we, then, to believe that show-jumping is itself a form of escape? At what point does one insist that involvement with the 'real' world is 'real' and not 'escape'?

Again, does one take the possible motive of one-upmanship as obvious or problematical? Thorstein Veblen has of course given the classic description of conspicuous consumption in *The Theory of the Leisure Class*:

The quasi-peaceable gentleman of leisure, then, not only con-sumes of the staff of life beyond the minimum required for subsistence and physical efficiency, but his consumption also undergoes a specialisation as regards the quality of the goods consumed. He consumes freely and of the best, in food, drink, narcotics, shelter, services, ornaments, apparel, weapons and accoutrements, amusements, amulets, and idols or divinities. In the process of gradual amelioration which takes place in the articles of his consumption, the motive principle and the proximate aim of innovation is no doubt the higher efficiency of the improved and more elaborate products for personal comfort and well-being. But that does not remain the sole purpose of their consumption. The canon of reputability is at hand and seizes upon such innovations as are, according to its standard, fit to survive. Since the consumption of these more excellent goods is an evidence of wealth, it becomes honorific; and conversely, the failure to consume in due quantity and quality becomes a mark of inferiority and demerit.[13]

Although it is necessary and important to try to achieve as explicit as possible a statement of motives and purposes, these may only perhaps be arrived at inferentially. It is for this reason that Merton distinguishes, as we shall see later, a concept of functional requirements. Indeed, the observable consequences of an individual or group using a cultural item may point to the possible motives for doing so. We turn therefore to Merton's third category.

Category 3: concepts of objective consequences (functions, dysfunctions)
Merton (p. 51) defines functions as those observed consequences which make for the adaptation or adjustment of a given system, and dysfunctions as those observed consequences which lessen the adaptation or adjustment of the system. He also notes the empirical possibility of non-functional consequences — ones which are simply irrelevant to the system being considered. He further distinguishes between manifest functions — those objective consequences contributing to the adjustment or adaptation of the system which are *intended* and recognized by participants in the system, and latent functions — those which are neither intended nor recognized.

In trying to organize one's observations of popular drama with a view to answering the major question (whether popular drama reflects or controls our perception of the social world), it is useful to try and specify what consequences manifest and latent are likely to follow from the consumption of popular drama. One might, for example, generate a hypothetical and necessarily tentative classification of objective consequences as follows:

Manifest function: enjoyment, relaxation.
Latent function: psychic orientation.
Manifest dysfunction: time-wasting, distraction from social duty.
Latent dysfunction: false picture of the world, or perversion — presumed effects of sex and violence in television drama.

One obviously will not know in advance what the consequences of consuming drama will be: the point of Merton's category is to suggest a framework of observation linked to other types of concept and observation.

Category 4: concepts of the unit subserved by the function
Clearly, drama may function differently for different people. For performers, it may have the manifest function of helping them make a living: for the audience it may have the latent dysfunction of narcotizing them, of making them acquiescent through purveying a false picture of the world. It is therefore necessary to specify in some detail for whom one believes the unit to be functional or dysfunctional.

This concept is particularly helpful when one's interest is *popular* drama. For whom is the drama popular? The utilitarian concept of the greatest happiness of the greatest number does not specify whether the emphasis should be on *happiness* or on *greatest number*. For example, a drama series like 'Colditz' may offer a diffuse satisfaction to 18 million people. By contrast, a series (unlikely ever to be screened) featuring flagellation by drunken monks of naked nuns to soft psalm music in Serbo-Croatian monasteries might produce intense satisfaction for sado-masochists.

Emphasis on the question 'Popular for whom?' may point up whole new areas for study. For example, institutional pressures of ownership and control may limit what drama is available in any given time or place. A necessary preliminary to the study of popular drama might, therefore, be a detailed study of the organizational and institutional features of, for example, broadcast organizations or theatre companies so that one could take account of the inhibitions or biasing emphases which they might introduce.

Category 5: concepts of functional requirements (needs, prerequisites)
Perhaps the most difficult concept of all in functional analysis is that of the functional requirements of the system under observation. All forms of uses and gratifications research in mass media studies involve some such conception, whether it is made explicit or remains implicit. It is here that one needs to state as clearly as possible whether the requirements one has in mind are universal or specific. For example, a universal need for the individual to have a sense of his place in society may be posited. If society represents nomos, failure of the individual to perceive his place in an orderly society may result in 'anomie' and action may follow to reduce the tension thus generated — suicide, or perhaps the widely noted heavy use of fiction, radio, etc. by those who feel themselves to be socially deprived. A recent Independent Television series, 'Upstairs Downstairs', featured the lives of domestic

servants in an Edwardian household. Was the evident popularity of that programme a result of a nostalgia for the subtle gradations of social hierarchy with their nomic (if alienating) features temporarily induced by conditions of social upheaval in the world outside — the threat of petrol rationing and acute shortages of lavatory paper? Or do the children of the welfare state long for a more personal form of paternalism? Or, is some deeper and more permanent need revealed by such audience interest?

In positing concepts of functional requirements, one may be forced to work backwards, with all the attendant dangers of arguing in a circle. But even *ex post facto* reasoning may help one to generate hypotheses for future study — particularly if one attends to Merton's sixth category of analysis.

Category 6: concepts of the mechanism through which functions are fulfilled

What description can one give of the mechanisms which operate to perform a designated function? Merton mentions such social mechanisms as rôle-segmentation, insulation of institutional demands, hierarchic ordering of values, social division of labour, ritual and ceremonial enactments. If popular drama is believed to control our perception of the world, does it do so by embodying social values in rôles and displaying the behaviour appropriate to those rôles? Does it induce in us a sense of the 'normal' by contrasting appropriate and inappropriate behaviour? Indeed, if it does this, can we really show that the contrast in a play of alternative behaviours actually *changes* or systematically reinforces our beliefs, rather than simply reflecting an underlying gestalt? When we watch a play, are we, as it were, mentally putting a finger in the water to see what sort of behaviour works or is approved of? Or are we, by our appreciation or rejection of the symbols used, simply displaying the structure of our perceptions?

It is this sort of question which points up the appalling difficulty of empirical investigation. It is valuable for precisely this reason — it makes one wary of social generalizations which are not amenable to systematic exposition.

Category 7: concepts of functional alternatives (functional equivalents or substitutes)

There is a danger in any form of functional analysis of gratuitously assuming a particular social structure to be permanent and all the items in it to be indispensable. Once one abandons that hypothesis, Merton points out, we immediately require some concept of functional alternatives, equivalents or substitutes.

To take a simple example, once one acknowledges that a human being can survive with a wooden leg instead of a normal one, one can investigate the functional equivalents of wood — plastic, metal, etc. Each equivalent or alternative serves the function of the leg in maintaining the viability of the person. As a further effort in defining one's cultural item and in specifying its operation, one must try to see what other cultural items could possibly serve the same function. We have already seen the difficulty of distinguishing in practice between drama and sport. By thrusting emphasis onto the moral content of drama, one may distinguish it from some aspects of sport. However, one may thereby stir up a hornets' nest of other problems. If popular drama serves to control our perception of the world, to give us a sense of right and wrong, do law-courts do the same? Indeed, the 'theatricality' of law-courts, and the frequent appearance in popular drama of scenes set in law-courts, suggests that one must here be rather careful in what one specifies. Again, if one's hypothesis concerns the possibility that patterns of consumption of popular drama reflect and express the deep structure of our perception of the world, are not other cultural products equally expressive? Newspapers, magazines, fair-ground side-shows, etc.? In all these cultural items, the normal world is contrasted with the abnormal — bearded women, giants, hideous murderers, etc.

Category 8: concepts of structural context (or structural constraint)

As Merton points out, the range of variation in the items which *can* fulfil designated functions in a social structure is not unlimited. How narrowly, Merton asks, does a given structural context limit the range of variation in the items which can effectively satisfy functional requirements? Particular forms of theatre may be rooted in particular social environments — as, for example, Jean Duvignaud has suggested in *Sociologie du Théâtre*[14]. But are the forms of theatre which arose at a particular time and place the *only* forms which could have arisen? If not, what is the validity of one's analysis linking a specific type of theatre to a specific time and place?

Category 9: concepts of dynamics and change

There is a danger in functional analysis that social equilibrium may be emphasized at the expense of social disequilibrium. Can one anticipate the direction of social change? And can such anticipation point in any detailed way to the likely changes in theatre practice — and consequently in what becomes popular drama? I do not intend to deal with this category in any detail. Suffice it to note that this necessary category of functional analysis can draw attention to many social factors affecting the form and content of popular drama which might otherwise be neglected. For example, could it be that inflation accounts for the form and content of 'Colditz'? The BBC possesses large studios in which much capital is tied up: it must be highly tempting to mount a drama series of thirteen episodes using the same (rather sparse) set and costumes — rather than mount thirteen separate one-shot plays, each requiring a separate set, etc. Again, did the period of Selective Employment Tax induce theatre directors to select plays with small casts, thus placing a restriction on what was available and what was potentially popular? Small details, I will admit; but necessary if one's description of what is 'popular' is to be accurate — and more so if one's account of the reasons for this popularity are to be coherent and systematic in a way appropriate to social science.

Category 10: problems of validation of functional analysis
Merton's tenth category requires a rigorous statement of the sociological procedures of analysis which most nearly approximate to the *logic* of experimentation. In most social investigations, this means a systematic review of the possibilities and limitations of *comparative* (cross-cultural and cross-group) *analysis.*

In most of this paper so far, I have been stressing the crucial importance of precise definitions. The enviable success of the physical sciences is largely due to the efficiency with which definitions are achieved at an early stage and the consequential precision with which comparative study can be carried out. That is to say, one can compare the properties of an item under widely differing circumstances only if one can control in some systematic way the range of observables. The procedure is perhaps easier in the physical sciences than in the social sciences, for the physical world has a certain concrete 'given-ness', a certain coerciveness in its physical reality. This is not so of the social world. A social situation is an evanescent phenomenon — created by individuals only in a specific time and place. By the same token, a play is similarly evanescent. The conditions of performance and of appreciation on one day may differ wildly from those on another day. Theatre managers know all about weather forecasts! Doomed though it may be to ultimate failure, the attempt to arrange information about popular drama in the sort of positivistic model of functional analysis may be invaluable if one wishes to make cross-cultural studies of what constitutes popular drama, or indeed studies pertaining to one society at different historical periods. The comparative method, sometimes I think coterminous with the mythical Scientific Method, is for the social sciences, like music to the arts, the condition to which all aspire. Indeed, in pursuit of its many charms, Max Weber evolved his celebrated concept of the 'ideal type'. 'Ideal types' are historical constructions drawn from historical data which help one to see the extent to which any specific historical phenomenon approximates to or deviates from the idealized conception. Their purpose, as Weber himself emphasizes, is purely heuristic.

> Such constructions make it possible to determine the typological locus of a historical phenomenon. They enable us to see if, in particular traits or in their total character, the phenomena approximate one of our constructions: to determine the degree of approximation of the historical phenomenon to the theoretically constructed type. To this extent, the construction is merely a technical aid which facilitates a more lucid arrangement and terminology.[15]

The nearest equivalent in literary terms, in my judgment, is the typification of fictional modes evolved by Northrop Frye in *Anatomy of Criticism*[16]. 'Ideal typical' specifications of the characteristics of a specific type of drama help the process of conceptual clarification, with which I have been concerned in this paper, so that one may see what constitutes truly 'popular' drama.

Category 11: problems of the ideological implications of functional analysis
Throughout his paradigm, Merton is at pains to emphasize that functional analysis has no intrinsic commitment to an ideological position. However, *particular* functional analyses and *particular* hypotheses advanced by functionalists may, he suggests, have an identifiable ideological rôle. His final category deals with the need to try to detect and specify any ideological tinge in a programme of functional analysis. Value-free social analysis is a chimera. All one can perhaps do is to specify as clearly as possible the grounds upon which one makes a judgment. This does not, of course, involve removing oneself — with one's aesthetic sensibility and social predispositions and prejudices — from the process of dramatic criticism. Indeed, Weber himself uses the *'verstehen'* method of sympathetic understanding for sociological interpretation. The difference, as I see it, is that traditionally literary criticism is an art

form in which unique insight and original perception is highly valued; social science, by contrast, emphasizes universal agreement, detached observation — in short, a model derived from physical science where it should theoretically be possible for two people to reach the same conclusion from the same data simultaneously. Just as the insights of literary critics may help social scientists to sort out concepts and categories, so too, one would hope, might the obsessively systematic preoccupations of social science provide a platform from which the unique and penetrating insights of the literary approach might take off.

To return then to my original question: 'Why did more than one person in three of the United Kingdom population over the age of five watch "Colditz" at 9.25 p.m. on Thursday, 18 January 1973?' Do the British long for the secure and orderly world of prison? Indeed, one might think so when the Independent Broadcasting Authority, enviously watching the success of 'Colditz', run a series 'Within These Walls' dealing with a women's prison, and achieve singular success thereby. Why at this time in this place should we apparently have such a preoccupation with prisons? Order in a world of disorder? Conflict with a sense of purpose — escape or rehabilitation — when one's daily life is a misery of confused conflicts of apparent purposelessness? Nostalgia for a public school ethos revealed, as one critic has suggested, in 'Colditz' — with the Commandant a benevolent but severe headmaster frowning on 'dorm feasts'? A longing for the selfless devotion and paternal concern of the Governor and Deputy Governor shown in 'Within These Walls' at a time when the country seems to lack any coherent 'Government'?

It would, I think, be foolish to claim that approaches to popular drama through the social sciences have at this stage in time anything much more significant to contribute than the inspired intuition of literary criticism. However, I hope I have been able to suggest that behind every particular observation — involving a methodology — must lie a theory, and that every theory, if taken seriously, involves a methodology. The ever-present danger in social sciences is that social theorizing will become a self-generating process more and more remote from the social reality which it seeks to explain. By contrast, the danger I have found in some theatre history is of more and more refined attention to specific details to the neglect of any strategy (theory) which would render a particular observation meaningful in a wider sense. Somewhere between the two extremes must lie a programme of study which keeps a fruitful balance between theory and methodological detail. In my judgment, the functionalist model — provided it is conceived of as an heuristic tool — has life in it yet.

Notes

1   For these figures of audience size, I am indebted to Miss Joan Robinson, Audience Research Department, British Broadcasting Corporation.

2   G. Gurvitch, 'The sociology of the theatre', in *Les lettres nouvelles* (1956), Vol. 35, 196-210. Quotation from the translation by Petra Morrison — pp. 71-81 of *Sociology of Literature and Drama* edited by Elizabeth and Tom Burns (Harmondsworth, Penguin, 1973), 76.

3   Michael Lane (ed.) *Structuralism : A Reader* (London, Jonathan Cape, 1970), 18.

4   Claude Lévi-Strauss, *The Savage Mind* (London, Weidenfeld & Nicholson, 1966), 58.

5   Peter L. Berger and Thomas Luckmann, *The Social Construction of Reality* (1966) (London, Allen Lane The Penguin Press, 1967). Quotations from 1967 edition.

6   Elizabeth Burns, *Theatricality : A Study of Convention in the Theatre and in Social Life* (London, Longman, 1972), 105.

7   J.S.R. Goodlad, *A Sociology of Popular Drama* (London, Heinemann, 1971).

8   Robert K. Merton, *Social Theory and Social Structure* (Glencoe, Ill., The Free Press, 1957).

9   Johan Huizinga, *Homo Ludens* (1938), quotations from Paladin edition, London, 1970.

10   Roger Caillois, *Man, Play, and Games*, translated by Meyer Barash (London 1962). Chapter 3, 'The Classification of Games', is reprinted in *The Sociology of Sport*, a selection of readings edited by Eric Dunning (London, Cass, 1971).

11   John W. Loy 'The nature of sport: a definitional effort', in *Sport, Culture, and Society*, edited by John W. Loy and Gerald S. Kenyon (New York, Macmillan, 1969).

12   Burns, 149.

13   Thorstein Veblen, *The Theory of the Leisure Class* (1899); quotation from Unwin Books edition (London, George Allen & Unwin, 1970), 64.

14   Jean Duvignaud, *Sociologie du Théâtre* (Paris, Presses

Universitaires de France, 1965).
15 In 'Religious Rejections of the World and Their Directions', Chapter 13 of *From Max Weber*, translated and edited by H.H. Gerth and C. Wright Mills (London, Routledge & Kegan Paul, 1948), 324.
16 Northrop Frye, *Anatomy of Criticism* (Princeton, N.J., Princeton University Press, 1957).

DAVID MAYER

Towards a Definition of
Popular Theatre

I should imagine that our presence at this symposium arises from a set of contradictory circumstances and that we have a history in common, for I assume that many of us became interested in drama after having first encountered it in some popular form — in my own case the cinema western and a production of *Uncle Tom's Cabin* with real bloodhounds and clattering wooden ice-floes. Later, after we had first succumbed to the pleasures of drama and responded directly to the excitement of vicariously enacted life, we gradually came to realize that there were such things as better drama and worse drama, the comparative terms *better* and *worse* referring alike to aesthetic standards imposed by distant and unknown critics and to our own private standards of what gave us pleasure. Many of us, in the belief that aesthetic criteria matter, have gone on to teach drama. Only as we have become more secure in our knowledge of what is supposed to be aesthetically respectable can we admit to deep and passionate obsession with ¯popular forms, and our obsessions are no longer occasion for apology.

Our present and mutual concern is with certain kinds of dramatic experiences which most of us agree can be grouped under the label of 'popular drama' or 'popular theatre'. There are many things which may be said about popular drama, and one of these is that it is probably easier and more profitable to describe various popular genres than to define what we mean by the term 'popular theatre'. I am uncertain that a definition is possible because a definition must aim at limiting, at fixing boundaries, at excluding apparent irrelevancies, whereas our present experience with popular theatre emphasizes the contrary. We are extending parameters and disproving former irrelevancies.

Just how necessary these actions are is illustrated by our prolonged emphasis on the literary qualities of drama and by our dependence upon the playscript, both as a standard of excellence and as the foremost implement of theatre research. Two periods, perhaps the most prominent in the entire range of theatrical development, reveal the theatre historian held captive by the surviving literature and his judgment in matters theatrical swayed by criteria that are chiefly literary. The first of these periods is ancient Greece. Even the most casual tourist to that country encounters ruined theatres of varying sizes at sites throughout the southern two-thirds of Greece and learns that similar theatres are found on the Asiatic Litoral, the Italian Coast, Sardinia, Sicily, and North Africa. Some of these theatres, altered to meet successive tastes in production, tastes perhaps forced by occupying garrisons, have existed in one form or another from the 7th century BC. Surviving relics and occasional records show us that a rich tradition of theatrical production flourished in these theatres. But the surviving literature from the Greek theatres does not adequately represent these tastes. What remains of the Greek drama are some forty-odd plays, written between 485-395 BC, representing, perhaps, no more than a fifth of the period in which drama enjoyed widespread appeal. Moreover, these plays are alike in that, with few exceptions, they were written by Athenian playwrights for performance before Athenian audiences.

Confronted with the body of plays, with scattered theatres, with a considerable collection of sculptural and pottery illustrations, inscriptions, and fragmentary commentaries, theatre historians have strained at a reconstruction of five centuries of Greek dramatic experience in the light of Athenian comedies and tragedies from a ninety-year period and a few examples, chiefly fragments, of Greek 'New Comedy'. Understandably, Athenian drama has been declared the apex of Greek dramatic achievement, but the ubiquitous popular entertainments and sacred plays presented at regular intervals in consecrated theatres have been neglected. There is increasing evidence that archaeological interpretation of ruined theatres has been too often influenced by the Athenian literary models, whilst the likelihood that these theatres served as the venue for variety acts, combats, dramatic contests, concerts, recitations, and courts of law is too often slighted.

A similar imbalance until very recently has affected our appreciation of the theatre of the English Renaissance. Studies in this period rarely have been undertaken without, at the very least, a sideways glance at Shakespeare. The problems arising from his thirty-eight plays have provided one of the principal impetuses to research in theatrical practice, theatre construction, company management, licensing of revels and other entertainments. Critics have rigorously and legitimately investigated Shakespeare's work for meaning, structure, language, versification, texture, style, historic content, biographic and autobiographic information, and their work has as thoroughly and meticulously extended to the plays of other poets with whom Shakespeare associated and competed. Almost inevitably there has been comparison, direct and implied, between the plays of Shakespeare's predecessors and contemporaries and those of Shakespeare himself. Our knowledge of the Elizabethan playhouse — restricted in primary sources to a drawing in a traveller's notebook, a few maps and city views, an account book, some woodblock engravings on the title pages of plays and in a book of mnemonic systems — has been vastly augmented by a study of stage directions, actual or implied, in the many playscripts that survive from this period. But we have been slow to recognize that playhouses chiefly owe their form to entertainments other than literary pieces and that literary drama was the uncomplaining inheritor of a physical environment devised for combats, jigs and the baiting of bears and bulls[1].

The scholar's extensive reliance on playscripts, both Ancient Greek and Renaissance English, has been in the main helpful, and such dependence is thoroughly understandable in the light of limited primary sources and the further fact that research often first began in departments of Classics and English. But the effect of such literary-oriented research has also been detrimental to our understanding of the full range of theatrical experience of these periods. We have been conditioned to accept literary merit as the paramount test of dramatic excellence; we are intimidated into accepting a set of priorities for determining theatrical merit, chiefly derived from Aristotle's dicta that certain elements of drama take aesthetic precedence over others, and in so doing we exclude a vast range of theatrical forms which express the taste and interest of their period with great fidelity. Only when we accept the possibility that for every literary, philosophic, and consciously artistic theatrical piece there are some dozens of inartistic, energetic, mindless, unliterary dramatic genres which enjoy a vast popularity and which appeal, not necessarily to persons of refinement and educated taste, but to the greater part of the population, perhaps to the entire population, do we begin to see the theatrical expressions of an age in a more accurate perspective.

Yet we cannot entirely blame scholars for neglecting the 'popular theatre' tradition. The popular theatre is ephemeral. The very fact that it is not literary by intent means that written evidence is slight. Playscripts or libretti or scenarios, if they should survive, are all too often inadequate for the extensive task of reconstructing the popular theatre piece. Audiences are too caught up in what they are seeing to recollect and record the occasion in adequate detail. Frequently the popular piece has been given a single performance, and just as frequently interest is in the result of the performance rather than in the performance itself. Because much popular drama does not occur in what each culture recognizes as a theatre, some popular theatre goes unrecognized or, if recognized and recorded, it is the subject of interest by persons other than students of theatre. For these reasons it has been extremely easy to overlook the popular drama or to misinterpret it. The occasional reporters tell us very little about those involved in the performance: who they are, why they are engaged in their various rôles, how or if they are compensated for their efforts, whether they are professionals or amateurs, who composed their audience, how many performances were given, how much admission was paid, and many other facts relevant to the social, historic, and economic aspects of dramatic performance. Popular drama forms are often interpreted in the context of their relationship to literary drama. Even the *commedia dell' arte*, so clearly and defiantly a popular theatre genre, came to respectable academic notice as an influence on Shakespeare and Molière, and even such prominent scholars as Duchartre, Nicoll and Katherine Lea have felt obliged to connect the *commedia* with literary drama[2].

If popular drama resists definition, it nonetheless can be described, and my intent is to try to locate and to describe some of the ground common to much popular drama. I find that there are a number of characteristics that recur among popular genres. The presence of a single characteristic, or even two, in a dramatic form will not necessarily make that form popular drama, and, equally, the absence of any or all traits will not prevent something from being classified as popular drama. But I find that a majority of popular dramatic forms share some traits. It is more than likely that if one tenaciously explores a particular popular culture or a popular dramatic genre one will discover principles of popular drama that are neglected or merely suggested here. It is more important that in searching for popular drama we be flexible and imaginative, open to suggestion, to perception, even impetuous, rather than risk being rigid and doctrinaire.

The need for flexibility is demonstrated by the most important characteristic of all drama, popular drama included: drama requires some measure of imitation or representation. Virtually every form of drama depends upon the participants and, on occasion, the spectators engaging in imitative or representative action. By imitation is meant the temporary assumption of an identity, that of some sentient being or object, or abstract characteristic that is distinct from the participants' private selves, in order to act out a tale or to perform a rite or to amuse themselves. In instances where the performers do not impersonate, that is, do not oblige the spectators to temporarily accept the performers as the beings or qualities they present to their audiences, they merely represent without becoming. The situation is often as Robin Starveling sees it when, with dog, bush, and lantern, he greets the guests at Theseus' marriage feast:

This lanthorn doth the hornéd moon present
I the Man-in-the-Moon do seem to be ...[3]

These are the simplest descriptions of imitation and representation that are possible, and even these invite confusion. There is little difficulty in accepting the concept of imitation that occurs when an actor assumes a stage identity; or when a masked reveler or costumed celebrant in a rite surrender their own personalities to the beings or characteristics represented by mask and apparel; or even when the priest, in the act of saying mass, successively mimes the events of the Last Supper, the agony of the crucified Christ, and the consternation of the Disciples. But there are dramatic events — particularly those associated with public rites, state and municipal pageantry, 'managed' political confrontations, or even trials — that are more difficult to recognize as imitative or even representative in character.

The presence of a sovereign at a state occasion is illustrative of a simple form of unconscious representation. The sovereign is always ruler, even in private moments; but in his behaviour as he opens his parliament or reviews his regiments or conducts investitures or opens a day-care nursery, without consciously imitating he nonetheless personifies on these occasions distinct attributes, such abstract qualities as the sovereign-as-titular-governor, war-leader, source-of-honour-and-reward, and compassionate-father, qualities that his subjects are likely to forget unless reminded at intervals. In acting a rôle that reinforms his subjects, the sovereign symbolically reasserts his rights and duties, and his subjects confirm these rights by allowing these events to proceed. Similarly, members of the public may enact rôles on these same occasions to express their consent or to instruct the sovereign on some point of issue with his subjects.

A second characteristic of the drama is presence of a recognizable structure. Does the event in question show evidence of a planned or partially planned structure? That is, do events or acts follow a deliberate sequence, and would this sequence be followed if the dramatic occasion were repeated? Popular dramas, regardless of their antiquity or seeming spontaneity, have recognizable structures, and these structures, even when first appearance would seem to contradict, have an efficiency and economy that is central to the purpose for which the performance is realized.

A third characteristic, closely related, is the requirement that there be action. Something must happen in the presence of the spectators, and what happens will be visible, even if not audibly intelligible. What happens may be slight, apparently insignificant or of very limited duration, perhaps nothing more than a parade of symbols before the spectators, a sequence of 'turns' by singers, jugglers, acrobats, and comics. However, there is an action in the sense that these events occur and that there is both a beginning and an end to the events. But often the action is more complex. Not only does something happen, but something or someone is changed — a transformation in the character or qualities assigned the person, an alteration in the quality of institution presenting the drama. The performers and audience are brought together in an event that not only affects the performers but may alter the spectators as well, the nature of the transformation depending upon such factors as the kind of drama performed and the degree of mental or emotional involvement between performers and audience. Depending upon such circumstances, a performer may seem to be born; he may seem to die or, if we are witnessing a public execution, he will actually die; he certainly may be changed in psychological or physical characteristics. Similarly, the action produces changes in the spectator: laughter or acquiescence, vicarious association with terror, death, sexual licence, and the presence of the daemonic or the divine. The dramatic action may lull, excite, satisfy, or frustrate him.

A fourth and, for our immediate purposes, final characteristic of the drama is that there is some general distinction between performers and spectators. However, in popular drama this distinction is not a fixed one, and in numerous instances the spectators are encouraged to join the performers, not merely empathically, but in phases of the performance. Encouragement may come in the 'Everybody join in' call of the music hall artiste who invites her audience to join in the refrains of her songs and who exchanges jibes with the gallery. Or the invitation will be a call for communal dancing, joining a procession, or a sexual orgy. Whereas some theatre is formal and circumspect and the intrusion of any part of the audience into the dramatic action is a source of annoyance inimicable to concentration and to the development of dramatic plot, the popular drama often cultivates the spectators' awareness of themselves, reminding them of their power to approve or disapprove, power even to alter the outcome of the representation. The popular drama maintains the flexibility to cope with the spectators' verbal and physical forays into the action.

The above characteristics may momentarily satisfy our need for a definition of what is dramatic. We need now to identify some of the central characteristics and limits of the adjective *popular*. Popular, in its widest sense, is something 'of the people', for our purposes drama that is principally concerned with the widest reach of audience available at a given moment or place. We recognize that the population of any society is divisible on the basis of a variety of criteria. Wealth, education, occupation, political power, social rank all operate to produce static or fluid groupings. Popular drama is that drama produced by and offered for the enjoyment or edification of the largest combinations of groupings possible within that society. Often it happens that for these groupings the adjective 'lower' is significantly appropriate: lower per capita income, lower level of education and literacy, lower interest in or knowledge of aesthetic criteria, lower level of political influence. Those described by these terms are the farmers, artisans, factory workers, shopkeepers, labourers, the rural and urban poor and middle classes. They constitute the greatest number of the popular drama's audiences. Their theatres are the boulevards, sports palaces, exhibition halls, fairgrounds, market places, shearing grounds, threshing floors and forest clearings. Their dramas are not often preserved in written form; they are quite unlikely to be noticed and commended by the critics in the daily and learned presses. Their dramas survive whole or in part by word of mouth tradition, in diaries, memoirs, anthropologists' notebooks, and censors' files. But their dramas reflect with phenomenal accuracy the nominal ideals and values of the societies that produced them. In these dramas we find the valid myths and fantasies that express the dynamics and ethos of their society.

The general rule that popular drama originates with and is controlled by the popular audience is subject to significant qualification, for the very fact that the popular drama is appreciated by the largest number of citizens makes it of considerable interest to heads of government, the politically ambitious, those concerned with the orderly progress of government, and those responsible to educate the community in religious, ethical and political values. Their influence upon the popular drama works in at least three ways: they order public rites at which the symbols and personalities of authority are impressed upon the public; they likewise commission entertainments for their private pleasures; finally, they act as censors, placing limits upon what may be performed. Sometimes these persons in authority can end a flourishing dramatic tradition with a single edict, or equally give encouragement to another. If they privately patronize an entertainment that has been predominantly a pleasure of the popular audience, as repeatedly occurred with the *commedia dell' arte*, they may give that genre a unique prominence and longevity. In short, to the degree that their authority approaches the absolute, these persons both promote education in norms and values and determine the limits of this education. However, if the educated, moneyed, aristocratic, and professional classes wish, without exercising direct political or social authority, to become spectators at the popular drama, they are welcome, but the exercise of their aesthetic critical dicta is unlikely to affect either structure or contents of that drama. Their influence is chiefly indirect: only as their own values become acceptable as the standards of the groups socially and economically beneath them do these values obtrude into the drama to shape both form and contents.

One criterion for determining whether drama may be classified as popular is the relationship of the dramatic occasion to current literary and artistic values. Although discussion to this point has suggested that the literary is antithetical to the popular, this antithesis holds only when the terms for literary drama have been established.

Scripts are not an indication. I do not exclude from my discussion of popular drama plays that are devised with parts written out. Nor does use of a scenario rather than a script necessarily decide that the drama is popular. What counts is the author's and audience's conscious acceptance of, or indifference to, literary and aesthetic criteria. A few questions, asked in the presence of a dramatic event, are a litmus to whether the drama belongs to what I shall hereafter call the popular culture or, alternatively, to the aesthetic culture.

Several affirmative answers to the following queries are enough to indicate that the work in question is popular drama. Is the author unknown? Is the piece the work of more than one author? Is the playwright indifferent to his reputation as a poet? Is the author's identity of little importance to those who announce and present the play? If the author is known, is he known for a style of drama, for sensational scenes, for the use of character types who are amusing in their own right irrespective of the overall unity of the piece! Are plays of this sort favoured over situations that deal with immediate moral and social values in a meaningful way? Does theatrical effect take precedence over literary and artistic conventions? Do the exigencies of public rite, whether political, religious, or social, take precedence over aesthetic considerations? Is the piece intended for a large general audience rather than a select group of spectators? Does the piece give the undiscriminating spectator 'what he wants' at the expense of meeting the tastes and predilections of an educated class? Is the dramatic plot embellished with actions and displays offered as much for their own effect as for their relevance to the plot? Does the piece reassure the audience in the validity of traditional values and in the continuity of belief rather than reinterpret traditional attitudes, accepted facts, or mythologies? Is the piece traditional, or is much of the material in the piece of a traditional nature?

When these questions are sorted out, two profiles emerge — that of the aesthetic drama and that of the popular. The drama of the aesthetic culture is characterized by single authorship, by playwrights who would be known for their skills, by structural and aesthetic relevance, by willingness to face complex moral and social issues without blinking and to lead audiences to newer or different attitudes. It is intended for audiences sufficiently educated to insist upon artistic and intellectual coherence.

The popular drama presents a different, antithetical profile. Because the popular dramatist is not asking for recognition as a poet, we do not invariably know whether a piece originates with one man or from some sort of collaboration. Unlike works from the literary culture, the work of the popular craftsman is often as anonymous as the handwrought stoneware jug or the carved ramshorn shepherd's crook. And like these artifacts the drama may owe much to tradition. It is indebted to conventions of structure, plot, dance, dialogue and song passed down for generations and is refurbished with material borrowed from a wide variety of sources. Its audiences are representative of the society's population. Anyone who has the price of admission or who presents himself at the site of the event is a potential spectator. Popular drama is also determined by function, utility and amusement being the chiefest of these. It has utility in that it serves social needs through public rites or through plays that reinforce desirable social and moral conclusions. Or drama may be amusement, performed for the spectators' pleasure, simplifying the issues and conflicts in values with which a society must deal, presenting these issues in such a way as to make them appear harmless and of minor consequence. It offers the audience acts that require physical skills — horsemanship, encounters between men and beasts that exhibit disproportionate strength and human intelligence pitted against brute instinct, or actual battles between antagonistic animals, wire-walking, juggling, singing, magic, trick shooting, dancing, displays of Nature's aberrations, technical oddities, and wonderous scientific innovations: freaks, fireworks, and free-balloons — or such verbal skills as telling jokes, monologues, mock debates, story-telling, all of which lead the mind away from current problems. On such occasions popular drama functions as entertainment only. It beguiles and amuses, rests and relaxes the mind, encourages conviviality and satisfaction with things as they are.

Popular drama also diverges from literary drama on questions of aesthetics. We may expect to find many momentary effects, amusing, interesting, and exciting in their own right but artistically unnecessary, intruding into dramatic plots. Aesthetic judgments and standards are recognizable, but it is because they are instinctively present in the minds of the producers. The piece has not been devised to conform with aesthetic dicta. We may take it as a rule of thumb that in the popular drama aesthetic values are instinctive, whereas pragmatic reason is assiduously cultivated and consulted. Reason not only prudently determines financial expenditure and such matters as the utterance of religious or political sentiments, but counsels which effects are most likely to please the greatest number of spectators. Reason almost invariably will dictate that aesthetic qualities may be sacrificed to theatrical effect. On the other hand, the popular drama does not bar qualities that we term 'literary'. Poetry is often found in popular pieces; so are settings and costumes of exceptional quality and effect. But what matters is the emphasis placed upon these devices. Poetry is employed because it is found to be the language appropriate to the occasion, because rhyme is an effective means of presenting doctrine, and because it is easy for performers to learn, remember, and pass on by word of mouth to successive generations of performers. These profiles of the two dramas are useful, but only to a point. Their limitations arise from the fact that they describe literary and popular drama in general terms, whereas individual dramas and categories of drama are not likely to correspond at all points to the general profile. Many dramas, in fact, satisfy criteria in both popular and literary categories.

There are notable borderline cases. The plays of Aristophanes, Shakespeare, and Molière, to name but a few playwrights, were and continue to be enjoyed by audiences whose tastes ranged from the knowledgeably elevated to the uninformed illiterate. Their plays may be enjoyed by persons without pretence to aesthetic standards, and the plays themselves originally shared theatres with entertainments decidedly within the popular tradition. But the plays of these authors also show considerable literary consciousness and effort. Those of Aristophanes were submitted to dramatic contests in which judgments based on aesthetic as well as social, moral, and political criteria determined prizes; Shakespeare's and Molière's position is less defined, but both authors encouraged publication of their works, and both were immediately conscious of literary tastes in their audiences.

It is along the border between the literary and the popular that a high proportion of dramatic masterpieces are found. Those plays which have received the respectful attention of critics are those which reveal the material of popular culture worked and controlled by an artist. Comedy most easily balances between literary and popular, but this partially lies with comic impatience with pretence and artificial standards. In depicting action that asserts society's norms, comedy depends upon conclusions that are compatible with popular taste; the conclusion of the dramatic action must support existing values. Innovations are decried and ridiculed. In matters of style as well as content, this rule continues to hold true. The comic playwright, however much he longs to make his piece a literary or aesthetic work, knows that he cannot too far depart from the tradition in which his audience has learned to see dramatic experience presented. The comic playwright largely refines popular material, showing concern for the structure and language of his plays, giving them more edge, more polish than preliterary models. And if he is dissatisfied with traditional genres in which comedy is located, he can change only by locating his subsequent plays in another genre. Comedy deteriorates, becomes artificial, pedantic and vapid if it is located too far into the literary tradition and too far away from popular drama.

Writers of tragedy enjoy no greater liberty. Their pieces can be as vapid and as pedantic as bad literary comedy if they become excessively literary, but they can also be banal and commonplace if too close to the popular tradition. The history of domestic tragedy, from Lillo, Lessing, and Diderot to such present-day authors as Arthur Miller repeatedly illustrates the perils of too close proximity to popular taste. At the same time we recognize the triumphs of Ibsen and Strindberg who, working within the same domestic framework, infused the situations of family crisis with poetry and general significance.

It is also true that for many, more probably for all of us, membership in the aesthetic culture is only part-time. We can be unselfconsciously at home in both the popular and aesthetic cultures, for even if we are taught to prefer select pieces from the aesthetic drama, we never wholly outgrow our early and constant exposure to the mythologies expressive of the fantasies, goals, and values of our own popular culture, nor do we escape the influence of popular dramas that perpetuate these mythologies. I can learn to appreciate and to enjoy plays by Racine and Schiller, but I will forever be more susceptible to a drama or film built on variations of the mythology of the American West. Although there are such significant differences between the aesthetic and popular as seriousness of purpose and result and overall aesthetic quality (just to name a few points of comparison), enjoyment of the one culture does not preclude finding pleasure in pieces from the other. We can enjoy both circus and grand opera, rodeo and classical tragedy, public spectacle and poetic drama. Only the cultural bigot, the stuffed shirt, insists upon the absolute priority of the aesthetic over the popular.

Recognition of our place in both cultures along with the realization that there are nevertheless points of tension and friction between the popular and the aesthetic has led in recent years to work of considerable benefit and effectiveness in the drama, literature, and the visual arts, but which because of its very effectiveness further blurs the distinction between the popular and aesthetic cultures. This work arises out of authors, directors and artists deliberately exploring Western popular cultures and using extensively the techniques of communication and the mythologies that have emerged within those cultures. Those who work these veins and their audiences can testify to the currency and power of the mythologies, especially at such times as the myths are magnified, re-examined and turned against the societies that produced them. Myths thus treated can reveal the aggression, fears, banalities and devious foundations of a society. Setting them in distorted versions of popular dramatic forms raises further questions about the values and methods of that society. We know what that dramatic form was devised to tell us, and an ironic use of that form brings an ironic awareness of its habitual and traditional content.

If we accept that there concurrently exist a popular culture and an aesthetic culture, our view of the nature of theatre history is bound to change. Not only are we obliged to reduce the former emphasis on literary drama and to proceed more cautiously with the accustomed and still necessary task of fitting scripts to theatres or reconstructing playhouses from scripts, but we may also learn to relinquish one of the more cherished concepts of the post-Darwin historian — that drama, along with the other arts, is continually evolving; that it begins as a simple popular form and becomes increasingly complex and increasingly literary; that it grows, improves, progressing from the rudimentary and naive to the fully mature, articulated and sophisticated drama. This notion also encourages the concomitant assumption that if a dramatic form has once been widely enjoyed and has subsequently lost favour, its decline is attributable to its comparative crudity, simplicity and lack of sophistication when placed against newer forms, and that audience taste had reached levels where such deficiencies were no longer acceptable. These efforts to account for the rise of one genre or the decline of another are nothing short of fitting credible biological theory — the concept that biological organisms evolve or perish depending upon their capacities to adapt to changing environments — to the non-biological phenomenon of drama.

This view, at best, is but a small part of the truth. The drama is continually changing, but it does not have an evolutionary history, and even the concept of a consecutive history — a history of one form of drama budding, flowering, withering, dying, and eventually giving place to another genre following the same cycle of growth and decay — is dubious. We must instead look to patterns — particularly with respect to popular drama — that, although confirming that drama is constantly changing, suggest that the change is evolutionary only in the sense that it is constantly being adapted to prevailing needs, fantasies, sensibilities. Also, contrary to the pattern of biological evolution, individual dramatic genres develop both in purpose and in form from the complex to the simple. Further, we must recognize that the changing, the growth of a new genre or the fading of an old, often proceeds from events outside the drama, not necessarily from sentiment within the profession that it is time for something new or time to put an end to obsolescent forms.

The latter point requires amplification and although for brevity's sake I have hitherto resisted illustration, the example to hand is particularly appropriate to this conference and makes the further point that drama, although created by men in a changing environment, is only the expression of those men. Not a living entity, drama is only the reflection of life without capacity to change or to adapt or to survive, unless men cause it to change to meet their own changing social and psychological needs.

The example to afford me so much personal satisfaction emerges from Virginia Scott's clarifying study of the origins of English pantomime[4]. She demonstrated that English pantomime owes its origins to the action of the French police who in 1702 closed the theatres at Paris' Foire St Laurent. The *forains* then sought work in London, bringing with them pieces from their Paris *commedia dell' arte* repertoire. Probably because these dramas extensively depended on acrobatic and other physical skills and because the performers hadn't sufficient English to make effective translation, the pieces were played *en mute* and were described in the bills as dances or 'Italian Night Scenes'. According to Professor Scott these Night Scenes were fused with allegorical and mythological ballets which, if not native to this country, entered with other performers at an earlier time. These hybrid entertainments, now called 'panto-mimes', a mélange of *commedia dell'arte*, English knockabout, dance, song and mechanical trickwork, were recognized as an instrument of contemporary social satire. It was partly in this capacity that pantomime secured a permanent place in the eighteenth-century English theatrical repertoire.

In this instance (i.e. the curtailment in one place of an existing form and its reappearance as a creation of a new form in another, and its eventual change into still another form), the events in large part began because of pressures that were external to the theatre. Moreover, the new dramatic form did not develop from a dying or decaying antecedent. And, finally, there are no objective criteria for insisting that any one of these several dramatic pieces, fairground *commedia* play, Night Scene, or pantomime, is superior to the other. Each arose through the changing circumstances of the society that fostered it, each variant expressed values and attitudes of that society, occasionally in language, invariably in pictorial image and in dramatic action entirely comprehensible to that society. That these genres and the values expressed by them are no longer readily comprehensible or entirely aesthetically pleasing to later societies is of secondary importance, and our efforts to rank them good-better-best, or to speak of a progressive evolution, are meaningless. Although the sequence of pantomime forms is discernible, many genres within the popular drama are independent of one another. Obviously, there are many occasions when the devices or conventions of one dramatic form are transferred to another. Audience preference, managerial opportunism or authoritarian fiat may dictate the terms for grafting one dramatic genre to another, and no matter how permanent these unions turn out to be, they are usually begun in a shortsighted fashion for reasons that are immediate and often fugitive. The longer popularity of these hybrid genres is rarely anticipated, nor is there much sense of perpetuating or of renewing dramatic tradition.

However, once we accept the fact that dramatic genres are not necessarily dependent upon one another for origin and growth and that the history of dramatic genres is discontinuous, we find ourselves in possession of a considerable advantage: we are no longer obliged to pursue a study that is chronological. We may, if we wish, disconnect the study of drama from sequential time and instead view the various genres of popular drama from the point of view of structure, method, and intended purpose, characteristics that in orthodox histories of drama are accorded only secondary interest.

These characteristics become the connecting thread once we realize that frequently popular drama is not only non-continuous, but local: many similar specimens of drama occur quite independently of one another in civilizations separated by distance and in time. Even when we cannot demonstrate that a dramatic genre has been derived from a foreign model or recognize the conscious or unconscious use of earlier material in that genre (although the latter is more easily done), still we can identify and describe such recurring characteristics as similarities in dramatic structure, similarities of theme, and similarities in manner and context of presentation.

Our new categories, while allowing greater flexibility and accuracy in recognizing and analysing popular drama, invite new dilemmas, not the least of which is the range of dramatic events that now become available for investigation. However, if many examples of popular drama come to hand, we must respect the warning first expressed to social scientists by the French anthropologist Claude Lévi-Strauss. Lévi-Strauss cautions[5] against facile and superficial comparisons, particularly between apparently similar myths or artifacts or attitudes, or modes of expression which appear to be held in common by different cultures. The similarities, Lévi-Strauss suggests, are similarities only to our eyes and may spring from quite diverse impulses, from needs to express vastly dissimilar attitudes or thoughts. What appears generally similar is only so in isolated detail. The dissimilarities are far greater than the similarities. It is for this reason, for example, that we must avoid drawing comparisons between the popular dramas of Europe and Asia or the Americas and Africa, a practice so dear to earlier generations of writers on so-called 'primitive theatre'.

Our present knowledge of non-Western popular dramas and of the diverse civilizations that produce them is insufficient to explain *why* these dramas are produced, what they mean to the culture producing them, what their social and psychological functions are, what their symbolic and linguistic significance may be. Our knowledge of Western drama and of Western civilization, though often suspect, is somewhat less subject to misinterpretation. And there are examples enough of popular dramtic forms within this smaller circle.

We do have a reasonably good understanding and appreciation of Western mythologies. We recognize that drama, among other forms of expression, is a repository of many of the crucial myths of Western cultures. We also recognize that groups and individuals respond to drama to the extent that the drama presents the particular myths that have both social and psychological relevance at given moments in time. The myths themselves are the projection of peoples' conscious and unconscious values, of the structures of the societies that create the myths, and of various institutions and their places within each society. By myth I mean more than the formal folk-tale or a codified account of interaction between man and an immortal or supernatural being or among the immortals or the supernaturals, although these are myths of great power and significance. Myth may be defined with sufficient latitude to include the obvious and recurrent patterns of human behaviour and imagination that occupy story-tellers, joke-makers, iconographers and performers even when the identities and circumstances of the chief characters are constantly changed. For example, there are infinite stories of relations between the sexes, a vast number of the tales turning on three characters: a young woman, a young man, and an older man. Whether the older man is father or guardian to the woman or father to the young man and/or rival suitor to the young man, the behaviour of the characters is predictable within limits; everything possible will be attempted to insure a pairing between the young man and woman. Expectations relating to Western attitudes about who is the appropriate mate for whom must be satisfied. This multitude of courtings and pairings is very much the substance of myth and certainly a basic myth in terms of the frequency with which it is to be found in both the popular and the aesthetic drama. Who goes to bed with whom is a subject of concern to writers of farce and panto, of comic authors from Aristophanes to Peter Nichols, as well as tragic playwrights and grand opera librettists.

Other material, less developed and far less generally known, may also qualify as myth if it presents some portion of the psychological or social or moral pattern of a particular society. Every culture has its formal and highly articulated myths, informal myths and fragmentary myths. There are differences from culture to culture and from era to era in these myths, not only in the basic structuring of the myths, but in details, in nuances and inflections. Further, all societies and individuals within these societies live, that is, think and behave, in terms of these mythologies. However primitive or naive the myth may seem at first glance, it has enormous power to evoke reactions of assent and compliant behaviour from the groups to whom the myth belongs.

If we wish to understand the dramas in which these myths are found, we will do well to turn our backs on the performers and examine the spectators. The recurrent myths and the recurrent mythic structures that underlie so much popular theatre are present because the audience has come to expect these elements as much as because the playwright intuitively senses that the myth or the pattern is appropriate. The myth understandably functions as an expression of that society's ethos, instructing the audience, telling it how to respond to a set of circumstances, how to function both individually and as an informed collective. The audience, in turn, reinforces the validity of the myth by sanctioning and approving the drama.

Once we assess the audience, we are in a position, and I think a dangerous one, to make moral judgments about them and their societies' values. As someone with moral, social and political points of view, I sympathize with this temptation, but I sense that to submit to temptation may impair my objectivity as an observer of popular drama. I mention this point because of a letter I received from Professor Brasmer at a time when we were organizing the Conference agenda. Referring to the Wild West Show, Professor Brasmer wrote,

> Let me warn you, I would take a negative slant. I am convinced that popular entertainment substantiates fantasies, often immoral, of a particular society. Certainly the honouring of the Indian killers in the Wild West Show distorted the reality of the Indian and contributed to the case with which society ignored the 'Indian problem'.

Professor Brasmer is correct in every particular, and I have recently argued on behalf of the use and value of fantasy in popular drama[6]. However, I doubt that his statement takes into account the possibility that the Wild West Show was allowed to survive and to develop because a majority of persons, those very persons who were the popular audience for the Wild West Show, had already decided on a morality that was prepared to see the Indian as an inferior and frequently dangerous being. With mid twentieth-century hindsight we may condemn the dubious popular morality of an earlier period, but I suspect that our own moral viewpoint is entirely after that fact and useful to our understanding of the popular drama only if we can demonstrate that yesterday's popular morality was in some way opposed by the morality of a less influential faction.

A further aspect of the relationship of myth to popular drama is that characters invented by the popular drama tend to generate and to develop mythologies and traits of character that extend far beyond the life given to them in the dramas in which they first appear. Their grip upon the popular imagination is such that they are exploited in dramatic and non-dramatic media and can be put through further exploits without taxing credulity. Unlike the aesthetic drama which can rarely use its characters in more than one play, we can recognize a vast number of characters from the popular drama such as Harlequin, Sgnanarelle, Donald Duck, the Tramp created by Charlie Chaplin and the historical Buffalo Bill, who have passed through many dramas in the theatre and other dramatic media into popular folklore. Similarly, characters from the aesthetic drama and from other literary sources are drawn into the popular drama and given long lives and adventures never imagined by their original creators. Through the popular drama Lemuel Gulliver and Don Quixote, Don Juan and Doctor Faustus have long ago passed from the confines of the aesthetic culture into popular consciousness. Through this process their original value as symbols has been expanded so that the characters can now represent whatever their adaptors find appropriate to the general outlines, rather than specific detail, of their original characterization.

The very adaptability of characters to vastly different circumstances and dramatic modes illustrates a further trait of the popular drama: it is very often occasional drama. Occasional drama, as its name suggests, is drama that is devised for a particular occasion or for periodic occasions. It may come into being to celebrate or to commemorate a particular event, a marriage, an alliance, a coming-of-age. Or it may serve either as the rite or the accompanying display for events that a society is likely to experience at intervals, a coronation, change of season, change of administration, death of a ruler. What is significant about occasional drama is that its structure often reflects the occasion for which it is designed rather than meeting any formal notion of dramatic structure. On the other hand, a recognizable dramatic form may be evident even if the piece is performed only once. It needn't be repeated to have existed as drama. Its structure is evident and would be followed if the event were repeated.

The structure of popular drama is subject to a variety of conditions other than the necessities of plot and characterization. Not the least of these factors is that the structure and plan of a popular piece may result from the known abilities of the performers. Our assumption that plot, characterization and thematic values are the dominant considerations of dramatic production is chiefly applicable to the aesthetic drama. It is often the case that in popular drama plot, character and theme may be subordinated to the performers' skills. If a performer can sing or dance, juggle or ride a unicycle, play a musical instrument or do impersonations, or perform any of a number of entertaining feats, then the entertainment in which he appears may be devised or adjusted to accommodate these skills and to provide periods when he may take the rest necessary to regain his breath after performing them. The entertainment will display these skills at the expense of what might be called dramatic probability, with the characters and the scenarios tailored to the performers' special talents, with audiences at such entertainments tacitly agreeing to overlook lapses in probability in exchange for diversions afforded by the multiple skills.

The shortcomings of this practice have less to do with impeding or defeating dramatic probability than with the nature of the skills themselves. Performers whose egos demand a full display of their talents run the considerable risk of surfeiting their audiences with their presence on stage and with displaying skills that are unevenly developed or interesting. Moreover, a piece that is devised for the particular skills of one performer may suffer if performed by another. The modern musical comedy affords us an example of this problem for we frequently find a piece developed and produced for the skills of a certain performer subsequently performed by another actor. The replacement has the choice of subordinating his own talents to those of his predecessor and of giving performances that obscure his own abilities or, alternatively, of adjusting the structure and contents of the piece to his own requirements. Such is the nature of the popular drama that the latter choice occurs with considerable frequency, and we are obliged to understand the skills of the various performers who have been associated with a popular drama if we wish to account for its original form and to keep track of successive modifications.

It is not only the performer who determines the structure of the popular drama. Often there will be conditions wholly external to dramatic needs which, though secondary to the drama, exercise a dominating influence. Thus, the sequence of acts in a circus is determined, not necessarily by aesthetic or dramatic preference, but by the problems posed by the unloading of equipment, tenting and beasts from vans or trains and, similarly, by the logistics of erecting and striking the performers' and animals' special equipment. The placing of episodes within large-scale melodrama, fairground spectacle, pantomime harlequinade and extravaganza, to name just a few popular entertainments, may also be determined by the ability to shift scenes or to provide other effects rather than aesthetic preference for logical development. Thus it is axiomatic of popular drama that much of it is sequential rather than consequential: the sequences follow in order, but the order is not always dependent upon a coherent or dramatically plausible plot.

In the sequential nature of these entertainments a further and final point emerges. It is that scenario takes precedence over script. A scenario is an outline of the sequence of action with notations of technical requirements, properties, scenic effects, music, and all other needs of the popular piece. Verbal requirements, if there are any, may be extemporized from the action or may be so imprecise as to make a script unnecessary. A script comes into being only when the piece is to be repeated at intervals and where verbal precision is desirable or essential. But in the main, words are secondary to movement, sound, pageantry, visual symbols and the full range of technical effects. In literate societies, such as those of Western Europe and North America, where both popular and aesthetic works are likely to be written out and even to be printed for the benefit of performers, scripted drama is not an anomaly. In pre-literate societies, however, or in societies where literacy is restricted by rank and profession, the script is often an indication that the work is partially intended for the aesthetic culture, for words and their meanings, verbal nuances and rhetorical virtuosity are skills associated with the aesthetic culture. One consequence of the predominance of scenario over script, is the comparative dearth of popular scripts and scenarios which adequately describe settings, costumes, technical effects and movement. We return, in consequence, to my original concern that we look for evidence other than the script and that we recognize tests other than the aesthetic for the existence and viability of dramatic occasions.

The principles of popular drama that I have outlined point the way toward these new tests. But, although they may help to identify some of the more general characteristics of this enormous area of study, they do not bring us much closer to the dramas themselves or to the variety of persons involved either as performers or spectators. For these insights we must look to other papers and to work beyond this symposium.

Notes

1 Glynne Wickham, *Early English Stages, 1500-1660*: Vol. II, *1576-1660*, pt. 2 (London, 1972).

2 Pierre Louis Duchartre, *La Commedia dell' Arte* (Paris, 1955); Allardyce Nicoll, *The World of Harlequin* (Cambridge, 1968); K.M. Lea, *Italian Popular Comedy* (London, 1934).

3 W. Shakespeare, *A Midsummer Night's Dream*, V.iii.

4 Virginia P. Scott, 'The Infancy of English Pantomime: 1716-1723', *Educational Theatre Journal*, XXXIV, ii, 125-34.

5 Claude Lévi-Strauss, *The Savage Mind* (London, Weidenfeld & Nicolson, 1966).

6 *cf.* my 'The Sexuality of Pantomime', *Theatre Quarterly*, IV, 13, 55-64.

ん